T0288243

DIVIDING THE UNION

DIVIDING the UNION

Jesse Burgess Thomas and the MAKING of the MISSOURI COMPROMISE

MATTHEW W. HALL

Southern Illinois University Press
Carbondale

19 18 17 16   4 3 2 1

Jacket illustration: handwriting of Jesse Burgess Thomas on the report
(*detail*) of the Joint Committee of Conference on the Missouri Bill,
March 1–6, 1820. National Archives.

Library of Congress Cataloging-in-Publication Data
Hall, Matthew W., [date]
Dividing the union : Jesse Burgess and the making of the Missouri
Compromise / Matthew W. Hall.
    pages cm
Includes bibliographical references and index.
    ISBN 978-0-8093-3456-8 (cloth : alk. paper)
    ISBN 0-8093-3456-9 (cloth : alk. paper)
    ISBN 978-0-8093-3457-5 (e-book)
    ISBN 0-8093-3457-7 (e-book)
1. Thomas, Jesse Burgess, 1777–1853. 2. Legislators—United States—
Biography. 3. Missouri compromise. 4. United States—Politics and
government—1815–1861. 5. Slavery—Political aspects—United States—
History—19th century. I. Title.
E302.6.T43H35 2015
328.73′092—dc23
[B]   2015013815

To Louisa Warren Hall

A house divided against itself cannot stand. I believe this government cannot endure permanently half slave and half free. I do not expect the Union to be dissolved—I do not expect the house to fall—but I do expect it will cease to be divided. It will become all one thing, or all the other.

—Abraham Lincoln, speech to
Republican state convention,
Springfield, June 16, 1858

CONTENTS

ILLUSTRATIONS

ACKNOWLEDGMENTS

The State Historical Society of Missouri supported this project with a grant from the Richard S. Brownlee Fund in 2007–8. I also owe a large debt to Sylvia Frank Rodrigue, Julie Bush, and their colleagues at Southern Illinois University Press who had faith in the book and made it better. The maps contribute another dimension to the narrative, and Tom Willcoxson was both practical and creative in preparing them. I also owe thanks to the staffs at the Abraham Lincoln Presidential Library and all the other repositories I visited over the last nine years. Last, thanks are due to the many friends and family members who encouraged and assisted me, but I would like to particularly acknowledge my friends Walker Lewis and Bob Marshall, who supported the project early and late, and my daughter, Louisa, who kept me going in the middle.

DIVIDING THE UNION

Introduction

The Missouri Compromise of 1820 was an arbitrary construct cobbled together by Congress to deal with the issue of slavery in the rapidly expanding West. It drew a geographical line extending the southern border of Missouri westward and provided that there would be no slavery in any territory north of that line except for Missouri itself, which was to be admitted to the Union as a slave state. This was the line that divided the nation's house against itself, to use the same New Testament metaphor that Lincoln was later to use. The compromise was awkward and ungainly, thought at the time to favor the South and unlikely to hold for long. Instead it proved remarkably durable, lasting for thirty-four years and in the end standing as one of the last bulwarks of defense for Northerners committed to preserving the Union.

This book explores the sectional tensions in the three decades leading up to the Missouri Compromise, the critical period in which the compromise was formed and implemented, and its gradual evolution over the years until its repeal in 1854. The story involves many leaders from all parts of the country and delves into national and regional politics, but it centers on Jesse Burgess Thomas, one of the first two senators from the new state of Illinois and the author of the actual language of the compromise. Slavery was not a vital issue for Thomas, but in his career he was forced to deal with it every step of the way, in all its changing forms, and in the process he developed a vital understanding of the relationship between slavery and political power in the Old Northwest and the Louisiana Purchase. Always rational and pragmatic on the subject of slavery, he avoided the emotionalism of many of his colleagues.

After wrestling for thirteen years to contain the issue of slavery on the local and regional levels in both the Indiana and Illinois Territories, Thomas
moved to Washington just as slavery reemerged on the national stage. There
he proved ideally suited both by experience and temperament to break the
deadlock over slavery in the West.

Thomas's life also illustrates how the issue of slavery was intertwined with
other issues on the frontier, particularly the pursuit of land. It was ironic
that land, like slavery, was an economic resource that the young and hungry
American Republic seized onto as a free or almost free source of economic
value but which cost another culture dearly. Land and slavery were the central
ethnic tragedies of American life, the one centered on Native Americans and
the other on African Americans. Jesse Thomas was involved with both.

Students of history are often unaware of how easily it could have happened
otherwise. Most American schoolchildren know the Missouri Compromise
and the other mileposts in the history of slavery—the tacit understandings
of the Constitutional Convention that preceded it, the compromises and
upheavals of the 1850s that followed it, the climactic Civil War, Reconstruction, Jim Crow, and finally the civil rights era—but few have imagined the
key times along the way when things could have gone very differently. This
book is about one such time, at the turn of the nineteenth century, when
Americans, with their countrymen flooding westward into areas where slavery
had not yet put down secure roots, first faced the issue of what to do about
slavery in the West.

Thomas Jefferson was the first to tackle the issue of whether slavery should
be allowed to expand westward. In one of his last acts as a legislator, as a
member of the Continental Congress, he drafted Article VI of the Ordinance
of 1784. Famously known as his antislavery proviso, it provided that, after the
year 1800, there would be, in any new state in the American West, south as
well as north, "neither slavery nor involuntary servitude . . . otherwise than in
punishment of crimes whereof the party shall have been convicted to have been
personally guilty." The Continental Congress later cut this language from the
bill without Jefferson putting up much of a fight, but, under the stewardship of
James Monroe, it resurfaced in the same-numbered article of the Northwest
Ordinance of 1787, the document intended to establish American government
in the area north of the Ohio River and east of the Mississippi River.[1] Monroe
made the antislavery provision immediately applicable in the territorial stage
of government and tacked on a provision allowing slave owners to pursue and

reclaim slaves escaping into the territory. Much of America's later experience with slavery relates to the opportunities missed in formulating Article VI of both the 1784 and 1787 Ordinances.

Jefferson's words, though not passed as he proposed in 1784, reappeared, slightly modified from time to time, at many points in the struggle against slavery, starting with Article VI of the Northwest Ordinance and culminating in the Thirteenth Amendment of the U.S. Constitution. In this account, Article VI twists and turns behind the scenes—guided, in part, by the careful hand and keen verbal acuity of Jesse Thomas—until it emerges in the Missouri Compromise and finally in the Illinois constitutional convention fight to legalize slavery in 1823. If these twists and turns had gone only slightly differently, Illinois could have become a slave state, which would have dramatically reconfigured the nation's sectional balance.

The idea of drawing a geographical line dividing slave and free, as was done in the Missouri Compromise, was, at first, repugnant to most members of Congress. Many who favored the elimination of slavery argued instead for temporal solutions—that is, gradually dismantling slavery in steps delayed to future points in time, as Jefferson had first suggested. It proved, however, impossible to devise a temporal solution that would apply uniformly throughout the country, or even throughout the western territories. A temporal solution might conceivably have led to the gradual extinction of slavery and avoided the ultimate bloodshed of the Civil War; but, after months of fruitless argument, no such solution appeared feasible, and even the ungainly Missouri Compromise was agreed upon only at the eleventh hour, by a single vote, through the efforts of a group of dedicated and skilled negotiators.

It was an inelegant solution, as political compromises usually are, and particularly difficult to defend. Arguably, however, the $36°30'$ line of latitude established by the Missouri Compromise was not the first geographical line dividing slave and free. Without focusing explicitly on what they were doing, the authors of the Northwest Ordinance had in 1787 already introduced the notion of a geographical dividing line between North and South, in that case the aqueous line of the Ohio River rather than a line of latitude. Thirty-three years after this first experiment with line drawing, the Missouri Compromise marked the fateful turning point when a very conscious geographical dividing line was drawn between slave and free—a line that purported to apply only to the area west of the Mississippi River but that, in fact, was extended backward in the national consciousness along the Ohio River and then even farther along

Over time, a wealth of names in southern Illinois has grown out of its identification with Egypt, including Goshen, the village later renamed Edwardsville; Carmi, a village platted on the Little Wabash River and named after the nephew of the biblical Joseph; Thebes, the county seat of Alexander County; Cairo, at the confluence of the Ohio and the Mississippi Rivers; the failed town of Alexandria, laid out on the Mississippi River between Thebes and Cairo; Dongola, named after the ancient city on the upper Nile; the Lake of Egypt; and, finally, Karnak, which was not created until the early part of the twentieth century.

the Mason-Dixon Line, which extended roughly from the source of the Ohio to the Eastern Seaboard. The eastern extension of this dividing line came into focus only as slavery was gradually eliminated north of it in the opening years of the nineteenth century. The dividing line led ineluctably to the illogical and unsustainable conclusion that America's fundamental principles could be applied differently in different parts of the country. It may have been the only conceivable basis on which the argument over slavery could have been resolved in 1820, but it also contained within itself the seeds of the Civil War.

In meticulously crafting the Missouri Compromise, Jesse Thomas applied his hard-won understanding of Article VI. It was his careful language, drafted and redrafted in four separate versions during the deliberations, each one playing on different shades of politically expedient ambiguity, that finally served to draw Congress through one of its most flammable periods of stalemate. Not only was he, as a very junior U.S. senator, the author of the amendment that became the heart of the Missouri Compromise, but he also was later chosen chairman of the conference committee that finally resolved the issue.

The dividing line between slave and free that resulted from the protracted Missouri crisis gave the nation, and the North in particular, the time to develop the strength and cohesion to withstand the stress of the Civil War. If the crisis had come to a head in 1820 instead of being postponed for thirty-four years, the Union likely would not have survived and would have broken into two, or possibly three, parts; and no one who had lived through the Hartford Convention at the end of 1814 or would live through the Nullification Crisis in 1832 could doubt that the country was fragile enough at that early point in its history to come apart at the seams. The sectional stresses between North and South made the future of the new western states and territories critically important. This book is an account of how the theme of slavery was intertwined with the history of America's burgeoning western empire and the untrammeled pursuit of property and power that occurred there. Jesse Thomas, his older brother, Richard, and their younger half brother Michael Jones were all drawn to this new center of power at the confluence of the Ohio and Mississippi Rivers, to an area that came to be known as Egypt because it shared with the Nile a rich fertility and a perceived dependence on slave labor.

CHAPTER 1

From Maryland to Kentucky: First Steps toward Egypt

esse Thomas's forebears had lived on the American frontier for generations, from the time when that frontier had been on the Eastern Seaboard. He was descended from two well-established Maryland families. His mother, Sabina, had a pedigree reflecting the full range of Maryland history. On her mother's side, she was a descendant of George Calvert, the first Lord Baltimore, who, as an idealistic protector of persecuted Catholics, was the prime mover behind the colony. She was also descended from one of Maryland's most powerful early Protestants, Robert Brooke, and from Kittamaqund, the *tayac*, or chief, of the Piscataway tribe that controlled the part of Maryland where the colonists first settled. On her father's side, Sabina was a scion of the Semmes family, which had been in Maryland since 1662.

The first Jesse Thomas, Sabina's husband and the father of Richard and Jesse, had a difficult life. Although also descended from some of the earliest settlers of Virginia and Maryland, he had inherited a black sheep strain that had been in the family for generations. He was the youngest child in a family of eight, and his father died before he could revise his will to include Jesse. He was brought up by his brother Thomas, almost twenty-five years older than he, who treated him more like a son than a brother. Thomas Thomas had commercial interests in western Maryland and Kentucky, and so, with his help, Jesse went to work as a boatman and merchant on the Potomac moving goods up and down the river.

The elder Jesse Thomas led a peripatetic existence. His name cropped up in Shepherdstown, Hagerstown, Frederick, and Leesburg, all towns on the Potomac or its tributaries. He moved his cargoes in flat-bottomed boats known as scows, with square ends, one or more retractable keels, and sometimes a sail. Jesse probably carried upstream his brother's goods and other merchandise intended for the frontier, along with the occasional pioneer family, and then downstream the tobacco that was at the time the lifeblood of the Potomac. The cargoes were valuable, and working the river was a difficult and risky occupation. Jesse was well into his forties by the time he married Sabina, but he continued to lead a tenuous existence. In 1772, at about the time of his marriage, he was involved in an altercation over a boat and ended up in a Frederick jail, where his elder brother had to bail him out.[1]

The eldest son of Jesse and Sabina Thomas was born in Washington County, Maryland, in 1773, probably at or near Sabina's family home in the Antietam Valley, and was named Richard Simms Thomas after Sabina's father. Jesse Burgess Thomas, his younger brother, was born in nearby Shepherdstown, then in Virginia, now in West Virginia, two years later. Jesse's middle name suggests some connection with the Burgess family of Anne Arundel County, a connection of which he was so proud in later life that he gave that name to principal streets in two towns he helped organize.[2] Jesse the boatman, not yet forty-eight, died soon after his second son and namesake was born, providing as poorly for his sons as his father had for him. As was customary at the time, Sabina did not wait long after his death to remarry. On September 5, 1780, in Hagerstown, she married Michael Jones, a widower and Revolutionary War soldier with three small children of his own. He proved a good stepfather to Richard and Jesse, who were about seven and five at the time of the marriage. He took his new wife and her two sons, along with his own children, to the southeast corner of Pennsylvania just above the western end of the not-yet-surveyed Mason-Dixon Line. They lived on Muddy Creek in what was then Westmoreland County in a homestead Michael built and called Jones' Arbor. On May 19, 1781, not long after her arrival, Sabina gave birth to another son, who was named Michael after his father.

A few years later, the elder Michael took his growing family down the Ohio into Kentucky. They settled in the town of Washington in what was then Fayette County in trans-Appalachian Virginia and carved a new home out of the wilderness. All the children in the Jones family, including Michael's stepsons, Jesse and Richard Thomas, grew up on, or near, the land where he first settled in Kentucky, working on the family farm and attending the few schools available to them. Sabina and Michael had three more children in Kentucky. Then in 1794, a few months after Richard Thomas had reached

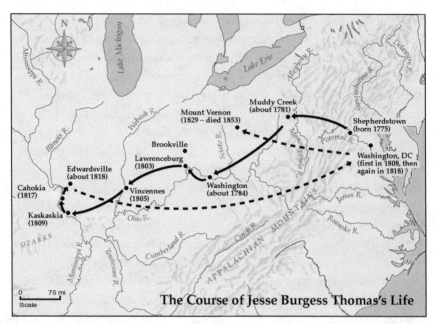

The Course of Jesse Burgess Thomas's Life

Jesse Burgess Thomas shared a typically American trait of moving on without looking back until he finally settled in Mount Vernon, Ohio, where he spent the last twenty-four years of his life.

the age of twenty-one, the elder Michael Jones died, creating a new sense of urgency and responsibility for Richard and Jesse and their half brothers to take on responsibility for their family and their futures.

After growing to adulthood in Kentucky, Richard, Jesse, and Michael moved north across the Ohio River and then westward in fits and starts to the area known as Egypt at the confluence of the Ohio and the Mississippi Rivers. They were drawn down the Ohio to the Mississippi by the lure of inexpensive, fertile land and the power and position that could come with it. The brothers proved to be ambitious and close-knit, looking out for each other with tenacity and ingenuity, and they were intent on establishing a significant base of power and influence in that promising part of the growing country.

The three brothers followed similar paths in Kentucky as they prepared to launch themselves on very parallel lives. All three sought out the best legal education available in a time when attending college was not a practical alternative. It appears Richard Thomas began his practice in Mason County, and Jesse Thomas studied law with him. Michael Jones then repeated the pattern, probably studying with both his half brothers. Instead of receiving the kind of academic training lawyers receive today, all three cemented their legal knowledge by becoming clerks of the county courts where they lived. In this role, they serviced and tracked cases as they passed through the court system, which was a superb way to learn the law while drawing a salary on which to live. They all learned their craft well.[3]

Jesse seemed intent on establishing a career that would not compete with his older brother, who was already one of the more established and well-regarded lawyers in Mason County. Jesse therefore began his practice of law in Brooksville, the county seat of the newly created Bracken County, which had been carved off of Mason County. As a first step toward independence, Jesse became the county clerk of the new county while continuing to read law with his older brother. In turn, Jesse mentored the young Michael Jones in this important role by making him the assistant clerk in Bracken County.[4]

So it was that, as the eighteenth century was drawing to a close, the two Thomas brothers and the younger Michael Jones were beginning their lives, competent and ambitious and thinking about starting their own families. In May 1795 Richard married Frances Pattie, known as Franky, and shortly afterward Jesse also married. He had been wed scarcely a year when his wife died.

All three brothers, like their fathers before them, were growing restless and looking westward. Kentucky held no further fascination for them, even though the town of Washington, which had grown up with them, had by then twenty flourishing stores, two taverns, ten mechanics' shops, three rope walks, and three churches and had become the center of education and fashion in Kentucky, with visitors coming from Lexington and surrounding settlements to buy, sell, and socialize. Evidently, however, the three young men felt that there were going to be even greater opportunities for them farther west.[5]

In Jesse's case, the decision to move west was spurred by his wife's death. It is unlikely that this was the only impetus for his decision, but it clearly was a factor, just as Richard's growing family was a factor in holding him back and delaying his westward migration. Jesse departed for the Indiana Territory in 1803. A testimonial signed by nineteen of his Kentucky neighbors and intended as a reference for him stated that "as an officer he hath conducted himself with uprightness and integrity and to general satisfaction and that as a gentleman his character from his infancy hitherto stands unimpeached." The testimonial is a solid description of the qualities in Jesse Thomas that were to carry him to distinction later in his life, making him a successful politician and a convincing advocate.[6]

CHAPTER 2

The Northwest Territory: Organizing an Expanding Nation

During the time Jesse Thomas was growing up in frontier Pennsylvania and Kentucky, the part of the new country lying west of the original thirteen colonies was in limbo, which, in general, was a concern only to those Americans who lived on the frontier or intended to speculate in western lands. Seven of the original thirteen states had claims to western lands and six did not. This caused conflict among the seven so-called landed states and resentment on the part of the six landless states, which contended that all western lands belonged in common to all thirteen of the original states and that no state had the right to impose conditions when handing over those lands to the federal government. Since all these lands ended up belonging to the federal government, whether they were previously owned separately or in common may appear not to matter. However, if Virginia owned its western lands separately, it could validly argue its right to impose conditions on the cession of those lands. In the final Virginia cession treaty in 1784, the federal government accepted the view that a ceding state could impose conditions, and one of the conditions it agreed to was that the federal government would respect prior property rights, including property rights in slaves. This set up a conflict between Article VI's prohibition of slavery and the federal government's commitment to protect property rights.[1]

The subject of slavery in the western territories had at first been obscured by the all-consuming competition to control, and profit from, the cornucopia of western lands. Few could envision a future in which many new states would be added, much less one in which a prohibition on slavery might be imposed on the newcomers. Many, even in the South, honestly wanted to eliminate slavery in the years following independence. Few on either side of the debate had thought through the implications of territorial expansion for political control of the Senate and the other instrumentalities of a federal government that still seemed largely theoretical. Because of these uncertainties, there was a brief moment in the last decades of the eighteenth century when an open and generous prohibition of slavery in the West might have been possible.

The fractious colonies had only barely managed to ratify their independence from Britain in 1783, and they were even less prepared to deal with a new wrangle over the protection of property rights in slaves in the newly ceded territories; but settlers were pouring over the Appalachians, and the federal government had to organize them. Working out a way to administer new territories became critical to avoid dissension among the states and to deal with Native Americans on the frontier, so the ineffectual Continental Congress took up the issue and assigned it to a committee chaired by Thomas Jefferson. In the final, and arguably the most important, legislative work of his career, Jefferson led his committee to put forward two seminal proposals in the spring of 1784, both written out in his own hand. The first dealt with the organization of western government and the second with the survey and sale of western lands. Neither was enacted as Jefferson's committee recommended, but his proposals provided the foundation for later developments in those two areas.

The first of Jefferson's proposals, generally known as the Ordinance of 1784, demonstrated his occasional farsightedness on the subject of slavery. It dealt with all the western territories, both north and south of the Ohio River, and is critical to an understanding of the American West and its tortured history with slavery. He proposed that after the year 1800 there would be no slavery in any state created out of any of the western lands, including even those south of the Ohio River not yet formally ceded to the federal government by North Carolina, South Carolina, and Georgia. This provision, unlike most other concepts set forth in the Ordinance of 1784, had no precedent and was evidently the product of Jefferson's own thinking. The Ordinance of 1784 also lacked the specific language of the Northwest Ordinance protecting preexisting property rights (the provision later used to defend preexisting slavery in the Northwest Territory), although Jefferson may still have had in mind that existing slavery would be protected by other language in his ordinance.

Although Jefferson's antislavery provision was defeated by a single vote, the outcome would have been different had two delegates not been too ill to vote, and the provision would not have been stripped out of the bill before its final passage. But Jefferson did not seem to fight very hard to preserve it, and there is an ongoing debate about how serious he really was about his proviso. Jefferson's delay of his ban on slavery to the year 1800 or until after statehood, whichever was later, also created the real possibility that slavery would by that time have gained enough of a foothold that it would be difficult to dislodge. His idealism on slavery was uniformly trumped by hard realities on the ground, and he found it easier to confront the evils of slavery in distant locales than he did nearer home in Virginia. Nonetheless, if either of those two ill delegates had been well enough to vote and the antislavery proviso had passed, the nation's history might have been very different.[2]

Although Jefferson's antislavery proviso was an admirable initiative, his draft ordinance also set forth the principle that new territories would be admitted as states on an equal footing with the existing states, which had crucial implications for the slavery debate. Arguably the first time in the history of the world that vassal territory was given this right, the concept of "equal footing" carried over into the Northwest Ordinance. Inhabitants of new territories reasoned that, if they were to be on an equal footing with the existing states, property rights in slaves had to be protected as they had been in the thirteen original states.

Later in that spring of 1784, Jefferson was appointed to a diplomatic post in Paris, where he would remain until 1788, so his proposals had to be worked out by others as the Continental Congress faltered and the Constitution was being negotiated and implemented. The Ordinance of 1784, without the antislavery proviso, was passed by the Continental Congress but never went into effect, being replaced in its entirety by the Northwest Ordinance of 1787. Jefferson's antislavery proviso was later resuscitated by others, in slightly different form, in Article VI of the Northwest Ordinance, but it had provided for the first time the core words used later in the Northwest Ordinance and also in the Missouri Compromise and the Thirteenth Amendment, namely that there "shall be neither slavery nor involuntary servitude . . . otherwise than in the punishment of crimes whereof the party shall have been duly convicted to have been personally guilty."[3] Although ultimately cut from the Ordinance of 1784 before its passage by the Continental Congress, the proviso represented the highpoint of Jefferson's own personal idealism with respect to slavery. From that point on, he slid into temporizing and pessimism on the question.

In the years following the rejection of Jefferson's antislavery amendment, the issue of slavery in the West came into clearer focus, particularly in the area north of the Ohio with the overlapping claims. Of the four states—Virginia, Massachusetts, New York, and Connecticut—that had ceded overlapping claims, three were nonslave, but the fourth, slaveholding Virginia, was the only one with a claim to the entire area and the only one to have staked its claim on the ground. After Jefferson's departure for Paris, the more practical James Monroe became the new moving spirit behind territorial organization. The committee he headed drafted the Northwest Ordinance, the first operational blueprint for America's western expansion, which passed on July 13, 1787, as one of the last acts of the Continental Congress. Monroe recognized that slavery could not be effectively ended south of the Ohio and so limited the ordinance to the area north of the Ohio and east of the Mississippi comprising the present-day states of Ohio, Indiana, Michigan, Illinois, and Wisconsin and the eastern part of Minnesota, as contrasted with Jefferson's effort that had addressed all western territories, even those in the South and those that had not yet been ceded. It was ironic that just as the much sought after Union was being formed, it had already started a process of division that would find its final articulation in the Missouri Compromise.

Monroe's ordinance also complied with the requirement in the final Virginia Deed of Cession that the federal government commit itself to lay out the ceded territory in states that would be "distinct republican states, and admitted members of the federal union; having the same rights of sovereignty, freedom and independence, as the other states." Additionally, Monroe recognized the need to reduce the ultimate number of western states that could be formed north of the Ohio and convinced Virginia to alter its act of cession to provide for larger states; in the end, the ordinance mandated not less than three nor more than five states to be created in the Northwest Territory. Viewed in the larger context of trans-Appalachian America, balance was becoming important, and Monroe perceived that the western territories claimed by Southern states might form about as many new states as would be formed from the area north of the Ohio. It is no coincidence that four states (Kentucky, Tennessee, Mississippi, and Alabama) were ultimately formed from the Southwest Territory. Finally, Monroe also altered the political process that Jefferson had envisioned in 1784 for the western territories. Jefferson's committee had called for democratic participation from the beginning, but Monroe proposed a far more colonial form of government during the territorial period with a far more limited suffrage than Jefferson had envisioned. If this more colonial model had been actively implemented rather than ignored, the federal government could have exerted more control over how territories dealt with issues like slavery.[4]

The preamble of the Northwest Ordinance clearly stated the principle that new states would be admitted "to a share in the federal councils on an equal footing with the original States, at as early periods as may be consistent with the general interest," and its Article V ordained that new states "shall be admitted . . . into the Congress of the United States, on an equal footing with the original States in all respects whatever." By saying not once but twice that the new states were to be admitted on "an equal footing with the original states," the ordinance created an assumption of equality that must have influenced the Constitutional Convention as it drafted provisions relating to territories and statehood.

Monroe ensured that a new compromise on slavery was set forth in the Northwest Ordinance's Article VI to stand in place of Jefferson's antislavery proviso, which had been similarly numbered. Selectively echoing Jefferson's language, Monroe's Article VI provided that "there shall be neither slavery nor involuntary servitude in the said territory, otherwise than in the punishment of crimes whereof the party shall have been duly convicted." Monroe's provision gave up on Jefferson's prohibition of slavery south of the Ohio and added the fugitive slave provision recognizing the right of Southerners to pursue runaway slaves into the North and reclaim them—a provision that was to inflame abolitionist sentiment in the years ahead. There are other important differences between Article VI of the Northwest Ordinance and Jefferson's antislavery proviso. Monroe's Article VI went into immediate effect, whereas Jefferson built a postponement into his antislavery proviso (to 1800 or statehood, whichever was later), suggesting the possibility that, when push came to shove, the ban on slavery might be postponed further or dropped altogether. Even more significantly, Monroe's Article VI, by its terms, applied only during the territorial period, whereas the antislavery proviso would have applied only after statehood.

Both Jefferson's antislavery proviso and the new Article VI in the Northwest Ordinance offered hope to both sides in the slavery debate, but in different ways. Jefferson's proviso, by allowing slavery during the territorial period (or until 1800 if a territory became a state before that time), set the stage for a possible change in the rules if slavery became firmly enough established during the territorial period. Opponents of slavery, on the other hand, held onto the hope that, under the proviso, no careful slave owners would consider bringing slaves to a territory where they might face compulsory emancipation upon statehood. Monroe's Article VI, by contrast, held out the hope for antislavery activists that if there were no slavery in a territory up to the time of statehood, then it would be unlikely that the new state would choose slavery, whereas proslavery activists argued that a new state could amend its constitution and choose slavery if it wished. Both provisions were ambiguous in different ways, but the ambiguities were necessary to garner support. On balance, however, the ambiguity of the new Article VI was to prove more dangerous than that of Jefferson's proviso because it held out the hope that states, once formed, could change the rules on slavery without consulting Congress.

There were further troubling ambiguities embedded in the Northwest Ordinance that undermined antislavery activists' wishful interpretation of Article VI as a permanent prohibition of slavery in the Northwest Territory. For starters, there were the enigmatic descriptions of the threshold populations required to enter the second stage of territorial government and then later to become a state: in both cases the thresholds were based on the number of "free" male inhabitants. Certainly Congress would not have included this description if it had not also contemplated the existence of unfree inhabitants, and there is no question of who those would be. Second, in the three previous colonial governments in the Old Northwest, those of France, England, and Virginia, assurances had been given that the property rights of previous inhabitants would be protected if they pledged loyalty to the new government. The French had introduced slavery into Illinois as early as 1720, and, to the extent that French citizens and later slaveholders were willing to pledge their loyalty to successive governments, they believed their rights in their slave property would be protected.[5] Carrying this property rights argument to its logical conclusion, since all settlers were to be on an equal footing under the Northwest Ordinance and since earlier settlers were allowed to hold the slaves they already owned, then all settlers arguably should have the right to continue owning slaves possessed in 1787 or at such later time as they came to the Northwest Territory. All of this considerably watered down Article VI, making it hard to determine what categories of slavery had actually been forbidden. Thus Congress itself was the first author of ambiguity on slavery in the Northwest Territory, first holding out to antislavery activists the promise of the new Article VI and then protecting the owners' rights in existing slaves.

The Northwest Ordinance was hammered out earlier in the same year that the U.S. Constitution was negotiated. The latter's Article IV, §3, governing the administration of territories and the admission of states, was influenced by the country's already quite extensive experience with statehood. The Constitution's handling of territories and new states was part and parcel of the rough and pragmatic compromises on slavery and political power made elsewhere in the original Constitution. Those early compromises almost assured that later compromises would be necessary, similarly messy, and destined to come to a bad end. These unsatisfactory compromises were to reemerge in the Missouri debates.

The first constitutional compromise was the so-called three-fifths rule, which provided that in apportioning representatives, population was to be determined by "adding to the whole number of free persons, including those bound to service for a term of years, and excluding Indians not taxed, three-fifths of all other persons." The purpose of the three-fifths rule was to swell the population in the slaveholding states to give them more weight in the House of Representatives than justified by their white populations. It is interesting to note that Illinois' use of indentured servitude as a proxy for slavery also allowed it, as a territory and prospective state, to count all its slaves, not just three-fifths of them, in its population. The population of the North, however, had grown far more rapidly than that of the South, so the North by 1820 dominated the House even with the three-fifths rule in effect, but that just made it that much more important for the South to defend the rule. Northerners argued that the three-fifths rule deprived them of fair representation, while Southerners claimed that the rule had been a vital concession by the North in the Constitutional Convention. Though the three-fifths rule related to slavery, it is important to note that its real essence was the appropriation of an unfair share of political power by the South that the South deemed necessary for self-defense but that was deeply resented by the North.[6] Northerners had no wish to extend that injustice west of the Mississippi.

The second of the original constitutional compromises on slavery prohibited Congress from outlawing the international slave trade prior to 1808.[7] This provision put off the slave trade question for twenty years, thus giving slave states the time necessary to import enough slaves that further importation would be unnecessary. After these two awkward entanglements with slavery in the Constitutional Convention, the subject did not come up again until 1790, when Quakers in the Pennsylvania Abolition Society petitioned Congress to discourage the slave trade and slaveholding, producing an uproar in Congress. On that occasion the House resolved that the federal government had no power to regulate slavery in the states, and, before the eruption of the Missouri controversy, most members of Congress believed that to be the correct conclusion.

Under the system of governance set up by the Northwest Ordinance, each territory that was created was to pass through two distinct stages of territorial government on its way to statehood. During the first stage, the governor and three territorial judges, all appointed by Congress, were to have almost complete control, exercising virtual martial law.[8] It was only when the adult free male population of the territory reached five thousand that some limited democratic institutions could be introduced in what became known as the second stage of territorial government. Even then, only one house of the territorial general assembly was to be popularly elected, the governor had the absolute right to call and to dismiss the general assembly and to veto any legislation he found unacceptable, and the territory's only representation in Congress was a nonvoting delegate. This second stage of territorial government was to last until the adult male population reached the level of the least populous of the original states, which at the time was roughly sixty thousand; application could then be made for statehood.

During the first decade after passage of the Northwest Ordinance, there were very few Americans in the Northwest Territory, and its leaders struggled to implement even the first rudimentary steps of territorial government. Then, with the Treaty of Greenville in 1795, Americans finally had their entry wedge. In the years following, the floodgates of immigration opened into the area north of the Ohio River, first into what would become the state of Ohio and then into what would become Indiana. Settlers came down the Ohio River, and north across it from Kentucky, in droves despite the fact that the Native Americans were yielding ground only grudgingly. The federal government was not really prepared to protect the settlers or administer a government for them; and the unremitting pressure of settlement stayed consistently ahead of its ability to do so.

There were other obstacles standing in the way of the settlement of the Northwest Territory. In defiance of their undertakings in the treaty that ended the Revolutionary War, the British still refused to vacate their forts along the Great Lakes at Buffalo, Detroit, and Mackinac; and the Spanish denied free navigation down the Mississippi and through New Orleans. The issue of the British forts was not finally resolved until John Jay's treaty of 1794, and the Mississippi was not opened to navigation until the Treaty of San Lorenzo in 1795 (although it was to be shut down again in 1802 when Spain secretly ceded Louisiana to the French). The ability to ship down the Mississippi and through New Orleans was a critical factor for the development of the Northwest Territory because, before the advent of the steamboat, it was not practicable to ship goods upstream toward Pittsburgh. This economic fact of life was the reason early Illinois oriented itself to the South, and it was one of the principal catalysts for the Louisiana Purchase in 1803.

In the end though, it was not military victories or diplomatic breakthroughs that expanded the American frontier but rather the relentless pressure of the rising tide of new settlers, and it was as a part of that tide that Jesse Thomas, preceded by Michael Jones and followed by Richard Thomas, pulled up stakes in Kentucky and left for the promised land across the river. The brothers departed the relative security of Kentucky in the reverse order of their ages, which was logical since the depth of their professional roots in Kentucky was related to the length of time they had practiced law there, thus making it harder for Jesse to leave than for Michael, and harder for Richard than for Jesse. In addition, Michael was the only one who had not yet married and Richard the only one with children, so the ties of family also played a role. The opening of the Northwest Territory for large-scale immigration was, however, an irresistible lure. All three brothers had been well on their way to establishing successful legal careers in Kentucky, but none of them could resist the clarion call of cheap and plentiful land in a new country where ambitious and accomplished men were going to be few and far between.

CHAPTER 3

In the Shadow of Slavery

Michael Jones crossed into Ohio in 1802, a year before it split off from the Northwest Territory to become a state. Although not yet twenty-one, he was already experienced enough as a lawyer to be appointed a justice of the peace for Hamilton County soon after his arrival. Less than two months later, and still shy of his twenty-first birthday, he was elected an associate judge of the Eastern Circuit Court of Common Pleas in Hamilton County, which then sat in Cincinnati.[1]

Jesse Thomas was the next brother to cross the Ohio River. Not yet thirty, Jesse had grown into a man of sound intellect and persuasive charm. He was usually calm and thoughtful, and he possessed analytical and political skills that were respected by his neighbors in the new territory. His ability to be dispassionate, objective, and discreet made him a sought-after presence. He was an imposing figure, six feet tall and weighing over two hundred pounds, with a dark but ruddy complexion, dark hazel eyes, and dark brown, almost black, hair. His physical presence was part of his hold over other men. Already there was a dignity about him that would be a feature throughout his life, even though his plain features and his hair, cut straight around his neck, gave him a simple, direct look. He came across as a man of the people—plain in dress, language, and manners; sociable and affable; and consequently popular with all classes—however, he just as clearly projected a sense of entitlement and position. His courteous and respectful bearing won and retained the loyalty and confidence of his friends and others with whom he came in contact. John Reynolds, a future governor of Illinois, looking back on his association with Thomas, described him as "a gentleman of fine appearance and address" who had a saying on which he acted considerably: that "you could not talk a man down, but you could whisper him to death." Thomas Ford, another future governor, made reference to the same saying and described Thomas as "a large, affable, good-looking man, with no talents as a public speaker; but he was a man of tact, an adroit and winning manager."[2]

Jesse settled in the town of Lawrenceburg in what is now Indiana, about sixty miles downstream from the part of Kentucky where he and his brothers had grown up. With the formation of Ohio as a new state that year, the remainder of the Northwest Territory, including Lawrenceburg, became the Indiana Territory and suffered the indignity of slipping back from the second to the first stage of territorial government.[3] The area around Lawrenceburg was formed into a new county named after Secretary of War Henry Dearborn. Although not the most populous county in the Indiana Territory, Dearborn County was the territory's link with the East, and as the first town encountered coming down the Ohio into the Indiana Territory, Lawrenceburg became the principal entrepôt into the new region. The new county seat in a new county in a new territory about to enter the second stage of territorial government looked to be fertile ground for young and ambitious lawyers, which is why Michael soon left Ohio to join Jesse there, beginning the brothers' pattern of leapfrogging westward.

Jesse eagerly renewed his practice of law in Lawrenceburg as one of the first three lawyers in the new town. He lived in a house looking over the river, a near neighbor of Captain Samuel Vance, the original proprietor of the town. By 1806 Michael Jones had also purchased property near Lawrenceburg while living in the town itself in space rented from the Fitch Livery and Undertaking Establishment. Michael shared rooms with James Hamilton, who was to become his friend and business partner. Hamilton proved an important connection for both Michael and Jesse. In 1802 he had been one of the founders of Lawrenceburg, as junior partner first to Vance, who failed in launching the town, and then to Benjamin Chambers, Vance's successor and Jesse's chief rival in Dearborn County, who succeeded. In Lawrenceburg, Hamilton acquired an intimate knowledge of town building and promotion that he later shared with Michael, Jesse, and Richard, to their great advantage.[4]

The area where Jesse Thomas and Michael Jones settled in the southeast corner of the present state of Indiana became known as the Gore. This long, narrow triangular wedge was the one part of land opened to settlement by the Treaty of Greenville that was not included in the new state of Ohio and was, therefore, the only part of the Indiana Territory where settlement could then legally occur. It appeared destined to be the most densely populated area of the Indiana Territory and thus a logical place for Jesse and Michael to set up their legal practices and start their political careers. It also was the part of the Indiana Territory with the strongest links to Ohio and New England and thus had more antislavery settlers than the rest of the Indiana Territory.

In the early years of the Northwest Territory, there were repeated attempts to eliminate, or postpone the effect of, Article VI of the Northwest Ordinance. The first came in 1796, when four slaveholders in the Northwest Territory presented a petition to Congress to permit the introduction of slavery north of the Ohio. Six years later, in 1802, territorial governor William Henry Harrison, believing untrammeled immigration of Southerners and their slaves was necessary to bolster population both for defense against the Indians and to qualify for statehood, called a special convention to petition Congress to suspend Article VI for a period of ten years with the understanding "that the slaves brought into the territory during the continuance of this suspension, and their progeny, may be considered and continued in the same state of servitude, as if they had remained in those parts of the United States, where slavery is permitted, and from whence they may have been removed." Harrison and his allies apparently also believed that Article VI's prohibition on slavery would have only prospective application and that any slave held at the time the Northwest Ordinance was passed in 1787 would remain a slave thereafter.[5]

In response to the passage of Harrison's petition, a meeting was immediately called in Clark County, recently formed next to Jesse Thomas's Dearborn County, at which an opposing memorial to Congress was passed asserting that many people had immigrated to Indiana because it was a place free of slavery and requesting that Congress take no action to alter Article VI. To their credit, the Congresses during Jefferson's two administrations were opposed to the temporary or permanent suspension of Article VI, and no action was taken on these proslavery petitions. If Jefferson himself had any part in rejecting them, it would have been an admirable follow-up to his original authorship of the antislavery proviso in 1784, but there is no record that he was involved. When the U.S. Senate committee to which the 1802 petitions were referred concluded that it was not expedient to suspend Article VI, the governor and judges of the Indiana Territory promptly responded by passing an indenture statute like Virginia's, which was very close to slavery.[6] It was the best they could do at the time, though it fell short of the expectations of proslavery advocates.

As the issue of slavery evolved in the Indiana Territory, Thomas Jefferson surprised his countrymen and the world with his purchase of Louisiana in 1803. With the stroke of a pen, Jefferson transformed the country's concept of itself and reordered all considerations of slavery in the western territories. Missouri, as part of the Louisiana Purchase, was an entirely new type of colonial frontier for the young American Republic. None of the original states had any claims there, and the only limitations on federal power in the purchase were the constitutional provision on the administration of territories and the terms of the treaty with France by which the new territory had been acquired. The constitutional provision stated simply that Congress "shall have Power to dispose of and make all needful Rules and Regulations respecting the Territory or other Property belonging to the United States," and the 1803 treaty with France provided that "the inhabitants of the ceded territory shall be incorporated in the Union of the United States and admitted as soon as possible according to the principles of the federal Constitution to the enjoyment of all these rights, advantages and immunities of citizens of the United States."[7]

These provisions had to be interpreted in the context of earlier initiatives to mold American territories east of the Mississippi, which had called for the unorganized territories to be admitted when feasible on an equal footing with the original states of the Union. The meaning of "equal footing" would prove as elusive on the western bank of the Mississippi as on the eastern. Some believed that the federal government, having negotiated the Louisiana Purchase with a foreign power, would have more power to set the rules there than it had in the Northwest Territory or in the other earlier territories east of the Mississippi that it held under agreement with the original states. Jefferson toyed briefly with the notion that Congress might make new rules in the Louisiana Purchase. He certainly considered keeping the new territory under firm military control, barring further settlement by Europeans and using it instead as a place to settle Eastern Indian tribes being displaced by American settlers streaming westward. The French and the other white settlers already in Missouri were upset, however, by any talk of the territory's transformation into an Indian reservation or of any limitation on slavery and wasted no time in pressing for a different solution, more like what had been worked out in earlier American territories.[8]

By 1803 Jefferson had been president for two years and had been transformed from an idealist into a pragmatist. He soon concluded that it made no sense to waste political capital on idealistic gambits to protect Native

Americans or slow the spread of slavery. Congress agreed. In the end, the white settlers in Missouri succeeded in having the basic structure of the Northwest Territory, minus the prohibition on slavery, instated in Missouri. Thus Missouri was allowed to follow the same roadmap Kentucky had followed in 1792 and Tennessee in 1796, and an opportunity to redefine the role of the federal government in dealing with slavery in the territories was lost. The talk about Indian preserves and prohibitions of slavery had, however, poisoned relations between the new citizens of Missouri and the federal government. Destabilizing suspicions had been sown in the hearts of the Missouri elite, and these suspicions would give rise to a streak of independent stubbornness that was to wreak havoc over time.[9]

The Louisiana Purchase suddenly transformed the Indiana Territory from America's westernmost frontier into a backwater, and all calculations about the future course of slavery were altered. The settlers along the Ohio now had to face the possibility that the territory and future state of Missouri, which had had slavery for a century, might ultimately come into the Union as a slave state. This was uniformly perceived at the time as giving Missouri an unfair economic advantage. By failing to extend Article VI's ban on slavery, even with all of its faults, to the newly purchased territory, the United States lost one of its last realistic opportunities to dramatically expand the area where there were at least some barriers to slavery.[10]

After three years in the first stage of territorial government under the firm control of Governor Harrison and its three territorial judges, Indiana had considerable support to enter the second stage of territorial government. Although Harrison was initially opposed to an initiative that would curtail his prerogatives, he was eventually persuaded to support the transition. The standards for moving to the second stage of territorial government had been relaxed, and instead of the five thousand free adult males called for by the Northwest Ordinance, the Indiana Territory was allowed to move on to second-stage government when its governor was satisfied that it was the wish of the majority of freeholders. At that point, the benefits of democratically elected government, including a general assembly and a territorial delegate to Congress, were restored to its citizens, who had briefly enjoyed them during the second stage of the Northwest Territory. But, for proponents of slavery in the Indiana Territory, the strongest argument for advancing to the second stage of territorial government was that it would improve the territory's chances of legalizing slavery. It was believed that, if the citizens' rights and interests "are properly represented to Congress, by a delegate, that we will readily obtain what for years, we have solicited in vain," including the repeal of Article VI.[11]

The organization of the territory's first General Assembly was a momentous event for its residents. On January 3, 1805, Jesse Thomas, although a relatively new arrival, was elected the sole representative of Dearborn County, which was one of the smaller of the six counties in the new territory. The assembly was set to convene at Vincennes, an old town with much charm and history on the east bank of the Wabash River that had been one of the original French outposts in North America and was still largely peopled by French settlers living quiet and leisurely lives. The town's only connection with the outside world was a post rider who came once a week over a well-worn buffalo trace winding through the forest from the falls of the Ohio near Louisville.

The House met for a preliminary session in the beginning of February to nominate members to serve in the upper house of the General Assembly. Thomas, though representing one of the smaller counties in the new territory, was chosen to preside as Speaker. It was an auspicious start to his political career, although one that must have been daunting to a young lawyer with no previous experience making laws or conducting the business of a legis-lature. Nonetheless, he clearly possessed a presence and political skills that impressed others. When the preliminary session broke up, Thomas returned to Lawrenceburg. The General Assembly of the Indiana Territory convened for its first regular session at Vincennes on July 29, 1805, and Thomas was again chosen as Speaker.

The legislature kept its sessions to about a month a year, usually right before or after harvest, so members could be at home to get the crops in or otherwise earn a living. Legislators were unpaid, and service in the legislature was a financial sacrifice. Thomas, anxious about how he would make ends meet during his time in Vincennes, was seeking business opportunities at the same time that he was launching his political career. He decided to invest in a sizable piece of property in the northern reaches of Dearborn County. Along with Amos Butler, a neighbor in Lawrenceburg, he established a town in the middle of what would soon become Franklin County and claimed the honor of naming it Brookville after his grandmother Mary Brooke.[12] He was an absentee property owner, apparently brought into the investment to provide political muscle in Vincennes. In that he succeeded admirably, helping to establish the new county and making sure that Brookville would be its county seat. This course of action was accepted practice for political leaders on the frontier who regularly organized towns, counties, and states to benefit lands they had acquired as private citizens.

Meanwhile, Thomas carefully nurtured the relationships that would advance his political career. From his first arrival at Vincennes, he had been a favorite of Governor Harrison. The long, and mostly warm, relationship between the two men likely began even before Thomas arrived for the First General Assembly in 1805; Thomas could not have been elected so quickly to the critical post of Speaker without already having Harrison's confidence. Harrison showed his support in a number of ways. Soon after Thomas arrived in Vincennes, Harrison appointed him deputy attorney general and then captain of the militia, and he continued to make such appointments during the remainder of Thomas's time in Indiana. These appointments came with modest stipends that were important to Thomas.

Harrison, who would go on to be the nation's ninth president, was possibly the most powerful and effective territorial governor in the country's history, as thoroughly in sympathy with the settlers he governed as he was out of sympathy with the Native Americans who were the rightful inhabitants of the frontier. Although not noted for brilliance, his role in the formation of the Whig Party and his subsequent campaigns for the presidency make him an important figure in American history. He likewise remained a significant presence in Jesse Thomas's life. Harrison is known for his heavy-handed dealings with the Indian tribes of the Old Northwest, but of equal importance were his efforts to reshape the policies of the young Republic dealing with public lands. The reform of the country's policies on the sale of public lands is an issue on which Harrison and Thomas, at different times, both had great impact, and it was by far the most vital issue on the frontier, far more important than slavery. This shared interest was the primary reason the two men maintained regard for each other despite antagonism on most other fronts.

Harrison's most significant involvement in public lands policy came at the time of his insurgent campaign in the fall of 1799 to become territorial delegate from the Northwest Territory. He had organized his candidacy around a promise to improve the existing land law, which was not working as envisioned. Upon his arrival in Philadelphia in 1800, Harrison was appointed chairman of the House committee to consider changes in the law. Remarkably, this twenty-seven-year-old nonvoting territorial delegate, working closely with Jefferson's talented secretary of the treasury Albert Gallatin, promptly reported out a new bill that transformed America's land law by proposing a reduction in the minimum size of land sales from 640 to 320 acres, putting ownership within reach of more yeoman farmers. Credit terms were much relaxed, allowing payment over four years instead of one, which allowed a settler to apply the expanding profits from four years of harvests to the purchase price instead of the slim or nonexistent profits to be expected in the first year. Harrison's actions that year won him the respect on which the rest of his career rested and served as a model for other ambitious young men like Jesse Thomas. His one disappointment was his failure to lower the price of lands offered for sale, which Congress insisted on keeping at two dollars an acre. Jesse Thomas was to remedy that twenty years later.

The mechanics of buying public land from the government were also simplified. The Land Ordinance of 1785 had not specifically provided for how or where sales were to occur, and it was a real hardship for settlers, both in time and money, to travel to land auctions at the very few official land offices. At Harrison's urging, Congress in 1800 created four new land offices in the Northwest Territory at Steubenville, Marietta, Chillicothe, and Cincinnati. Although still not easily accessible, this was a great improvement, and offices at Vincennes, Kaskaskia, and Detroit were to follow in 1804 and many more in subsequent years. In addition, each land office was to have a register and a receiver, and their duties were spelled out, with the former responsible for description and documentation of land sold and the latter for receipt of purchase money. The separation of these functions was intended to ensure the independence and integrity of both.

In addition to the new offices of register and receiver, the law also provided for the appointment of panels of land commissioners to work out problems with preexisting titles before lands were offered for sale by the federal government. Usually the register and the receiver of the relevant land office were named as commissioners, and often a third person was named as well. Congress had resolved to take the untangling of land titles out of the hands of overworked territorial governors because of the complexities of the issues with preexisting titles and the governors' lack of time and expertise to do the job properly. This was particularly the case when Harrison became governor of the Indiana Territory, because he, unlike many later territorial governors, was not a lawyer by training and did not have the time necessary to unravel the land issues, being responsible for an immense geographical area undergoing rapid settlement. In fact, he was soon to give up being governor altogether as he became overburdened fighting Indians during the War of 1812.

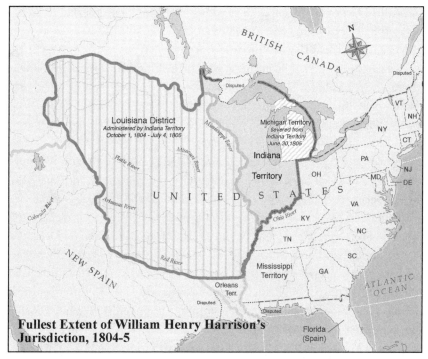

Fullest Extent of William Henry Harrison's Jurisdiction, 1804-5

For a brief time in 1804–5, William Henry Harrison governed a vast area, enclosed on this map by a heavy dark gray line. The western and northern borders of the Louisiana District were at first indeterminate, reflecting uncertainty about the extent of the Louisiana Purchase that would not be resolved until the Treaty of 1818 with Britain and the Adams-Onis Treaty of 1819 with Spain (see map, page 137).

Familiarity with public lands policy formed the basis for the strong relationship between William Harrison and Jesse Thomas and likely also informed their attitudes toward slavery. Neither of them was particularly enamored of the institution of slavery, but both put their trust in Southerners to develop the western regions and likely shared a belief that a system that protected slavery in some fashion was necessary to attract and retain substantial Southern settlers. Slaves may not have had the same economic significance on the frontier as in the South, but Harrison and Thomas respected Southern values and believed that accommodating slavery was a critical step in promoting those values.[13]

Aside from the various offices to which Harrison appointed Thomas, the most important token of Harrison's esteem was his enthusiasm for Thomas's marriage to the widow of John Francis Hamtramck, a distinguished American general whose estate and children had been left in Harrison's charge. Ham-tramck had been a larger-than-life figure, casting his shadow over many of the events that had shaped life on the frontier. At his death in 1803 at the age of forty-six, he had been the second highest ranking officer in the U.S. Army, responsible for holding together its honor and discipline during the tenure of its first ranking officer, Brigadier General James Wilkinson, who many thought had been a coconspirator during Aaron Burr's ill-fated filibuster into the Southwest.

The drowning of his first wife in 1794 had left Hamtramck with two small children, and a year later, at the age of forty, he married the twenty-one-year-old Rebecca McKenzie, reputed at the time to be the "*belle* of Detroit" and characterized later in her life as "a lady of marked and distinguished character." She had been born at the outbreak of the American Revolution on December 1, 1775, in Crown Point, New York, a fort on the shores of Lake Champlain that was hotly contested between Royalists and revolutionaries throughout the war. Her father was a British army officer who died shortly after her birth. Rebecca was brought up by her older brother, Alexander McKenzie, who, like his more famous namesake, the great Canadian explorer, was a fur trader with the North West Company. He took Rebecca with him to Montreal, where he was based, and provided her with a good education that gave her all the accomplishments expected of a well-bred young woman. She then accompanied her brother to Detroit, where he had been sent to oversee one of the North West Company's key outposts. Hamtramck's successful courtship of Rebecca was a victory of romance over politics, culminating as it did in the marriage of the Anglican daughter of a British officer who had fought against the Americans with an anti-British, Catholic officer who had left British Canada to fight on the American side. The one factor they presumably shared was the French language they had both grown up speaking.[14]

In addition to the two daughters from his first marriage, Hamtramck had three more children with Rebecca: John Francis Jr., born in 1798; Alexander McKenzie, born a year later; and Rebecca, born in 1802. All five children were left in Rebecca's care at the time of Hamtramck's untimely death on April 11, 1803, on the eve of his departure to superintend the construction of a new fort at the portage at Chicago. Harrison, as governor and an old battlefield colleague, was named administrator of Hamtramck's estate, along with his widow, and also guardian for his children. Harrison had been visiting Michigan country at the time of Hamtramck's death, and he prolonged his stay there to take charge personally of the administration of the estate. Rebecca may have stayed on briefly in Detroit, but there was a devastating fire there in 1805 that destroyed most of the town and many of Hamtramck's household effects.[15] If she had not already left Detroit, she did so then and went to Vincennes, where it was easier to communicate with Harrison about Hamtramck's estate and the upbringing of his five young children.

It may have been Harrison himself who introduced Jesse Thomas to the young widow, possibly thinking that marrying her to a capable lawyer would be the best way to relieve himself of some of the responsibilities of administering her late husband's estate, or it may have been John Rice Jones, an intriguing character in Indiana and Illinois who had close connections with the Thomas family. Jesse was apparently successful in winning Rebecca's affections during the month-long second session of the First General Assembly. On December 2, 1806, as the session drew to a close, they were married in Vincennes. They were both thirty-one. The courtship may have been brief, but the attachment proved enduring. Jesse and Rebecca were to have a very happy marriage, spanning many years and places. Although they never had children together, Thomas became attached to Rebecca's children by her first marriage, and he and Rebecca were devoted caregivers to the children of his elder brother, Richard, when he died in 1828.

The bridegroom, and perhaps the bride, left a few days after their marriage for Dearborn County to seek his reelection to a second term in the territorial House. Thomas had Harrison's backing in this election because he had lined up with him on most issues of importance during the First General Assembly. The one issue on which Thomas's position was not totally clear was slavery. In both 1805 and 1806, in the first and second sessions of the First General Assembly, a majority of the members of the Legislative Council and the House approved resolutions to be submitted to Congress to suspend Article VI. Thomas, representing a county with pronounced antislavery views, was by this time inclined to go against Harrison and oppose slavery. As Speaker, however, despite the title, he rarely spoke on the merits of any proposition and did not have to vote unless there was a tie. Thus he never had to go on record on slavery in the territorial assembly, while his rivals were often forced to take definite positions.[16]

On February 2, 1807, Jesse Thomas was reelected as representative from Dearborn County in the House. Harrison, for one, believed that, though Thomas had distinguished himself in the General Assembly, his reelection had been in doubt. Soon after the election he wrote Thomas, saying, "I congratulate

you on your election. We had heard that you were not elected." Apparently
Harrison's perception was that Thomas was out of tune with his constituents,
perhaps because of the slavery issue. Thomas was still listed as a resident of
Dearborn County in the territorial census taken that same year but shortly
thereafter changed his residence from Lawrenceburg to Vincennes. It may be
that Rebecca preferred Vincennes, a town she was familiar with. Whatever the
reasons for the move, it weakened Thomas's ties to the antislavery district that
had first elected him. When the first session of the Second General Assembly
convened on August 16, 1807, Thomas was once more chosen Speaker of the
House and was again elected to that post when the second session convened
on September 26, 1808. Thomas thus was Speaker in all four sessions of the
territorial legislature in which he served, from July 29, 1805, to his resignation
on October 24, 1808. He was diligent in his duties, and his signature appears
on almost all the laws passed during that time.[17]

During the first session of the Second General Assembly, the territorial
legislature strengthened the system of indentured servitude that had been
devised to circumvent the prohibition of slavery in Article VI. This was the
first time that the territorial legislature had considered the indenture laws that
had originally been put in place by the governor and territorial judges during
the first stage of territorial government. The new legislation was titled "An act
concerning the introduction of negroes and mulattoes into this Territory" and
was approved by Governor Harrison on September 17, 1807. The first section
of the law provided that "it shall and may be lawful for any person being the
owner or possessor of any negroes or mulattoes of and above the age of fifteen
years, and owing service and labor as slaves in any of the States or Territories
of the United States, or for any citizen of the said States or Territories purchasing the same, to bring the said negroes or mulattoes into this Territory."
The second section required that, within thirty days after bringing a slave into
the territory, the owner must take the slave before the clerk of the court and
negotiate an agreement as to how long the slave should be obligated to serve
his or her master. The negotiation was, however, entirely one-sided, as, if they
disagreed, the master could take the slave to another state and sell him or her.
The third section provided that, if the slave refused to enter into the indenture,
the master could remove that slave to a state where he or she could be held
without complying with such a condition. The thirteenth section required
that a son born in the Indiana Territory of a parent of color serve the master
of such parent until age thirty and a daughter until age twenty-eight. Harsh

though these laws were, it is interesting to note that proslavery frontiersmen in 1807 were willing to adopt a system of gradual emancipation similar to what had been done in New York and other eastern states. If proslavery legislators could have agreed on this approach thirteen years later, the slavery question could conceivably have been resolved without bloodshed.[18]

Two days later the House again approved resolutions to be submitted to Congress to suspend Article VI "for a given number of years." The petition, after candidly recognizing that there existed a difference of opinion on the subject in the territory, laid out two arguments. The first was that the imminent prohibition on further importation of slaves into the United States, which was to go into effect the following year, meant that no further slaves would be added to the existing population and that existing slaves should be dispersed as widely as possible to ease the transition away from slavery. The second argument was that the climate and agriculture in the Northwest Territory made it unlikely there could be any large-scale use of slaves. That petition, passed on September 19, 1807, was typical of its predecessors, proclaiming that "it is not a question of liberty or slavery. Slavery now exists in the United States, and in this Territory. It was the crime of England and their misfortune; and it now becomes a question, merely of policy in what way the slaves are to be disposed of, that they may be least dangerous to the community, most useful to their proprietors, and by which their situation may be ameliorated."[19]

Thomas, as Speaker, was again not required to vote; but there appears to be some evidence of his taking a position opposing the petition and therefore opposing slavery. John Badollet, land register in Vincennes, wrote his friend Albert Gallatin, secretary of the treasury, on December 21, 1807, about the petition, noting that "the former unanimity of the Legislature exists no more, two members of the lower house, in compliance with instructions from the Counties of Dearborn & Clarke [*sic*] have seceded & opposed the measure."[20] Thomas, the sole member from Dearborn County in the lower house, could have demonstrated his lack of support by speaking against the bill, even though he was not required to vote on it. Thomas went on to sign the memorial as Speaker of the House, but that was merely a ministerial act indicating only that the petition accurately reflected the action taken in the House.

As the second session of the Second General Assembly drew to a close, the pace of the slavery debate picked up, and there was an even greater flurry of pro- and antislavery petitions in the General Assembly. General Washington Johnston, chair of the House committee established to consider them and an ardent opponent of slavery, claimed that there were in all these petitions a majority of six hundred persons opposed to the admission of slavery into the territory. Johnston particularly objected to the act passed in the previous session that offered black and mulatto slaves introduced into the Indiana Territory the alternative of either signing a long-term indenture or being sent back to be sold in a slave state. In a moving report that Johnston submitted to the territorial House on behalf of his committee on October 19, 1808, and that was subsequently characterized by Jacob Piatt Dunn as "entitled to rank among the ablest, if not the ablest, of state papers ever produced in Indiana," Johnston proposed legislation banning slavery in the Indiana Territory. The House was swept away by the report and passed his proposal without even a roll-call vote; but, by the time the legislation reached the Legislative Council five days later, the spell was broken, and the bill failed to pass its first reading.[21]

As Jesse Thomas was juggling the issue of slavery, trying to satisfy both his antislavery constituents and his proslavery political allies, he was also drawn deeply into the administration of the 2,363-acre military tract in Ohio that had been awarded to John Francis Hamtramck and inherited by his widow, now Thomas's wife, and her elder son. This property would remain central to Jesse and Rebecca for the rest of their lives, becoming one of the focal points for the entire Thomas family. It was difficult to run the property as an absentee, yet Thomas understood that it was vital to his family's future. Following up on the successful model of Brookville, he worked hard to have a new county created, centered on this large tract, and to have a town established there and made the county seat. He was aided immeasurably in this process by his brother Richard, who was serving in the Ohio senate during the critical time when Knox County was being formed and Mount Vernon was designated as its county seat.

Richard Thomas had moved with his family in 1804 to Lebanon, Ohio, and quickly emerged as a powerful political figure there, assertive, proud, and less likely than Jesse to make compromises. Within two years of his arrival in Ohio, he was elected a state senator in the Fifth General Assembly, which opened in the state capital of Chillicothe on December 1, 1806. Richard, like Jesse and most other political figures on the frontier, was a Republican, although he was not as eager as most other Republicans to put his faith in the popular will and the legislative branch of government to the detriment of the executive and judicial branches. One manifestation of Ohio's extreme democratic outlook was that all state legislators, senators as well as representatives, were elected for one-year terms, answering yearly to the electorate. Richard himself successfully stood for reelection in 1807.[22]

In particular, Richard rejected the extreme distrust of the judiciary that was becoming an article of faith for the more democratic wing of the Republican Party in Ohio. This distrust became particularly intense when the judiciary had the temerity to question the constitutionality of an act of the legislature. Richard believed in the importance of the judiciary and stood up against multiple attempts to impeach or otherwise limit state supreme court judges. He himself was several times an unsuccessful candidate for a seat on the Ohio Supreme Court. Despite his disappointments with the supreme court, Richard Thomas later in 1809 reached the apogee of his political career when he narrowly missed being elected U.S. senator.[23] Despite these political travails and near misses, Richard chose to stay on in Lebanon for several more years and in that time helped to defend Jesse's family property in Knox County from attempts to alter the county boundaries and move the county seat. The two brothers continued to solidify the position of Mount Vernon by seeing to it that the county courthouse was built in 1810 on land Jesse had donated.

Jesse, meanwhile, was doing his best to extricate himself profitably from his initial foray into real estate development in Brookville, Indiana. Although he gradually reduced his role there over the next few years, he was still involved and spent the time necessary to protect his interests. He and Amos Butler hired a surveyor, and he supervised the laying out of a town plat, which was duly recorded on August 8, 1808. He also named the principal street Burgess, after the family that had given him his middle name.[24] While Thomas pursued his on-and-off campaign to market the town from the relative comfort of Vincennes or from his home in Lawrenceburg, Butler actually moved to Brookville and engaged in the more substantive business of building a town.

Butler came to suspect Thomas's commitment to the project. Things came to a head when minor disagreements degenerated into a complete falling out between Butler, Thomas, and other new arrivals. After that it was a free-for-all, with various owners building mills and trying to promote the development of the town on land where they had the greatest interest. But Thomas, with a half interest in the prime real estate and the upper hand in political clout, appears to have had the advantage. His involvement in Brookville and Mount Vernon indicate that land and power remained principal themes for Jesse Thomas.

CHAPTER 4

The Next Slippery Rung on the Political Ladder

In the Second General Assembly in the Indiana Territory, strains began to show between the legislative and executive branches, marking the end of the spirit of cooperation that had previously prevailed. Only three of the five members of the Legislative Council bothered to appear for the session, and William Henry Harrison for the first time vetoed bills passed by the General Assembly. The primary reasons for the friction were personal and again had their roots in the competition for land and power in the territory, but there were also substantive issues, the most important being slavery and a developing tug-of-war over making Illinois a separate territory. As these conflicts intensified, Benjamin Parke, Indiana's first territorial delegate, resigned unexpectedly on March 1, 1808. The strains in the territorial government were to reach their height in the election to replace Parke, and Jesse Burgess Thomas was to defy his governor and risk his political career in hopes of seizing that post and carving out a larger destiny for himself, as Harrison himself had done nine years before in the original Northwest Territory.

By 1808, the Indiana Territory had been independent of the original Northwest Territory for eight years and had been in the second stage of territorial government for three; but it was still in its infant stages. Thomas, without rocking the boat, could have looked forward to a long and promising career in Indiana. He had been from the start a prominent leader in the territorial General Assembly, and some road to advancement would surely have opened before him, even without any active intervention or risk on his part. But slavery was beginning to be a difficult issue for him in Dearborn County, where his constituents were becoming more pronouncedly antislavery. He finally decided to pursue Parke's seat by allying himself with those who wanted to establish a new territory in the sparsely populated Illinois Country, where he could play an even larger role, though he would be trading his antislavery backers in Indiana for proslavery backers in Illinois.

The most influential residents in the Illinois Country had for several years wanted a separate territory to be formed, and Thomas, in his role as Speaker, was familiar with their situation and motives. Harrison was appalled by the initiative. The breakaway territory would be immense, encompassing not just the modern state of Illinois but also all of Wisconsin, part of Minnesota, and part of the upper peninsula of Michigan. Harrison had already seen the Indiana Territory diminished by the loss of the Michigan Territory in 1805, and there had been other erosion as well: four years before, in 1804, when the Louisiana Purchase had been divided into the Orleans Territory, for the area around New Orleans, and the District of Upper Louisiana, for all of the purchase north of the 33rd parallel, Congress had briefly put Upper Louisiana under Harrison's authority, giving him virtual martial law authority over a wider swath than had been assigned any U.S. territorial official before or since. That lasted only a year before Congress created an independent Missouri Territory.

In the previous session of the U.S. Congress, a select committee chaired by Parke had received petitions both supporting and opposing the creation of the Illinois Territory, but Parke, dutiful to Harrison, made sure no action was taken. By 1808, the Illinoisans were again pressing to separate, and Illinois was becoming more strategic and valuable by the day: the British had withdrawn from their forts along the northwestern frontier; the Mississippi River was once again open to American shipping; and Illinois was going to be the entrepôt to the new American West. Although all recognized that Illinoisans would one day have a separate territory and state, Harrison wanted to delay that day as long as possible so that he and his allies in Vincennes could dictate its future. On the other hand, if the Illinois insurgents were successful, Harrison knew he would be left with an Indiana Territory reduced in size to the boundaries of the present state of Indiana, which would be galling. Having reveled in the exercise of power and the extent of his territorial hegemony, Harrison resisted the creation of further territories with his every sinew.[1]

The Illinois separatists were centered in the town of Kaskaskia, which was the hub of political and commercial activity in the Illinois Country. It and its neighboring town of Cahokia were the earliest settlements of the French in the Mississippi and Ohio River valleys during their time of ascendancy, and they continued to flourish until the middle of the nineteenth century. These towns were the essence of the Illinois Country at the time and were the world within which the early territorial history of Illinois unfolded. Kaskaskia began as a French town and a Catholic one, replete with churches and convents, and retained that aura during the rest of its existence. Founded long before Pittsburgh or Cincinnati had even been conceived of, it at one time had a population of seven thousand and was rivaled only by New Orleans in the Mississippi basin. The town was located on a small peninsula on the eastern bank of the Mississippi about fifty miles south of where St. Louis would later be founded. It had been situated on the peninsula to make it more defensible against Indian attack, but the water that protected it also left it vulnerable to the floods that periodically, and ultimately, destroyed it.

By the early 1800s, Illinois' French community, having suffered through fifteen years of British domination, a few years of active control by George Rogers Clark and his Virginians, and then almost twenty years of passive, absentee American government under the Northwest Ordinance, was in a period of serious decline. The earliest American arrivals had been sympathetic with the French culture they found in Illinois at the same time that they looked to profit from its decline. They now actively bought up French land claims and sought the creation of a new and independent government for Illinois that they would dominate. The most active leaders of this faction in Kaskaskia were John Edgar and William and Robert Morrison. They and their allies had been in the area, known generally as the American Bottom, for a long time and had come to believe that the Illinois Country was theirs, to be disposed of as they saw fit.

Those of the Edgar-Morrison clique considered Harrison an interloper with no right to interfere in their affairs. They also had the misfortune of being identified as friends of the Federalists at a time when the political tide in the Northwest Territory was running heavily to the Republicans. They thought that it was likely because of these political differences that Harrison had, by their lights, done so little to protect the scattered settlers in Illinois. For his part, Harrison had resisted Edgar and the Morrisons at every turn. Though never articulated, the most vital issue underlying the separation initiative was the question of who would control the settlement of Illinois' many disputed land claims, a priority that far outweighed the issue of whether Illinois would permit or prohibit slavery. Those in the Edgar-Morrison group had actively bought up claims, both good and shaky, of French settlers and had bolstered them in every way they could think of, some honest and some not, and they were now desperately fighting to defend their claims.

Harrison had earlier convinced Jefferson to appoint a man named Michael Jones as register in the newly created Kaskaskia land office and as land commissioner, along with Elijah Backus, its receiver, to resolve the disputed land claims. John Reynolds described this Michael Jones, who was born in Pennsylvania and is referred to hereinafter as Michael Jones of Kaskaskia, as being "a sprightly man, of plausible and pleasing address. He possessed a good English education and was, in his younger days, well qualified for business if . . . excitable and rather irritable. His mind was above the ordinary range; but his passion at times swept over it like a tornado." The latter part of this description would prove accurate in his dealings with Edgar and the Morrisons.[2]

By 1808 Jones and Backus had already been working for several years on the disputed land titles. As the Edgar-Morrison faction redoubled its attacks, its efforts to end Jones and Backus's work and establish a separate territory took on a new urgency. Michael Jones of Kaskaskia, using his two offices as a springboard, had become the Edgar-Morrison group's nemesis, and matters only became worse when Harrison, without informing Thomas or the Illinoisans, subsequently settled on Jones as his candidate to be Indiana's territorial delegate and oppose the efforts to create a separate Illinois Territory. Meanwhile, Thomas's antislavery constituents in Dearborn County were of two minds as to whether Illinois should be allowed to split off and form a new territory. Sometimes they felt there was a clear antislavery majority in all of the Indiana Territory, at which times they opposed separation, thinking that they had the leverage to prevent slavery in both Indiana and Illinois. On other occasions, when they felt less securely in the majority, they were concerned that Harrison and his faction were going to succeed in sanctioning slavery in the entire territory, and at those times they supported separation, thinking that, if the more virulently proslavery Illinois Country could be carved off, then Indiana, at least, could be safely preserved free of slavery. It is fair to assume that Thomas's views on separation in his early years in the territorial House were as ambivalent as those of his constituents.[3] Somehow he managed to retain the loyalty of his neighbors, who were committed to opposing slavery, while at the same time winning the loyalty of the Illinoisans who wanted to preserve slavery. To the very end he kept the loyalty of the other legislators from Dearborn and Clark Counties, and their support was to prove crucial in his campaign to become territorial delegate. As in Thomas's early days in the General Assembly, his position as Speaker allowed him to avoid going on record on the issue of slavery. However, with all the major territorial leaders and most of the other counties in the territory actively proslavery, and Thomas representing one of the two antislavery counties, he faced a difficult balancing act, not unlike what he would deal with in the Missouri crisis twelve years later. It was probably his first successful effort to straddle the fence on the subject of slavery and taught him much about political nimbleness and the usefulness of ambiguity.[4]

As the time approached for both houses of the General Assembly to meet together to select the new territorial delegate, Thomas felt optimistic. With the pledged support of the representatives and legislative councillors from his home county of Dearborn and the neighboring county of Clark and still believing that Harrison supported him despite his having decidedly different views on slavery from Harrison's other backers, Thomas agreed to attend a caucus on the evening of October 21 to select the Harrison party's candidate for the following day's election, with the implicit understanding that all who attended would be bound by the caucus's choice. But Harrison stunned Thomas by backing Michael Jones of Kaskaskia, who became the choice of the caucus. As Thomas left for his lodgings after the meeting, he viewed this as a personal betrayal, almost as a trick intended to take him out of the running for territorial delegate.

Meanwhile, John Rice Jones, legislative councillor from Knox County and trusted advisor to the Edgar-Morrison faction, was despairing of his chances to elect a pro-separation delegate, even though he knew he was only a few votes short. The morning of the election, as the pro-separation forces met at his lodgings, there was a discussion of what had happened at the caucus the night before, and the Illinois separatists agreed to invite Thomas to attend their meeting. When he arrived, they hammered out an unusual agreement in which, in return for the backing of their group, Thomas signed a document pledging "his honor that he would use his influence to obtain a division of the Indiana Territory to the west of the Wabash, and also use his endeavors to further the interest and wishes of the inhabitants of the Illinois Country conformably to the instructions that might be given him by the members from those counties."[5]

This all happened so close to the time of the vote for territorial delegate that the Harrison faction had no time to react, and with his own vote and that of the other legislators from Dearborn and Clark Counties, Thomas was elected with six votes to three for Jones and one for Shadrach Bond. Tellingly, the *Vincennes Western Sun* of October 29, 1808, asserted that his election came from the fact that "while he opposed the admission of slavery he favored a division of the territory."[6] Both Thomas and Harrison believed themselves double-crossed, and a fissure opened in their friendship that did not resolve itself for several years. Harrison's reaction seems unreasonable because, in 1799, he had been elected as the first territorial delegate from the Northwest Territory in a contentious election (very like the one Jesse Thomas had just gone through in 1808). In that election, Harrison had defeated the son of his territorial governor, Arthur St. Clair, and then persuaded Congress to carve out five new, almost certainly Republican, states from the Northwest Territory rather than the three favored by the Federalist St. Clair.

John Rice Jones, who engineered Thomas's victory, was a fascinating character and a worthy antagonist for Harrison. Born in Wales in 1759 and educated at Oxford in both medicine and law, he came to America in 1784. He spent time in Philadelphia, where he practiced law and made the acquaintance of Dr. Benjamin Rush and Benjamin Franklin. He then decided to move farther west to Kentucky, where he joined General George Rogers Clark's expedition against the Indians on the Wabash in 1786. For four years he lived in Vincennes, serving as commissary-general for Clark's campaigns. Jones's role in the army had brought him into close contact with General Hamtramck, and he knew Rebecca as well. He had gone on to Kaskaskia, on the Mississippi, in 1790, staking a claim as the first English lawyer to practice in Illinois, and had remained a resident of Kaskaskia for eleven years, establishing close relationships with Edgar and the Morrisons. He was aided immensely by being fluent in French, and in 1792 he translated the laws of the Northwest Territory into French for the use of French-speaking judges. He later served as official interpreter and translator for the land commissioners appointed to resolve land titles in Illinois.[7] In 1801 Jones was commissioned attorney general of the Indiana Territory and moved back to Vincennes, where he also was a founder of Vincennes University. In 1802 he served as secretary of the democratically elected convention held at Vincennes that composed and presented to Congress the memorial seeking a ten-year suspension of Article VI of the Northwest Ordinance. He had been an ally of William Henry Harrison during the early part of his career and, with Harrison's support, was elected a legislative councillor from Knox County, which included the territorial capital of Vincennes, but his innate conservatism and his commitment to Illinois soon caused him to grow apart from Harrison.

His son, Rice Jones, was as exceptional as his father, possessing both an intelligence and a political drive that made him a formidable adversary in the struggle over Illinois land rights. Still in his twenties, he was energetic and incisive but also dangerously arrogant. Both Rice and his father were highly competent men, famed for acting with pride and dispatch. Born in Wales and having come to America with his parents, Rice had acquired considerable disputed property with his father, and the two had become the main spokesmen and political operatives for the Edgar-Morrison faction. It was Rice Jones's success in one of the special by-elections for the lower house of the Indiana territorial assembly that put him squarely in the forefront of the impending contest for the control of Illinois, where the Edgar-Morrison group faced off against Michael Jones of Kaskaskia and the diminishing group of Harrison's supporters in Illinois.

Though securing Jesse Thomas's election as delegate was a great victory for the Edgar-Morrison faction, the position Thomas had won was relatively powerless, at least on paper. The post of territorial delegate had not been mentioned in the Constitution and had been created out of thin air by the Continental Congress. The position, mentioned for the first time in Jefferson's Land Ordinance of 1784, had been modeled on the British colonial agent in the pre–Revolutionary War era. The existence of colonial agents was considered one of the safety valves that had prevented an earlier explosion of revolution in the American colonies, and Jefferson envisioned the same sort of role for territorial delegates in the feisty and assertive American West, except that they would play the role in America's capital rather than in London.

A territorial delegate serving in the U.S. House could not vote and therefore seemed consigned to play only a marginal role. It was, however, a position that had its own kind of power. Despite lacking a vote, the delegate could be appointed to committees and was routinely appointed to committees dealing with issues related to his territory, often being designated chairman. The territory's delegate was also its only representative in Washington and was therefore the conduit for all territorial business that needed to be conducted there. Jesse Thomas was certainly cognizant of the way Harrison had used the position of territorial delegate from the Northwest Territory as a springboard to become governor of the newly created Indiana Territory. But Harrison had had a full two-year term to work with, whereas in 1808 the new delegate from the Indiana Territory would be elected only to complete the remaining four months of Parke's term. To further complicate Thomas's calculations, to gain his new position he had defied many of those who had up until then been his political friends. He could therefore expect his erstwhile allies to be lined up in the regular election for territorial delegate the following year to make sure that he was not reelected.

Despite later protestations by John Rice Jones, the so-called bond executed by Thomas seems highly unusual from our perspective. It was accepted practice for state legislatures to instruct their representatives in Congress how to vote on particular measures, though, as was to be the case with the Missouri Compromise, many in Congress disobeyed their instructions, but here Thomas was offering carte blanche, in the form of a binding contract, on matters not yet specified. His commitment was not legally enforceable, since a legislator cannot allow others to exercise the judgment he is supposed to exercise himself; but it was a commitment Thomas would be honor-bound to respect, and he had no clear idea of the true extent of his commitments to the Illinoisans. They were strong men with strong opinions, and Thomas probably felt drawn further into their world than was comfortable for him. He was certainly forced to take a more definitely proslavery stance, at least temporarily, once he had committed himself to the Edgar-Morrison faction. Slavery was far more entrenched in Illinois than in Indiana, and its inhabitants had provided much of the impetus behind the agitation in the early days of the Indiana Territory to limit Article VI.

During the brief time the entire Louisiana Purchase north of what is now Louisiana was placed under the control of the governor of the Indiana Territory, more questions had arisen about slavery in the West: did the assignment of this new territory to the Indiana Territory mean that Article VI of the Northwest Ordinance was to carry over and apply to Upper Louisiana, or was slavery to continue as a sanctioned activity, as it had been under the French and Spanish? Congress no doubt recognized that this was an issue to avoid if possible and within months established a separate Missouri Territory outside the framework of the Northwest Ordinance, which removed Missouri from the shadow of Article VI and protected slavery in the newly acquired territory.

Although the issue of slavery continued to simmer in the territories, it was temporarily put on the back burner following Congress's passage of an act prohibiting the importation of slaves in 1807, the year before Jesse Thomas served his brief tenure in the House of Representatives. The U.S. Constitution had forbidden such an act going into effect before 1807, and its passage in the first possible year, when combined with the almost simultaneous passage of a similar act in England, led many abolitionists to the complacent conclusion that, with the abolition of the international slave trade, domestic slavery would soon be snuffed out. The British Royal Navy did its part to bring about this result. In the period from 1810 to 1860, its West African Squadron seized 1,237 slave ships, freeing 125,830 Africans who were aboard, and took direct action against African tribal leaders who refused to give up the trade, all at tremendous cost in matériel and sailors' lives lost to disease.[8]

There were, however, forces at work in the United States that were about to revive and transform the slave economy. Although slaves were, in theory, no longer imported, the invention of the cotton gin and the rapid expansion of the cotton economy in the Deep South soon led to an expanded internal slave trade. Cotton was not a factor in Missouri, but the cultivation of hemp was growing rapidly and was perceived as requiring slave labor. Unnoticed by Northerners, Virginia and other states with depleted tobacco lands began selling superfluous slaves into these new areas. With the supply of slaves from Africa limited to the small number who could be smuggled into the country, the slaveholders of the Upper South found they had stumbled upon a profitable business. Support for slavery in both the Lower and Upper South experienced an upsurge. Between 1800 and 1810, the slave population grew by 33 percent and then increased an additional 29 percent between 1810 and 1820.[9]

Taking advantage of the brief lull in antislavery activity, the citizens of the territories of the Old Northwest continued their low-key campaign to protect and extend slavery. Some proslavery advocates, including Harrison himself, thought that slavery could be best protected prior to statehood by continuing to present petitions encouraging Congress to amend or delay Article VI and fine-tuning the territorial laws protecting indentured servitude. Thus, in the Second General Assembly, as in the First, the proslavery party adopted a memorial to Congress requesting the suspension of Article VI, which was adopted both in the House and in the Legislative Council by two-thirds majorities. Thomas did not vote but certified the memorial in his capacity as Speaker, but his Dearborn County neighbor Benjamin Chambers, then serving as president of the council, was more loyal to his constituents and refused to sign it. Chambers finally agreed to leave the chair, and Samuel Gwathmey, appointed president pro tem, signed in his stead.[10] No doubt others, likely including Jesse Thomas, felt that the safest and surest way to establish slavery was after statehood. They believed that the antislavery prohibition in the Northwest Ordinance was meant to be effective only during the territorial period and that thereafter, according to accepted states' rights doctrine, it was a matter for each state to decide for itself.

Regardless of whether they thought success more likely before or after statehood, Illinoisans believed that the prohibition of slavery could be more easily neutralized in an independent Illinois than in a united Indiana, where the strong and rapidly growing antislavery contingent in eastern Indiana would weigh against them. Although those same antislavery elements in eastern Indiana had provided crucial support for Jesse Thomas's candidacy for territorial delegate, some of them, as noted, did so only because they believed they would be better off without the more virulently proslavery Illinois. Slavery, however, was not pivotal to most westerners in the thick of this political battle and was only one factor among many in the campaign to establish a separate territory. Land, not slavery, remained the most important issue on the frontier. It was also a critical part of Thomas's personal and political life and the first subject pressed upon him by his Illinois allies as he set out for Washington.

CHAPTER 5

Into the Fray in Illinois

J esse Thomas transferred his allegiance from Indiana to Illinois with a rapidity that was a tribute to his pragmatism and resourcefulness. No one, including himself, could have foreseen how far and how fast he would move or how securely he would establish his initial position in Illinois. He had been adopted by the Edgar-Morrison faction, but, as their insistence on a bond attests, its members were not sure of him, and he never really became a part of their group. Thomas's new political partners may not have made immediately clear to him that land was going to be the nub of their relationship with him. But they were imperious, ambitious, and thoroughly driven, and the subject certainly came to the fore quickly, for they were playing for very high stakes and under extreme time pressure. Thomas understood that land was the sine qua non in Illinois, as in the rest of the frontier, and quickly became attuned to the intricacies of Illinois land issues.

Land titles in Illinois were very confused, as all the controlling powers that had preceded the Americans, starting with the various Indian tribes and proceeding through the French, the British, and the various colonies that had claimed authority, had all made conflicting land grants. Edgar and the Morrisons and other early settlers had placed their bets on the validity of early French claims, buying up as many as they could, though some were quite shaky, and pinning their hopes on early assurances given to French settlers that their claims would be respected if they remained loyal to subsequent regimes.[1] Whoever could control, directly or indirectly, the appointment and supervision of the federal officials who would determine the validity of contested land titles in the Illinois Country would hold the keys to immeasurable wealth and influence, and those in the Edgar-Morrison clique knew it would be far easier to seize that control in a newly separated territory. As long as the Illinois Country remained a part of the Indiana Territory, territorial governor William Henry Harrison could oppose the validity of their land claims and instruct his handpicked land commissioners to stand up to them. He sought to keep firm control over the process of settling old disputes and making new grants, keeping close tabs on the appointments of land office registers and receivers, even though those appointments were technically in the hands of the president, with the advice and consent of the Senate. Harrison was able to exert this kind of personal control because President Jefferson in effect had made him his proxy in the Indiana Territory.

When Jesse Thomas departed Vincennes in the late fall of 1808 to serve as Indiana's territorial delegate in Washington, the two land commissioners, Michael Jones of Kaskaskia and Elijah Backus, had already been hard at work for four years in Illinois in proceedings that were strewn with allegations of perjury and marred by violence between the two factions. The embattled Edgar-Morrison faction lodged numerous complaints in Washington, and the slow and painful resolution of those issues, mired in charges and counter-charges, were to delay the initial sales of public lands in the Illinois Territory for an additional six years. But at the time Thomas set out for Washington, his marching orders were clear—his primary goal in seeking separation was to establish a new and independent territory not for its own sake but rather as a stepping-stone to dismantle or discredit the work of the land commissioners then at work in Illinois.

On Monday, November 14, Joseph Varnum, the Speaker of the U.S. House, presented a certificate from the Legislative Council and House of the Indiana Territory declaring that Jesse Thomas had been elected to fill the remainder of Benjamin Parke's term as territorial delegate. Thomas was likely already in Washington, but he could not take his seat because, as a delaying tactic, his political enemies had made sure that the certificate was referred to the House Committee on Elections. Varnum also laid before the House two other communications from Indiana. The first was a letter from Benjamin Chambers, president of the Legislative Council of the Indiana Territory, presenting General Washington Johnston's eloquent report opposing the admission of slavery in the territory. Chambers, a former neighbor of Thomas's in Lawrenceburg, probably resented the much younger man and also felt Thomas had betrayed Dearborn County by supporting separation and the possible establishment of slavery in an independent Illinois. The second batch of communications Varnum presented was made up of several resolutions intended to make territorial politics more democratic by allowing popular election of the Legislative Council and limiting the terms of councillors to four years. Both sets of documents complicated the situation Thomas had to deal with, intertwining the themes of slavery and the extension of the suffrage with the unspoken concerns about land. Finally, on December 1, Thomas was seated and went to work on all these issues in the three months he had remaining in his term. He was no doubt frustrated by the two-week delay, but he was determined, from that point on, to make every day count. Unable to vote himself, he had to succeed solely through the power of persuasion, which he exerted largely behind the scenes.[2]

In these circumstances it was critical to form alliances quickly, and Thomas was fortunate to become friends almost immediately with William Harris Crawford, who was five years his senior and had just completed his first year of service as a senator from Georgia. Crawford was a product of the Southern Scotch-Irish frontier. If anybody surpassed Harrison in his influence over Thomas, it was Crawford. Crawford went on to serve in a dazzling variety of legislative, diplomatic, and executive offices, but he and Thomas became friends before all of that, in the simpler time of 1808. Won over by Thomas's pragmatic, balanced approach to politics, Crawford recognized in the younger man an up-and-coming frontier leader who had the potential to become an important ally. Crawford's mentorship would, ten years later, contribute to Jesse Thomas's effectiveness as a leader in the U.S. Senate. In the short run, however, Crawford was likely a key Senate supporter in Thomas's effort to make Illinois a separate territory.[3]

The Constitution was vague in describing the process by which new territories would be created. It apparently contemplated a gradual and orderly process by which a new territory would be carved off shortly before the rump territory was ready for statehood, which is exactly what happened when Ohio was ready for statehood. Under this view, a territory would remain largely unchanged until, when populations had grown sufficiently in the more settled part of the territory, it would be divided in two, with the more populous part becoming a state soon thereafter and the balance remaining a territory that reverted to the first stage of territorial government. However, the mechanism had not worked in this way in the next separation that occurred. Instead of waiting patiently for populations to grow, settlers in Michigan wanted to jump the gun and carve off a new territory before there were enough inhabitants to qualify the more established part of the Indiana Territory for statehood. The Ordinance of 1787 had provided for the possibility of dividing the Northwest Territory into two districts ("district" apparently being a term used synonymously with "territory" in the ordinance), but that language appeared to mandate that a territory could not be divided into more than two parts at a time. Thus, as Jesse Thomas sought to create the Illinois Territory, he had to contend with the fact that he too would be seen as moving too fast: the Indiana Territory had already been divided in two, and neither of its constituent territories was anywhere close to becoming a state.

At the same time that he sought a separate territory, Thomas intensified the attack on the land commissioners. As Michael Jones of Kaskaskia continued his dogged campaign to undermine the claims of the Edgar-Morrison group, the group clamored ever more loudly for him to be fired or at least for the terms of the commissioners not to be extended as Jones and Backus had requested.[4] Under the terms of their original appointment, the two were scheduled to make their official report to Albert Gallatin, the secretary of the treasury, at about the time that Jesse Thomas was elected delegate from the Indiana Territory, but the commissioners were not yet finished and wanted more time to continue their investigations. Drafts of their report were already circulating, and its proposed contents, very damaging to the Edgar-Morrison group, were well known by the fall of 1808. Therefore, the bill in Congress to extend the terms of the commissioners, which was wending its way through the legislative process at the same time as the bill to create a new Illinois Territory, was deemed by the Edgar-Morrison group to be even more of a threat.

At that point, the Edgar-Morrison faction was fighting for property and honor. The date to which the commissioners' terms might be extended was left blank when the bill was first introduced in the U.S. House, and Thomas must have decided that, if he wanted to succeed with the territorial separation, he would have to agree in principle to an extension of the commissioners' terms and then do battle to make the extension as short as possible. In the end, he was able to establish a new cutoff date for the commissioners of January 1, 1810, which under the circumstances was a victory. The competence and reliability of Michael Jones of Kaskaskia has always been an issue for those interested in the early history of Illinois. He was considered by many then and since to be able and honest, if somewhat edgy. It certainly can be said by looking at the reports he authored that he was thorough and apparently knowledgeable and that Edgar, the Morrisons, and their allies may in a number of instances have overreached; but Jones also, and perhaps understandably, had a chip on his shoulder. One reason, of course, was his defeat in the election to become Indiana's territorial delegate. From then on, he became even more assertively a Harrison ally, making it his prime business to push back against the tight-knit group that opposed Harrison. John Edgar and the Morrisons understood that they were in a nasty fight and relied more and more on John Rice Jones and his son Rice Jones, who became the point man in Illinois to discredit the work of the land commissioners. The contest became so tense that Rice Jones, suspecting that the mails were being tampered with, instructed Thomas to send mail for him in care of others.[5]

The history of early Illinois unfolded in an atmosphere of violence unusual even for the frontier. For the Edgar-Morrison clique and the pro-Harrison group the violence first erupted in a duel between Rice Jones and Shadrach Bond Jr. Jones's sharp tongue, high spirit, and Welsh sense of honor were well matched in Bond, another young man with a reputation for impetuosity. Bond's friend Dr. James Dunlap charged that Rice Jones had addressed a meeting in Kaskaskia on August 7, 1808, at which he "threw out many invectives against several respectable characters," going on to say that Bond was the tool of Governor Harrison and had been opposed to the interests of St. Clair and Randolph Counties in the Indiana General Assembly. Bond challenged Jones to a duel, and the two met the next day on an island in the Mississippi between Kaskaskia and Ste. Genevieve, presumably choosing the site because it would provide some privacy and perhaps some confusion about whether Illinois or Missouri would have jurisdiction in the event of a fatality.[6]

Jones's pistol discharged just as the men were taking position. It is not clear why, but it apparently had a hair trigger, a common adjustment meant to give a duelist an advantage. Dunlap, serving as Bond's second, insisted that the accidental discharge count as Jones's first shot, allowing Bond, in his view, the right to take a careful shot at Jones. No one else saw it that way, and a settlement was arranged. But in the aftermath of the affair, different accounts of the duel and the settlement were put forward, and the incident continued to fester. Dunlap, angry and belligerent and possibly egged on by others, never let up. His threats against Rice Jones's life became so loud by late November that the elder Jones responded in a note to Elijah Backus, one of the pro-Harrison land commissioners: "Sir—I have just heard your threats of yesterday, that if my son did not go out of the country, he should in a few days be put out of existence—'it will be done, it shall be done.' I now inform you that he will remain here, and if he should be murdered either by you or through your instigation, I shall know where to apply. I must, however, confess that the threats of poltroons can be considered in no other light than as those of assassins."[7]

John Rice Jones appears to have been more intent on staking out the family honor than on protecting his son's life, and his note only added fuel to the fire. The final showdown occurred as Rice Jones walked out of William Morrison's house on December 7, 1808. The horror of the incident is clear in a letter from Robert Morrison to Jesse Thomas describing Dunlap approaching Jones from behind and shooting him in the heart as he turned around. The event caused outrage in the community, and Dunlap fled to New Orleans. When Nathaniel Pope, the newly appointed territorial secretary, arrived in the Illinois Territory, he was the first territorial official on the scene and therefore was acting governor. One of his first acts was to issue a demand on April 29, 1809, to the governor of the Orleans Territory to arrest and return Dunlap. Ironically, he did so under the statute titled "An Act respecting fugitives from justice and persons escaping from the service of their masters," thus demonstrating that the fugitive slave act that was to cause so much controversy in the years ahead could also be used by a Northern state to reach into the South. Dunlap, however, faded from view, and those intent on avenging the death of Rice Jones had to look elsewhere. The urge to hold someone responsible for the cold-blooded murder was irresistible. Some may earnestly have believed that Michael Jones of Kaskaskia and others in the anti-separation party had incited Dunlap to commit the act, but it is just as likely that Michael Jones's enemies sensed that they might be able to harness the bitterness of the community to convict and remove Jones and possibly also Robert Robinson, an anti-separation activist serving as clerk to the land commissioners.[8]

Although news of the violence and conflict of late 1808 in Illinois certainly drifted back in bits and pieces to Washington, it was in marked contrast to the quiet efficiency of Jesse Thomas's campaign to establish Illinois as a separate territory. It was remarkable that he so quickly overcame the objections to seating him and temporarily defused the antislavery and prosuffrage documents that had been presented along with his certificate of election. If seriously considered, these certainly would have weighed in the balance against separation. So it was impressive that in the two weeks after he was allowed to take his seat on December 1, Thomas was able to take total control of all three issues. On December 13, he organized a resolution to appoint a committee to inquire into the expediency of dividing the Indiana Territory and had four presumably pliable representatives appointed to the committee along with himself as chair. He then succeeded in having the various anti-slavery resolutions that had arrived with his certificate of election referred to his committee, where they could be safely buried. Three days later he dutifully presented to the House a petition from various residents of Knox County opposing separation but saw to it that this petition too was referred to his committee, where it went nowhere.[9]

Thomas worked tirelessly for separation, and at the end of his first month in the House, in a Saturday session on December 31, he presented the report of his committee, which he had authored. Not surprisingly, the report indicated that the committee found itself "convinced that it is the wish of a large majority of the citizens of the said Territory that a separation thereof should take place" and deemed that it was "always just and wise policy to grant to every portion of the people of the Union that form of government which is the object of their wishes, when not incompatible with the Constitution of the United States, not subversive of their allegiance to the national sovereignty."[10] Along with the report, Thomas's committee efficiently provided a bill to implement its recommendations. The bill, which wisely avoided any mention of slavery, was committed for consideration on the following Monday, January 2, by a committee of the whole, a mechanism used often in the early years of American government to permit the entire House to function more informally while considering difficult topics. Thomas's bill did not come up on that Monday, however, apparently because of ongoing behind-the-scene altercations that were certainly made more contentious by the arrival of news of Rice Jones's death.

It was not until January 16 that Thomas was finally able to move that the House, as a committee of the whole, take up the bill. Willis Alston, a seasoned and reliable Republican from North Carolina, was made the chair of the committee of the whole and helped guide the bill through to passage. The House's bill was then passed successfully in the Senate on January 31, under the guidance of John Pope, the Kentuckian who chaired the select committee formed to consider the creation of the new territory. The law was signed by the president on February 3 to be effective on March 1. The new territorial capital of Illinois was to be at Kaskaskia, and the act included provision for the president to make recess appointments of the territorial governor and judges if the U.S. Congress were not in session. The entire exercise had been a tour de force of efficient management of legislation, and in the process Thomas received an education in congressional lawmaking on the House side that was to serve him in good stead in his later career in the Senate.

Once the act to divide the Indiana Territory was safely through and signed by the president, Thomas set out to pass another act that, though not trumpeted to the same extent, was considered almost equally important by the new citizens of the Illinois Territory and particularly the Edgar-Morrison clique. The bill reduced the property requirements for voting in the Indiana Territory and gave its citizens the right to elect directly not only their delegate to Congress but also their Legislative Council. It further gave the territorial General Assembly, rather than the governor, the important right to apportion districts for the Legislative Council and the House. Thomas had overseen the start of this initiative in his final days in the General Assembly of the Indiana Territory. The intent was to make newer territories more attractive to settlers from more established eastern states, where many adult males still did not have the franchise. Though the bill pertained by its terms only to citizens of the Indiana Territory, it was twinned in Congress with a similar bill extending the suffrage in the Mississippi Territory, and together these bills virtually guaranteed that these rights would be assured for all future territories reaching the second stage of territorial government, including Illinois. In addition to broadening the franchise, the resolutions of the Indiana House also sought to limit the power of the territorial governor. The Indiana assembly had appealed to Congress to repeal "that part of the Ordinance which vests in the Governor of this Territory an absolute negative on all acts; and also that part which confers on him the power of proroguing and dissolving the General Assembly." With that part of the program of democratization, Thomas and his allies were not successful.[11]

Thomas's actions as territorial delegate offended his antislavery constituents and angered the status quo in Vincennes to such an extent that he was burned in effigy there. Realizing that he had quite literally burned his bridges in both Dearborn County and Vincennes, Thomas determined that his future lay in Illinois. In an effort to stay one step ahead of his political enemies, he was able before leaving Washington to obtain from the incoming president, James Madison, an appointment as one of the three federal judges for the new Territory of Illinois. His new ally George Poindexter, Mississippi's territorial delegate, signed the petition from members of Congress to President

Madison recommending Thomas's appointment, a harbinger of their future close political friendship. In nominating him, the president described Thomas as "being of the Illinois Territory," and this was perhaps an acceptable stretch as he was already deeply involved in the politics of Illinois and, besides, intended to move directly to the new territory without stopping in Indiana.[12]

Thomas had made many friends in Washington and for a brief moment was in a position to be the dominant power in determining the initial federal officials in the new territory. Even after obtaining one of the territorial judgeships for himself, he had enough sway left with Madison to prevail on him to offer John Boyle of Kentucky the appointment as the first territorial governor in Illinois. Boyle had served with Thomas in the House of Representatives and was leaving the House that year. Boyle, however, after first indicating his willingness to accept the appointment, turned it down.[13]

This opened the way for John Pope of Kentucky, chair of the Senate select committee considering the new territory, to exert his influence over the choice of governor. Pope, who acquired the sobriquet One-Arm Pope after losing an arm in a childhood accident on the family farm, was the mainspring of a formidable political organization in Kentucky that served as a counterweight to Henry Clay's. Pope had wanted badly to install his younger brother Nathaniel, who was also a friend of Jesse Thomas's, as governor in the new territory but had to settle for the appointment of his first cousin Ninian Edwards. Madison appointed Edwards governor and Nathaniel Pope secretary on March 7, 1809, the same day that Thomas was appointed territorial judge.

Edwards, who was to become Jesse Thomas's principal adversary in Illinois, was the same age as Thomas and, like him, had been born in Maryland, where his father, Benjamin, had been a member of the Maryland convention that ratified the U.S. Constitution and his uncle John had been one of the first two U.S. senators from the new state of Kentucky in 1792. Although he had many good qualities, most astute observers thought little of him:

> Kindly, charitable, generous, and at the same time pompous, over-bearing and affected, he had many warm friends, many enemies too, and perhaps many associates who humored his foibles, so long as doing so would promote their own advantage. The quality of mental balance was almost completely lacking in Edwards. By turns he was bold and overcautious, headstrong and vacillating, now plunging rashly into an enterprise . . . now hesitating between

two courses and striving to follow both when an irrevocable decision between them had to be made. A mental shiftiness sometimes
led him into equivocal positions which he could justify only by
elaborate explanations.[14]

Edwards had been educated at Dickinson College, where he was swept
up in a short late-adolescent binge of dissolute behavior involving gambling
and drink; but, before he was twenty, he had reordered himself and set off for
Kentucky to clear a new farm for his father. He then applied himself to the
study of law, reading William Blackstone and becoming involved in politics.
As with other frontier intellectuals like John Rice Jones, Edwards read medical
treatises as eagerly as he did legal ones. In 1795, before completing his legal
studies, Edwards was elected to the first of two terms in the lower house of
the Kentucky legislature. When first admitted to the bar in Kentucky, he had
done extensive legal work for Henry Clay, who was roughly a contemporary.[15]
In 1806 Edwards was a candidate for the U.S. House of Representatives but,
before the election, was appointed a judge of the Court of Appeals, Kentucky's
highest court. He eventually rose to become chief justice of that court. After
holding that post for two years, he induced Henry Clay to join One-Arm Pope
in putting him forward to be governor of the Illinois Territory in the place of
John Boyle, after Thomas's candidate withdrew. With Clay's support added
to Pope's, Edwards was a certainty and was appointed in 1809 at the age of
thirty-four. Edwards and Thomas were to prove perfect foils for each other.

Jesse Thomas used his remaining influence in Washington to procure the
appointment of Obadiah Jones as one of the two territorial judges in Illinois
besides himself. Obadiah Jones was a close friend of Georgia senator William Harris Crawford, and Jesse presumably supported this appointment as
a favor to his new friend and future ally.[16] Once again, however, Thomas's
efforts to install potential allies in the new territorial government were frustrated—Obadiah Jones never set foot in Illinois, preferring instead to resign
as a territorial judge in Illinois in order to accept the same post that opened
up in the Mississippi Territory, much nearer his Georgia home. Thus Thomas
had few allies at the outset in Illinois.

Over the next few months Kaskaskia served as a magnet for strong and ambitious men drawn to the opportunities opening up there. As noted, Nathaniel
Pope was the first of the territorial officers to arrive in Kaskaskia after taking
the oath as territorial secretary in Missouri on April 25, 1809, and crossing

the river a few days later. Jesse Thomas presumably came during May and started looking for a place to live near Kaskaskia. He was much applauded on his arrival that spring, both for his success in gaining Illinois' separation from the Indiana Territory and for the expansion of political power he had engineered for territorial citizens. Alexander Stuart, another of the three original territorial judges, arrived at about the same time. With the third of the judgeships left temporarily open by the resignation of Obadiah Jones, the only territorial official not yet there was Ninian Edwards, and he came at his leisure, in true patrician manner, on June 11, with a train of slaves and livestock. With the exception of one of the three federal judgeships, which was vacant on and off throughout the entire territorial period, the full complement of federal appointees was on hand and ready to create a government for the territory.

CHAPTER 6

Gathering Forces

Jesse and Rebecca Thomas cut their ties with the Indiana Territory to start over again in Kaskaskia, the new territorial capital of Illinois, where all issues, including slavery, would be seen in a different light. Rebecca, so recently uprooted from Detroit and happily resettled in Vincennes, was undoubtedly upset to move again; but Kaskaskia, as a major landing point on the Mississippi and the county seat of Randolph County, was the new territory's most important town and probably much like Vincennes in character. At about the time of their arrival, the bustling town contained "forty-five houses, many of them well built, several of stone, with gardens and large lots adjoining," and boasted "467 inhabitants, of whom 47 were slaves."[1] Under the terms of the Northwest Ordinance of 1787, each of the territorial judges received "a freehold estate in 500 acres of land while in the exercise of their offices" to be chosen by them from any land not previously reserved or claimed. In addition to this generous grant of land rights, judges were to receive an annual salary of $1,200, for that time a considerable sum. These emoluments put Thomas and the other territorial officials among the local elite.

Their new home was ten miles north of Kaskaskia in the American Bottom, the fertile alluvial plain where early European settlement was centered. From there Jesse and Rebecca could see across the Mississippi to Missouri, which had recently been acquired by the United States in the Louisiana Purchase. Ninian Edwards settled nearby, establishing a large farm called Elvirade, after his wife, Elvira. In these early years the Thomas and Edwards families were socially close. Julianne, the elder of Rebecca's stepdaughters, was married on

November 27, 1809, to Elvira's younger brother Dr. Harvey Lane, who would soon move across the Mississippi and become influential in Missouri politics.[2]

On their arrival in Illinois in the spring of 1809, the governor and the territorial judges turned immediately to the business of passing territorial laws, meeting frequently thereafter until the territory moved into the second stage of territorial government three years later. On June 13 they adopted a resolution declaring "the laws of Indiana Territory of a general nature" to be in force in the new territory.[3] It was logical that the laws of Indiana should be used as a starting point since the two territories were similar in circumstances and those laws had themselves been adopted in the more or less recent past and had been applicable in Illinois prior to separation; but it is notable that the governor and judges chose laws that Jesse Thomas had himself been intimately involved in creating and that had been carefully crafted to preserve much of the institution of slavery.

As a territorial judge, Jesse Thomas was once again thrust into a role with which he had no experience, just as had occurred with his election as Speaker of the territorial House in the Indiana Territory. One of the first cases that came before him and fellow judge Alexander Stuart was the accusation that the land commissioner Michael Jones of Kaskaskia had been involved in the murder of Rice Jones. Thomas was certainly under considerable pressure from the Edgar-Morrison clique to secure Jones's conviction. On September 12, 1809, the two judges summoned a grand jury of twenty-two local citizens to present the case against James Dunlap and Jones. The grand jury, after bringing in an indictment against Dunlap for murder, also indicted Michael Jones, because "he did, on the 6th of December, 1808, incite, move, abet, etc., feloniously and with malice aforethought, the said James Dunlap to commit the crime of murder."[4] Following this incendiary allegation, tempers began to cool. The prosecuting attorney moved for a continuance of the trial on the affidavit of an important witness who claimed to be sick and unable to attend court. A continuance was granted, and Michael Jones, who had insisted on a speedy trial, was admitted to bail in the sum of $3,000 on the declaration by six prominent citizens of Randolph County, including Shadrach Bond Jr., that they would see that he appeared for trial. He was finally tried and acquitted seven months later before a twelve-member petit jury that included two of the six men who had stood security for him. In an unusual move, the court also exonerated the complaining witness, John Rice Jones, from paying the costs, as it found there were probable grounds for seeking the indictment.

Several years later, Michael Jones brought suit against John Edgar and the Morrisons for defamation in letters they wrote to Washington and released to newspapers; his victory in these suits was a black eye for the Edgar-Morrison faction, but Jesse Thomas had distanced himself by then.[5]

The first year of territorial government ended with the release of the land commissioners' long-delayed report at the end of 1809. It was a virulent attack on those of the Edgar-Morrison clique, finding that they had suborned witnesses on a massive scale and invalidating 370 of their land claims. There was another side to the story, which came out more fully fifteen years later when John Edgar submitted a claim to the U.S. Senate's Committee on Private Land Claims, at a time when Jesse Thomas was serving on that committee. The committee found that many of the land grants the commissioners had taken from Edgar had been confirmed to him between 1791 and 1796 by then governor Arthur St. Clair, relying on records that had been subsequently destroyed. Michael Jones had ignored these confirmations by the then governor and instead insisted that Edgar be forced to rely on such testimony as it was in his power to procure in 1813, more than twenty years after his claims had been examined and confirmed by the territorial governor. In the meantime, Edgar had taken possession of the properties, had them surveyed at his expense, and paid property taxes on them. Congress in 1825 determined that Edgar be awarded new land grants in compensation.

The commissioners were well aware that they were stirring up a hornets' nest and concluded their report with these words: "We close this melancholy picture of human depravity by rendering our devout acknowledgements that, in the awful alternative in which we have been placed of either admitting perjured testimony in support of the claims before us, or having it turned against our characters and lives, it has, as yet, pleased that Divine Providence which rules over the affairs of men, to protect us both from legal murder and private assassination."[6] Given all that occurred in the previous two years—from the burning of Jesse Thomas in effigy to the murder of Rice Jones—this thanks to Divine Providence was more than a rhetorical flourish. With the release of the report, those of the Edgar-Morrison faction may have hoped that they were finally rid of the mercurial Michael Jones of Kaskaskia, but it was not to be. Jones and his supporters in Vincennes succeeded in convincing Congress to create a new commission to continue looking at different aspects of the title controversies in Illinois. Jones was again appointed a commissioner, this time along with Thomas Sloo and John Caldwell, both of Shawneetown, and this second commission did not send its report to Washington until 1812, where it languished for two more years before finally being approved.

As had occurred in Indiana, the residents of the new Illinois Territory were touchy about sliding back into the first stage of territorial government in the new territory. Moreover, many thought the second stage, and the broader voting rights that went with it, was essential to attract a continuing flow of immigrants and to encourage the settlers already there to stay. Congress, as its experience with the territorial process grew, and prodded by Jesse Thomas and others, continued the progressive relaxation of the requirements for passage to the second stage of territorial government. As in the Indiana Territory, the governor of the Illinois Territory was authorized to advance to the second stage of territorial government when convinced that a majority of the freeholders wished to do so, notwithstanding that there might not yet be five thousand of them. That was a particularly important concession in Illinois because, on account of the controversies over property titles, public land was not available for sale until 1814, and it was impossible to become a freeholder without owning land. The governor had the power to inaugurate the second stage of territorial government by proclamation, but he chose first to submit the question to a vote that was held in April 1812 and was almost unanimously in favor.

During these early years when Judge Thomas and Governor Edwards were neighbors and friends, Thomas supported the Pope-Edwards group in some patronage decisions, even going against the Edgar-Morrison clique. He had, for example, supported President Madison's appointment of Nathaniel Pope as territorial secretary and then joined with Edwards in 1810 in backing Pope for a territorial judgeship.[7] This cooperation, however, was not destined to last long, and Thomas soon chafed at Edwards's unbridled power to make appointments. Seeking new allies, Thomas reacted to this breach by urging his brothers to join him in Illinois. His older brother, Richard, moved in 1810 from Ohio to Ste. Genevieve, Missouri, directly across the Mississippi from Jesse, and within two years their younger half brother Michael Jones pulled up stakes in Indiana to join Jesse in the Illinois Territory. With Illinois preparing to enter the second stage of territorial government in 1812, the number of political offices multiplied and patronage battles loomed. Thomas wanted his brothers with him, not just for them to benefit from his power and prestige in Illinois but also to help him consolidate his position there. The brothers were at the peak of their powers as they converged on the fertile area known as Egypt, with Richard on Jesse's western flank and Michael on his eastern.

Richard had made his decision to move farther west within two years of losing the election for the U.S. Senate in Ohio. He had grown disenchanted with his prospects in the turbulent politics of that pivotal first state in the Northwest Territory. He decided, however, to bypass the Illinois Territory and to make a new and independent start in Missouri, which promised to be just as pivotal in the Louisiana Purchase as Ohio had been in the Old Northwest. It also suited Richard that Missouri appeared even more Southern-leaning and conservative in its outlook than Illinois. Ste. Genevieve, where Richard first settled, served as a depot for the substantial amounts of lead mined each year along the Maremeg River, and it was growing rapidly. It would soon swell to more than three hundred houses and would boast an academy and a dozen stores.[8] An active intercourse existed between Ste. Genevieve and Kaskaskia, allowing the older Thomas to be close to his younger brother without having to compete for political office. The brothers had easy contact with each other over the next few years, evidenced, for example, by Richard witnessing in Ste. Genevieve the conveyance to Jesse Thomas of the slave James. Jesse and Rebecca also occasionally went to Ste. Genevieve to visit her stepdaughters Julianne, the elder, who had married Harvey Lane, and Harriet, the younger, who, after a divorce and remarriage, lived next door to Julianne.

Missouri was in the doldrums when Richard Thomas arrived and remained so until the end of the War of 1812. Thomas was fortunate to establish himself as a leading figure in the territory during this lull and was well positioned by the time the postwar surge began. Between 1814 and 1820 the population grew from twenty-five thousand to sixty-five thousand, and it was no longer just huddled along the Mississippi but was spreading into the interior parts of Missouri.[9] Richard's new life west of the Mississippi centered first on Ste. Genevieve and then on Cape Girardeau, both long-established French towns and the oldest in what became the Missouri Territory. They were the principal towns in two of the five districts organized long before under the Spanish and French. Under American administration these districts became counties, and by July 1811 Thomas was admitted to practice law in both. His entry into Missouri's legal community was eased by the presence there of John Rice Jones, who became a staunch ally of Richard's as he had earlier been of Jesse's.

There were very few lawyers in the territory in Richard's early time there, and even in 1815, four years later, there would still be fewer than two dozen. Their life, riding the circuit from town to town along with the judge, required vigor and resourcefulness. As he rode on the alternately muddy and dusty

wilderness roads, Thomas came to know thoroughly not only the backwoods
and rivers of the new territory but also his fellow lawyers, like Thomas Hart
Benton, who would play important roles in Missouri's future. On his arrival in
Ste. Genevieve, Richard Thomas again took up his political career. Since the
Missouri Territory was immediately advanced to the second stage of territorial
government on its organization in 1812, it was to have a general assembly from
the beginning, and Thomas was elected one of three representatives from Ste.
Genevieve County to the House that November. He was a part of a coalition
of large land claimants and established commercial interests that dominated
that first territorial General Assembly. Thomas played an active role and was
reelected in 1814, the only one of the three original representatives from Ste.
Genevieve to serve in both the First and Second General Assemblies.[10]

Even as he was reelected from Ste. Genevieve, he was making the decision
to move to the newly organized Cape Girardeau County, sixty miles to the
southwest. In November 1814 he purchased at a sheriff's sale about 400 acres
to the northwest of the town of Cape Girardeau on the White Water River,
about ten miles upstream from where it empties into the Mississippi. Some
six months later, in May 1815, he purchased 350 additional acres nearby in the
center of what would soon become a new town.[11] The town was the first to be
named after Andrew Jackson, to commemorate his victory at the Battle of
New Orleans, which was a small irony given the bitter relations that were to
develop between Jackson and the two Thomas brothers.

The town of Cape Girardeau, a long-established outpost on the Mississippi
River, was the logical candidate to become the seat of the new county Richard
Thomas had chosen as his future home, but, mysteriously and during Thomas's
time in the General Assembly, defects were discovered in the deeds for the
land that its promoters had given the new county for the construction of a
courthouse. Thomas immediately reiterated an offer he had previously made
of fifty acres for construction of a courthouse and jail in the northwest corner
of his new 350-acre tract in the town of Jackson on condition that Jackson be
made the county seat. With Thomas training a microscope on the problems
with the deeds in the town of Cape Girardeau, the county was induced to
accept the offered land in Jackson and make that the county seat instead. The
General Assembly affirmed the designation, and Thomas proceeded to break
up his property into town lots that became the core of his wealth. He was
soon involved in purchasing additional lots in the town and even persuaded
his brother Jesse and son-in-law George Bullitt to join in purchasing a lot

near his property. This pattern, of course, repeated what Jesse was then doing in Mount Vernon, Ohio, and what Jesse and Michael had already done in Brookville, Indiana.

Part of what prompted Richard's move to Cape Girardeau County was his decision to leave the legislature and become a judge. Like his involvement with land, his move to the bench appears to have been a calculation based on ambition. When Missouri's territorial General Assembly met for the first time in 1812, one of its first objectives had been to simplify the administration of justice. Under the influence of Thomas and a few other similarly minded individuals, the Missouri Territory's five circuits were simplified into two, each to be placed under a single circuit court judge earning the princely annual salary of $1,200 (at a time when the annual salary of the territorial governor was $2,000 and when Richard Thomas, as a representative, was receiving only $300 for each session of the territorial House). Thomas was appointed by the governor as the first judge to serve on the Southern Circuit, composed of the counties of Ste. Genevieve, Cape Girardeau, and New Madrid and the other southern parts of the Missouri Territory that were to become the Arkansas Territory when it was split off in 1819. Predictably, Richard was subjected to a barrage of criticism when he resigned from the General Assembly to take this lucrative post that he had helped to create. He clearly believed he could use the judiciary to advance his interests and those of his allies but soon found aligned against him a phalanx of committed Democrats who distrusted the aristocratic tendencies of judges and believed them more interested in protecting property than people. This tension over the proper role of judges was to dominate the balance of Richard's life.[12]

Jackson may have been a remote court town when Richard first purchased property there, but it was centrally located in the middle of the new Southern Circuit over which he presided; and, just as St. Louis would soon eclipse Ste. Genevieve, Jackson was on its way to bypassing Cape Girardeau to become the principal business and political center of the southern part of Missouri. When the time came to begin sales of public lands in Missouri in 1818 and the first three federal land offices were opened in the territory, one of them was put in Jackson, marking it as a place where up-and-coming businessmen would gravitate. The town was to remain Richard Thomas's home until his death.

As he solidified his place in the legal community, Thomas was also the head of a growing family that was described as cultivated and accomplished.[13] He and Franky brought with them to Missouri two sons, Claiborne and Jesse, and four daughters, Sabina, Nancy, Mary, and Eliza. Once settled in their new home, the family continued to grow, with the arrival of Catharine, then Frances, and finally, in 1817, the youngest, Richard. The household, like his brother Jesse's, likely also included a few slaves.

Two years after Richard Thomas had made his move to Missouri, Michael Jones joined his half brothers, bringing with him to his new home not only his skills as a lawyer but also, even more important, his experience as a real estate investor, and he rapidly eclipsed his brothers in this most important of pursuits in the lives of almost all ambitious men on the American frontier. Michael made his home in Shawneetown on the eastern edge of the Illinois Territory, just below the point where the Wabash flows into the Ohio. The town had received its name because for a short time in the mid-eighteenth century the Shawnee Indians had a village on the same site. The northern part of the town was built on one of a number of prehistoric Native American burial mounds that rose along the bank of the Ohio River. The federal government laid out the town and surveyed the surrounding area, and the first American settlers reached Shawneetown about 1800, a decade before Michael arrived. The town soon became a bustling trading post and the principal point of entry for Americans emigrating from the East down the Ohio to the Illinois Territory.

Shawneetown's greatest early advantage was its proximity to the U.S. saltworks known as the Salines, about fifteen miles to the northwest. The Salines consisted of two salt springs and a series of salt wells running along the Saline River in Gallatin County from the town of Equality south to the saltworks themselves. These saltworks were the oldest west of the Alleghenies. The Indians had made salt there long before the first settlers appeared but, in 1803, ceded their "great salt spring" to the United States by treaty. Because it was easily portable and essential for preserving and seasoning meat, salt was one of the West's most valuable commodities. The salt produced near Shawneetown was used throughout the western territories and was known as "white gold" because it paid such significant royalties to the federal government. In the 1785 Land Ordinance, Congress determined that it would maintain control over this subsurface bonanza and the associated mines, salt springs, and water mill sites. Accordingly, the government refused to sell the salt lands but did authorize the secretary of the treasury to let the lands to individuals at a royalty under leases requiring the holder to produce a certain quantity of salt each year or pay a penalty. In 1818, as part of the process of making a new state, Congress gave the Salines to Illinois but forbade the sale of the land.

The state continued to lease out the springs until about 1837, when the low price for salt made the expense of extracting it from the brine prohibitive.[14]

At the peak of production under the Americans, the works produced about five hundred bushels of salt a day. The salt royalties, and the patronage connected to the salt operations, were under the direct control of the territorial governor, which made the Salines an important focus of attention for territorial politicians. Isaac White, the federal agent in the Salines, was one of Ninian Edwards's most important political allies, which made it doubly important for Jesse Thomas to have Michael in Shawneetown to look after his political interests.

Salt and the Salines were also an important element in Illinois' experience with slavery, and the government's ownership of the Salines involved it directly in the practice. The making of salt was backbreaking work, and it was generally thought it could not be done without slave labor. As a result, the need for labor in the saltworks was one of the major arguments in favor of slavery in the territory. During the early years of the second stage of territorial government in Illinois, Shadrach Bond Jr., the first territorial delegate, carried to Congress several resolutions related to slavery and captured the almost flippant nature of the debate in writing Governor Edwards that the "one respecting the partial introduction of negroes to carry on the salt-works, I suppose, will make a fuss with some." Special territorial laws, and later special provisions in the Illinois state constitution, permitted exceptions to Article VI allowing slavery in the Salines. The census of 1818 for Gallatin County listed 236 slaves and indentured servants, almost a third of the total number in Illinois, most of whom had been brought in by the lessees of the Salines to manufacture salt.[15]

To make his initial move to Illinois, Michael had had to give up, in large part, his stake in Jesse's real estate venture in Brookville in the Indiana Territory. Michael's primary aim with the town had been to promote and develop Jesse's investment as rapidly as possible and then to liquidate it in order to have a grubstake to invest in Illinois. Brookville, thus, was just one of the money-making real estate initiatives that were typical of the brothers and most other frontier politicians. It was also, however, a constructive and useful initiative, since by the time Michael left Brookville it had become an important town, second in Indiana only to the territorial capital at Vincennes. At the same time that Michael Jones was exiting Brookville, he was courting Mary James, the daughter of John James, another frontier real estate maven who, like Michael, had been born in Maryland and moved to southwestern Pennsylvania, then to Kentucky, and finally to Ohio and Indiana. John James was also a town builder, founding Rising Sun, Indiana. Michael and Mary were married on August 6, 1811, in Lawrenceburg, the town in the Indiana Territory where he and Jesse had first lived.[16]

Meanwhile, Jesse Thomas was laying the groundwork for Michael's arrival in Illinois. He remained confident that he could persuade Edwards to give his half brother a political job. A new land office was being discussed for Shawneetown, which would require a register and a receiver, and three new counties were to be formed when Illinois entered the second stage of territorial government, each of which would need a sheriff and a clerk. Surely Edwards could be persuaded to find a job for Michael, who was imminently well qualified. Edwards, however, seemed to take delight in turning aside Thomas's requests. Thomas wrote Edwards on March 23, 1812, displaying a rising irritation with the governor. Jesse declared that his brother "was here in time. . . . He has made considerable sacrifice in disposing of property in Indiana which under other circumstances he would have retained, and removed his family to this country prepared to settle in it. He will now certainly settle near me on the Ohio—Several years back he studied under myself the duties of a clerk and I have no doubt by the time the county is established he will be well qualified to fill that office which would be as agreeable to him as that of sheriff."[17] As spring wore on, Thomas came to realize that Edwards intended to deny Michael any significant government job. Edwards did eventually appoint him to the unpaid post of justice of the peace in Gallatin County on Christmas Eve, 1812, but this was purely a sop.

Despite the cold shoulder he received from Edwards, Michael Jones decided to remain in Shawneetown, a choice that proved fortunate from every point of view. As the second most important town in early Illinois, Shawneetown proved an ideal place for Michael to settle. Not only could he serve as Jesse's eyes and ears in the eastern part of the territory, but he also found it a good place to practice law and make his initial real estate investments. The first record of Michael acquiring property there is the purchase of 160 acres outside of the town on July 25, 1814, followed by three town lots in October and November of that same year. Over the next fifteen years Jones purchased twenty-five additional town lots and almost 2,000 acres of property outside of town. In addition to these private transactions, he acquired more than 1,000 acres in direct purchases from the federal government between 1824 and

1838. It was clear that Gallatin County was going to provide ample business opportunities to keep Jones fully occupied, and he eventually became one of the largest landowners and wealthiest men in Illinois.[18]

In addition to his legal skills and the capital on which he built his real estate empire, Michael also brought with him a tribe of family and friends, including not only his own relatives but his wife's as well. Perhaps most important among these was Jeptha Hardin, who in 1813 married Sally James, his wife's sister. He was a scion of a powerful Virginia family, a half brother of Benjamin Hardin, who served five terms as a U.S representative from Kentucky, and a cousin of John J. Hardin, who was later to serve a term as a U.S representative from Illinois before being killed in the Mexican-American War. The brothers-in-law had both followed the same route to Gallatin County so almost certainly knew each other earlier. In the same year he was married, Jeptha became the first lawyer admitted to practice before the recently organized courts in Gallatin County. Both Jones and Hardin had been fortunate in arriving in the very early years of Shawneetown, and both went on to become successful lawyers and large landowners. Jeptha was to become an important, though thorny, ally of Michael's in the years ahead.

The sought-after land office for southeastern Illinois was finally established in Shawneetown in early 1814 and made its first sale of public lands in July of that year. Michael may have been denied one of the lucrative appointments he and his brother had sought in the land office, but he contrived to make money from its creation in a different way. All land purchases from the land office had to be transacted in gold or silver, and Jones, together with John Marshall, who ran a wholesale merchandise business in Shawneetown, and a number of their friends, recognized the need for some mechanism for settlers to turn their salt and buckskins into specie that could be used to purchase land. And once the purchase of land was completed, the receiver of the land office needed a secure place to deposit the specie received and a mechanism for transferring those funds eastward. Clearly what was needed was a bank, and Michael's friends gave notice through the newspapers of Kaskaskia, Frankfort, and Nashville that they planned to apply to the legislature of Illinois to establish one in Shawneetown. Michael was not part of the original committee, but he was certainly involved.[19] Another of Jesse's allies who backed the bank was John McLean. The Bank of Illinois was the first bank in the territory and was used by Jesse and Michael as a stepping-stone. It opened its doors in 1817, thereafter doing a proverbial land office business. Michael Jones was one of the bank's officers along with John Marshall and John Rives, and these three remained the only officers of the bank until it faded out and suspended operations in the aftermath of the Panic of 1819.

The founding of the land office and the bank was among the earliest intimations that Shawneetown had possibilities beyond the wealth flowing from the Salines. The bank gained an important head start in establishing itself as the principal bank in Illinois, making Shawneetown the territory's financial center. It later constructed an elegant Greek Revival stone building, which still stands as an Illinois landmark. Jesse Thomas, his brother and half brother, and their political allies had a clear sense of how such an institution could support successful political careers and vice versa. They also understood that a strong bank could make a town preeminent. These were lessons that Ninian Edwards and his allies were slow coming to, although Edwards did later win the loyalty of bank president John Marshall and director John Caldwell by helping them obtain federal depositor status for the bank, thus making sure it could continue to handle the proceeds of federal land sales.[20] Despite this gesture by Edwards, the bank was always more closely associated with Thomas's supporters and consistently competed against the younger and less solid Bank of Edwardsville, where Edwards put his main efforts.

All three brothers were now firmly established in the rich and promising regions near the confluence of the Ohio and Mississippi Rivers, ready to live independent lives but also prepared to assist each other. The focus on land and politics in Illinois, however, was temporarily overshadowed by the War of 1812, a war that was as much about control over frontier areas as it was about British abuses on the high seas. As in the Revolutionary War, the new conflagration fell particularly heavily on those living on the frontier, where the British again enlisted mistreated Indian nations as allies. During the war, Edwards led the Illinois militia against the British and the Indians with great energy until charges of atrocities against the Indians led to his replacement by a more professional military officer. With Oliver Perry's victory of September 10, 1813, in the Battle of Lake Erie, the British gave up their support of the Native Americans, and William Henry Harrison, who had resigned his governorship in order to resume his full-time military responsibilities, thereafter had carte blanche to seize whatever territory he could. Edwards also served as a commissioner in negotiations with Indians, at various times with Auguste Chouteau; his close friend Benjamin Stephenson; and William Clark, former colleague of Meriwether Lewis and then governor of the Missouri Territory.

His varied service made Edwards the most prominent public figure in Illinois before statehood.

Accused of having aristocratic tendencies, Edwards nonetheless espoused Jeffersonian principles. He expanded the scope of democracy in Illinois, from the beginning, by making county and militia appointments according to petitions and other expressions of local preference by citizens of the territory. It is likely Edwards followed this course in part to avoid being caught up in the pro- and anti-Harrison factions at the time of separation, but it must also have been his natural inclination. Though his patron Senator John Pope criticized him for this course of conduct, Edwards appears even to have been amenable to accepting this mode of appointment as a more formal system.[21]

In the first several general assemblies, the structure and duties of the judiciary continued as a major theme. After the initial excitement of the trial of Michael Jones of Kaskaskia for the murder of Rice Jones, judicial business slowed to a snail's pace. Thomas and his fellow territorial judge Alexander Stuart, perhaps distracted by their quasi-legislative function during the first stage of territorial government or by the first squabbles over patronage, never focused on their judicial work as Ninian Edwards and others thought they should. Edwards, asserting expertise as a result of his short service on Kentucky's high court, had clear ideas about how he thought the judges ought to do their jobs. Thomas had his own ideas, believing that the General Assembly should create a full panoply of inferior courts like the ones he had helped to set up in the Indiana Territory. This would have the incidental benefits of saving him and the other territorial judges from some of the rigors of riding circuit and giving them more time to pursue other interests. Edwards, on the other hand, wanted to keep the territorial judges busy and out of politics and therefore encouraged the General Assembly to pass laws detailing their responsibilities. There ensued a bitter debate about whether the General Assembly had the power to regulate the territorial judges, with Thomas and the other judges arguing that their authority flowed from the U.S. Congress and only that body had authority to control them. What was really going on, though, was a struggle for political power in Illinois.[22]

During these early years in the Illinois Territory, Thomas was sorting out where he stood politically. His relationship with Harrison was still in tatters. Since he and Harrison still shared the responsibility of administering the estate of Rebecca's late husband, it was essential for Thomas to establish some new modus vivendi for the sake of his wife's considerable property.

Thomas also probably recognized the need to mend the rift between them to mollify Harrison's many friends among his new neighbors in the Illinois Territory. Unfortunately, however, relations between the two men remained frosty for several years more, as evidenced by Thomas's writing to Harrison on August 11, 1810, in response to a sharp communication from Harrison six months before: "I have no hesitation in saying that I feel no less reluctant at renewing a correspondence with you than that expressed by you in your letter to me of the 14 Feby last, for experience has already taught me that I have neither profited by our former correspondence nor by my acquaintance with you; and this opinion is bottomed on a belief that you were the prime mover of the plan laid in 1808 to crush me, and that too when we were in the habits of intimacy—."[23] The two men must have eventually agreed to cooperate but remained uneasy coadjutors of the estate. Neither was on the scene in Ohio, the location of the land that was the critical element of the estate, and vital matters were left undone. There was even the threat at times that part of the property would be sold for taxes. The fate of John Francis Hamtramck's property was something that mattered much more to Thomas than to Harrison and probably became a means for Harrison to needle Thomas.

As time went by, Harrison's influence in Illinois faded and new factions coalesced, one supporting Governor Edwards and one opposed to him. Thomas eventually emerged as the leading figure in the faction opposed to Edwards, and the two men gradually evolved into enemies. It was clearly a matter of personality and power as they were in essential agreement on the pivotal issues of land and slavery.

The largely pointless competition between Thomas and Edwards would later be played out on the national stage in the so-called A. B. affair, but, at the start, the main source of tension was local patronage. Thomas, harking back to the more harmonious times at the start of the territorial government, seemed genuinely to believe that a sharing of patronage would continue. On February 21, 1812, he wrote Edwards, confessing "that I was not a little surprised at the manner in which that cordiality which had heretofore existed between us ceased on your part, feeling as I did conscious that I merited not only your respect but your friendship. And if my mind had been employed in reflecting on that subject ever since I discovered your coolness, I should have been as far from knowing the real cause as I was at first."[24] As the feud with Edwards deepened, Thomas adjusted by cementing alliances that would help him face a new and difficult stage in Illinois politics. These new alliances were possible only because Thomas was moving away from John Edgar and the Morrisons, who were increasingly perceived as an older generation with unfortunate Federalist leanings. Standing with him in the emerging anti-Edwards faction were Elias Kent Kane and John McLean, both of whom later joined Thomas in the U.S. Senate; Shadrach Bond Jr. and his uncle of the same name; and even the troublesome Michael Jones of Kaskaskia.

Perhaps the most critical of Thomas's new allies was Kane, the most brilliant and productive member of the group. Kane was a cousin of both Chancellor James Kent of New York and the intrepid Arctic explorer Elisha Kent Kane of Philadelphia. He had been born and grew up in New York City and graduated from Yale College in 1813. Admitted first to the bar in Nashville, Tennessee, he practiced briefly there before moving to Kaskaskia in 1814. While still in his early twenties, he was appointed a judge in the courts set up by the territorial general assembly and soon became Thomas's colleague and friend, going on to become the intellectual linchpin of the Thomas faction. He proved a nimble politician, but he was always enigmatic, operating behind the scenes and leaving behind not "one human touch, not one phrase that can endow the man with a living personality."[25] Also arriving in Illinois in 1815 and settling in Shawneetown was John McLean. McLean had been born in North Carolina and, like Thomas, came to Illinois by way of Kentucky. Once in Illinois, he read law for a year, was admitted to the bar, and soon allied himself with Thomas, using his skills as a lawyer and banker to advance his political ambitions.

Like other supporters of Harrison, Shadrach Bond and his uncle of the same name found themselves adrift after the creation of the new territory. They initially kept their distance from the emerging factions centered on Edwards and Thomas but, recognizing that Edwards had no inclination to help them, threw in their lot with his opponents. Shadrach Bond Jr. was a power in territorial Illinois, serving as receiver in the Kaskaskia land office and being elected Illinois' first territorial delegate. Edwards unsuccessfully petitioned Congress to investigate Bond's election, and, though the two men worked relatively closely during Bond's two-year term, the rift between them never healed. Michael Jones of Kaskaskia, another staunch Harrison man, tried to establish an independent political base, but he too soon fell in with the disparate Thomas faction.

John Rice Jones left Illinois for Missouri after his son's murder and ultimately became a member of the Missouri Constitutional Convention in

1820, one of the original three justices of the Missouri Supreme Court, and a recognized authority on lead mining there. As an original sponsor of Thomas and possibly the person who introduced him to Rebecca, he was an important supporter. He also helped Richard Thomas, a neighbor in Ste. Genevieve, by sponsoring him for admission to the bar. The cast of characters on both sides of the Edwards-Thomas political divide was now in place, and it was time to test each other's strength.

CHAPTER 7

The Political Divide

A s Illinois settled into the second stage of territorial government, it quietly addressed the issue of slavery. In 1813 the territorial General Assembly followed a course on slavery similar to Indiana's, prohibiting further immigration of free black people into Illinois, allowing the continued use of indentures, and requiring all black people in the territory to be registered with the clerk of the court of common pleas of the county in which they lived. A year later, it added an authorization to use slaves in the saltworks (the General Assembly used the term "slave" in this latter context rather than "indentured servant"), thus acknowledging that the concept of slavery persisted in Illinois. The 1810 federal census in Illinois showed 5,858 white residents and 629 African Americans living in the Illinois Territory, with 129 of the latter being slaves and 500 being indentured servants. The Illinois Territorial Census taken in 1818 immediately before statehood (and before being puffed up to reach the population required for statehood) showed the white population roughly quadrupling to 27,785 while the African American population roughly doubling to 1,068, of whom 751 were indentured servants or slaves and 317 were free persons of color.[1]

Members of both of the nascent political alliances owned slaves. Jesse Thomas brought with him to Illinois a twenty-year-old mulatto woman named Fanny who was an indentured servant, bound to eleven more years of service. By the time of the census in 1810, the household included, in addition to Fanny, two Kaskaskia Indians as slaves. Later that year he wrote a friend to determine whether a slave named Maurice belonged to his stepdaughters Julianne and Harriet or whether ownership had passed to the new owner when the small

farm on which Maurice worked was sold. On September 25, 1813, Thomas registered a twenty-eight-year-old black woman named Abigail who had come to
Illinois as an indentured servant from Kentucky and was bound for a term of
thirty years, the maximum then allowed under the Illinois statutes. In a pattern
that was apparently typical, Thomas crossed the Mississippi to Ste. Genevieve,
Missouri, on June 21 of the following year and purchased a twenty-seven-
year-old black man, known as James, for the price of $500. Thomas brought
James across to Kaskaskia that same day and filed an indenture showing him
to be bound in Illinois for a term of thirty years. Finally, in his last known
transaction in human bondage, Thomas filed an indenture on September 29,
1817, for a twenty-three-year-old black woman named Mary, showing a price
of $500. Thomas's involvement with the institution of slavery was typical of
early settlers in the Northwest Territory. The records show Ninian Edwards,
Thomas's principal rival in Illinois, as owning eighteen slaves.[2]

Jesse Thomas and Ninian Edwards may have had in common that they
were both slave owners, albeit on a different scale, and they agreed on the major
issues of land policy and slavery; but they disagreed on almost everything else.
The real issue between them was political power, an issue made more acute
by the diminution of power that both men suffered as Illinois passed from
the first to the second stage of territorial government. Thomas likely resented
having to give up the legislative function in which he had been almost equal
with the governor and to revert to a purely judicial role. Edwards, for his part,
had to share his powers and perquisites with a territorial legislature. To make
matters worse, both men now had to share the stage with Shadrach Bond Jr.,
Illinois' first territorial delegate.

The informal political parties that had started to coalesce even before
Illinois became a territory continued to evolve during the territorial period,
even in the absence of organized political parties. Most candidates were put
forward by small groups of friends rather than nominated in a more formal
party framework, and all candidates disavowed personal interest in obtaining
elective office, eschewing, or claiming to eschew, party politics as the worst
evil that could befall a republic. Candidates affected not to work together in
concert. There were no formal slates or party platforms; and even caucuses,
like the one in which Thomas had participated in Indiana in 1808, were rare.
Candidates were also required to strictly observe the fiction that there could
be no politicking on one's own behalf. The electorate was meant to be limited
to well-informed men of substance who knew the character of the candidates

and were capable of making their choice based on a candidate's personal qualities rather than on his positions on specific issues.

Political theory aside, however, there were clearly loose amalgamations of individuals acting together for common ends in Illinois, as elsewhere. As Jesse Thomas's group came together, another more established and cohesive group clustered around Edwards, composed in large part of relatives of the powerful Pope family in Kentucky. It included, among others, Daniel Pope Cook and Nathaniel Pope, the first a distant cousin of Edwards and the second a first cousin. Perhaps the most important person in Edwards's circle, however, was his close friend and political ally Benjamin Stephenson.

In 1814 Edwards backed Stephenson to replace Shadrach Bond as territorial delegate. The situation on the eve of this election was tense. Edwards, even though he was actively involved supporting Stephenson, never acknowledged that he was practicing party politics. When he interfered personally in any election, he truly believed it was a prerogative of his social station and his office, a dispensation he never allowed to Thomas or any other adversary. Thomas, on the other hand, was more flexible than Edwards in both temperament and intellect and instinctively understood the evolution of party politics then occurring in Illinois and elsewhere in the country. He did, however, share enough of Edwards's patrician outlook that he was never able to follow the new politics all the way to its logical conclusion. The younger men with whom he was associated could and would, but Thomas, like Edwards, would not survive the transition to full-blown party politics.

These differences in character and political outlook were nowhere more evident than in the election contest for territorial delegate in 1814. Born in Pennsylvania in 1769, Benjamin Stephenson immigrated to Virginia as a nineteen-year-old and then to Kentucky, where he became a friend of Edwards. For the rest of his life, his fortunes were closely tied to Edwards's, and their histories are intertwined in politics and business as well as in friendship. He came to Illinois with Edwards in 1809 and settled near him in Kaskaskia. On June 28, 1809, Edwards removed James Gilbreath from the office of sheriff in Randolph County and appointed Stephenson in his place.[3] With the coming of war against the British in 1812, Edwards commissioned Stephenson to lead one of the two regiments of militia assembled at Fort Russell to defend the territory against the British. Stephenson served as a colonel in two campaigns during that war. The following year Edwards appointed him adjutant general of the territory and then a year later put him forward as a candidate for territorial delegate.

When Thomas refused to support Stephenson, Edwards took personal offense and looked upon him as a traitor. Furthermore, Edwards considered it a personal insult when Thomas suggested that Edwards was supporting Stephenson in order to advance his own political objectives. It is hard for the modern reader, from the perspective of the present, to understand what the fuss was about; however, for three days at the end of June and beginning of July 1814, Thomas's suggestion that Edwards might be actively supporting Stephenson brought Edwards and Thomas to the verge of a duel. In the tension of this confrontation, the personalities of both men emerged in sharp relief.

The first salvo came in a June 28 letter from Edwards to Thomas, in which Edwards harks back to the patronage squabble in 1812, when Thomas was trying to find a job in Illinois for his half brother Michael Jones:

> In the year 1812 without any just cause of provocation on
> my part, you commenced war upon me. And while I was
> engaged on the frontier in defending my fellow citizens,
> you disregarding the dignity and delicacy of your office was
> in the honorable employment of riding about from place to
> place electioneering, and using the most unjustifiable means
> to injure me.
>
> On my return from Peoria you acknowledged your error,
> professed to be sorry for it, and as I had no desire to injure
> you, a peace was settled upon terms of your own proposing,
> one of which was that you were never to meddle as you
> had done in elections. You have now broken the truce &
> I think it candid and honorable to tell you that I intend
> freely and publicly to investigate your conduct towards me
> in 1812, and to exhibit to the world the motives by which
> you were governed.
>
> I had not intended to interfere in the least in the
> approaching election, but have been reluctantly dragged
> by the most unfounded insinuations from the repose in
> which I have for months indulged. And I will now defend
> myself against the attacks of a coalition—heterogeneous in
> everything except unprovoked hostility to myself. Nor can I
> doubt that their former open crimination and recrimination
> of each other will deservedly [reflect] upon the weight of

any accusations they might be disposed to make against me, for if they have for years persisted in making statements the most malignant & untrue against each other, it proves them unworthy of credit against me—and if their statements have been founded in truth, each establishes against the other charges of the highest magnitude. And you know it is fair at all times to use in ones favor the testimony of his adversary.

In me you shall find a fair and open antagonist and all I ask of you, is that if you have any charges to make against me to justify the course you adopted towards me, that you will appoint any day & place which may suit your own convenience to exhibit them and afford me a public opportunity of defending myself.

Before I conclude this letter, I must declare that every statement and insinuation that I had either directly or indirectly been instrumental in bringing Colo Stephenson forward as a candidate for Congress are false in fact & that I can prove them so to be by the Colo himself and by Mr. Sec'y Pope & [Leonard] White of the U.S. Saline.[4]

Thomas did not react well to Edwards's attempt to impose his will on him and responded with a coolness clearly calculated to goad Edwards on. The letters in the exchange were carried back and forth between the two men's houses, so there was little time for reflection or good sense to steer them away from a potentially deadly confrontation. Edwards's letters were long and rambling, and Thomas's were succinct and rapier-like.

In one response, Edwards said he wrote in haste and his full response would be delayed until after he had dealt with other business; but then, after his initial avowal, he went on, slightly incoherently, for three and half pages. Thomas egged Edwards on, toying with, without actually using, the terminology of dueling. He artfully avoided the demand for an explanation that would be the first step in invoking the rules of honor while at the same time asserting that he had every right to do so. There was clearly also an awareness on his part, more than on Edwards's, that dueling between two so senior members of the territorial hierarchy was counter to public policy (as reflected in a law both men had passed four years before) and would be potentially damaging to the career of whichever of them was so unlucky as to survive.[5]

The letters that followed were sequentially numbered and, if from Thomas, copied and certified by Elias Kent Kane, who was acting as Thomas's second, so that Thomas would have a record of all that transpired, whether it culminated in a duel or not. Even if a duel could be averted, it would be essential to demonstrate that Thomas had fully satisfied the code of honor. At one point, Edwards, in his choler, neglected to sign one of his letters, and Thomas refused to respond until it was properly signed. Edwards, finally realizing that a duel might be imminent, unsuccessfully attempted to lay on Thomas the onus of having commenced the formal etiquette of dueling.

The exchange of letters continued with Edwards lumbering on, somewhat awkwardly, and Thomas more successfully skating the thin line between political repartee and the code of honor while raising for the first time the propriety of senior territorial officials settling disputes with a duel: "Your singular communications . . . as you admit gave me the most unquestionable right to an appeal to what you term the laws of honor—with my pacific disposition and filling a highly responsible office under the Government of the United States—I would certainly have [waived] that privilege, although my letters to you have affirmed a becoming and independent character, the more so because the attack came from yourself, I did not intend a threat yet I cannot consent to withdraw any thing stated in my letters." Thomas then invoked the necessity of holding court in a distant county as a reason for temporary delay, probably understanding the importance of a cooling down period. He still stood ready to proceed with a duel if Edwards wished it but wanted Edwards to be responsible for initiating it.

The cooling off period worked, and the matter was finally put into a troubled abeyance as evidenced by the notice, dated August 3, 1814, prepared by Kane for publication in the local newspaper:

> The editor of the *Kaskaskia Illinois Herald* will please give the following an insertion in his paper:
>
>> Reports prejudicial to Judge Thomas concerning a
>> recent correspondence carried on between himself and
>> Gov. Edwards having gained an extensive circulation
>> I feel it my duty, in justice to the Judge, to state it
>> publicly, as a fact, that such reports are wholly without
>> foundation. On the contrary the communications on

the part of Judge Thomas if published would bear him
an honourable testimony of integrity and firmness.

Elias Kent Kane

After this bitter exchange between Edwards and Thomas, Benjamin Stephenson proceeded to win election as territorial delegate on September 3, 1814.
When he replaced Bond on November 14, 1814, his first priority was to marshal
support in Congress for Edwards's efforts to control the territorial judges in
Illinois. Edwards continued to push for Congress to pass a law authorizing
the territorial General Assembly to regulate the territorial judges as it saw
fit, but he first wanted to drive through the General Assembly a new law
defining the duties of the territorial judges along the lines he preferred. The
General Assembly passed the new law a month later, establishing a supreme
court of the Illinois Territory in the place of the general court. The three
territorial judges were to constitute the supreme court, but they were also to
ride the circuit and share the local workload with local county judges. Other
changes unpalatable to the territorial judges were also made. Judges Thomas
and William Sprigg responded to the new act immediately, addressing a letter
to the General Assembly setting forth their objections.[6]

The legislature, evidently seeking to duck a complicated and legalistic dispute between the two most powerful men in the territory, sent the letter from
the judges on to Governor Edwards, requesting his opinion, which he gave at
great length in a response dated December 12, 1814, in which he claimed that
the General Assembly had the right to prescribe the specific responsibilities
of the territorial judges provided they did not conflict with what had been
set forth by Congress. The territorial judges still refused to acknowledge the
validity of the law, and on December 21, 1814, the General Assembly for-
warded all the documents to Congress together with a memorial praying for
relief. The memorial innocently set forth that, "there being no intermixture of
party spirit or individual hostility with this proceeding, the objections of the
judges to executing the law doubtless arise, more from a conviction in their
own minds of the want of Power in the Legislature to pass it, than from any
indisposition on their part to perform the duties therein assigned to them."[7]

The argument between Edwards and the territorial judges now moved to
Congress, which also chose to duck the issue in a way that preserved its own
prerogatives. Instead of approving an act giving the General Assembly broad

authority over the territorial judges, Congress instead took the act that the General Assembly had passed and adopted it as its own with few substantive changes. Although this gave Edwards much of what he wanted, it was Congress setting the rules, which was what Thomas and Sprigg had insisted upon throughout. The most important change imposed by Congress was a provision prohibiting federally appointed territorial judges sitting with judges appointed in the territory. Despite the fact that the 1815 act was as much a victory for the judges as it was for Edwards, the governor claimed it as a great triumph, and Benjamin Stephenson, in an open letter to the citizens of Illinois, took full credit for ramming it through during his tenure as territorial delegate.[8]

Jesse Burgess Thomas was an impressive figure, standing six feet tall and weighing over two hundred pounds, yet he rarely tried to impose his will, one of his favorite observations being that "you could not talk a man down, but you could whisper him to death." *John Francis Snyder, "Forgotten Statesmen of Illinois: Hon. Jesse Burgess Thomas, Jesse Burgess Thomas, Jr., Richard Symmes Thomas, Jr.," Illinois State Historical Society Transactions 9 (1904): 514–25.*

William Henry Harrison was Thomas's most important supporter in the Indiana Territory until the two had a falling out in 1808. They later mended fences in time for Thomas to help elect Harrison to the presidency in 1840. *Library of Congress.*

Harrison completed his home, Grouseland, in the town of Vincennes in 1804, the year before Thomas arrived as a representative in the territorial House. Known as the White House of the West, its size and elegance were in stark contrast to the simplicity of the dwellings of most frontiersmen. Grouseland is on the National Register of Historic Places and is administered by the National Park Service. *Grouseland Foundation, Inc. (www.grouseland.org), 3 West Scott Street, Vincennes, Indiana.*

John Rice Jones negotiated the controversial deal that made Jesse Thomas territorial delegate, and he may also have introduced Thomas to Rebecca McKenzie, the woman who became his wife. *From Edward G. Mason, Early Chicago and Illinois (Chicago: Fergus, 1890), facing page 230; photograph collection (021468), The State Historical Society of Missouri.*

Thomas first met William Harris Crawford in 1808, when he went to Washington, D.C., as a territorial delegate. When the two met again ten years later, Crawford was the secretary of the U.S. Treasury and the leading contender for the presidency in 1824. From that point on, the two men's fates were intertwined. *Library of Congress.*

Ninian Edwards was Thomas's chief rival in Illinois, and their enmity carried onto the national stage in the A. B. affair, which played a major part in the campaign for the presidency in 1824. *Abraham Lincoln Presidential Library and Museum.*

Kaskaskia, shown here about the time that Jesse Thomas lived there, was one of the oldest towns in the Old Northwest and served as the capital of Illinois throughout the territorial period. *Abraham Lincoln Presidential Library and Museum.*

The territorial General Assembly met in this building in Kaskaskia. It is likely where Thomas presided over the state constitutional convention and where he was first elected U.S. senator. *Abraham Lincoln Presidential Library and Museum.*

At the age of twenty-four, Elias Kent Kane was the principal architect of the Illinois Constitution. He worked with Thomas to leave open the possibility of slavery after statehood. *Abraham Lincoln Presidential Library and Museum.*

Thomas moved to Cahokia shortly before statehood in 1818. Cahokia and Kaskaskia were the two towns in Illinois still redolent of French culture and customs. *Abraham Lincoln Presidential Library and Museum.*

Daniel Pope Cook was Edwards's ally and Thomas's enemy. Surprisingly for a frontiersman, he was also an admirer of John Quincy Adams. As the lone representative in Congress from Illinois, Cook helped deliver Illinois to Adams when the 1824 presidential election was decided by the House of Representatives. *Abraham Lincoln Presidential Library and Museum.*

James Monroe was as practical as Thomas Jefferson was theoretical. He implemented in a workmanlike fashion many of Jefferson's more speculative ideas on government in the West, and he played a careful but vital role behind the scenes in the Missouri Compromise. *Library of Congress*

Although Henry Clay played a lesser role in the first, and more contentious, Missouri Compromise, he did work with Jesse Thomas to engineer the piecemeal approach that allowed it to pass. He then prevailed in a parliamentary fencing match with John Randolph at the eleventh hour that saved the compromise. *Library of Congress.*

John Quincy Adams was a superb diplomat. The Adams-Onis Treaty with Spain and the Treaty of 1818 with Britain defined the area covered by the Missouri Compromise and included far more land than expected north of the 36°30′ line. But his uncompromising rigidity as president was the death knell for his allies like Jesse Thomas. *Library of Congress.*

Andrew Jackson, a fiery competitor, developed an implacable dislike for both William Crawford and Jesse Thomas. *Library of Congress.*

John C. Calhoun of South Carolina was a perennial presidential contender. Ninian Edwards became not just a supporter of Calhoun for the presidency in 1824 but also a hatchet man for him, attacking Jesse Thomas and William Crawford in the A. B. affair. *Library of Congress.*

The committee of conference of the Senate and of the House of Representatives on the subject of the disagreeing votes of the Two Houses, upon the Bill entitled an "Act for the admission of the State of Maine into the Union,"

Report the following Resolution.

Resolved.

1.st That they recommend to the Senate to recede from their amendments to the said Bill

2.d That they recommend to the two Houses to agree to strike out of the fourth section of the Bill from the House of Representatives now pending in the Senate, entitled an "Act to authorize the people of the Missouri Territory to form a Constitution and State Government and for the admission of such State into the Union upon an equal footing with the original States," the following proviso, in the following words — and shall ordain and establish that there shall be neither Slavery nor involuntary servitude otherwise than in the punishment of crimes whereof the party shall have been duly convicted; provided always, That any person escaping into the same, from whom labour or service is lawfully claimed in any other State such fugitive may be lawfully reclaimed and conveyed to the person claiming his or her labour or service, as aforesaid: Provided nevertheless, That the said Provision shall not be construed to alter the condition or civil rights of any person now held to service or labor in the said Territory:

And that the following provision be added to the Bill —

And be it further enacted, That in all that Territory ceded by France to the United States under the name of Louisiana, which lies north of thirty six degrees and thirty minutes North latitude, not included within the limits of the State contemplated by this act, Slavery and involuntary servitude otherwise than in the punishment of crimes whereof the party shall have been duly convicted, shall be and is hereby forever prohibited. Provided always, That any person escaping into the same, from whom labour or service is lawfully claimed in any other State or Territory of the United States such fugitive may be lawfully reclaimed, and conveyed to the person claiming his or her labour or service as aforesaid —

Thomas was chairman of the Senate managers appointed to the conference committee that fashioned the Missouri Compromise. The handwriting on the committee's report, shown here, can now be definitively identified as Thomas's, conclusively demonstrating that he handled every aspect of the negotiations. *National Archives.*

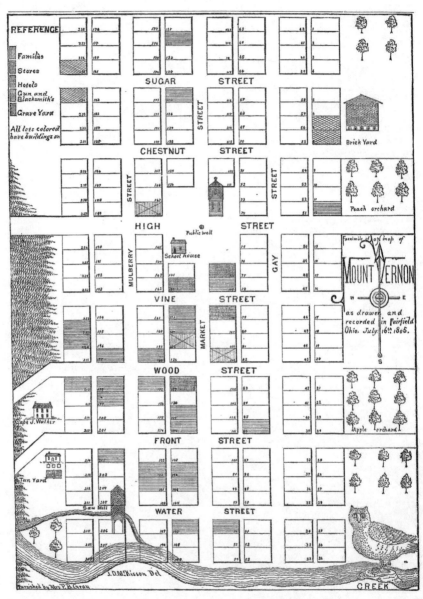

This 1805 map shows that the town of Mount Vernon, Ohio, was well established even before Jesse's marriage to Rebecca in 1806, but Jesse contributed mightily to its growth. *Library of Congress.*

Jesse and Rebecca built this comfortable Greek Revival house on East Gambier Street in Mount Vernon in 1837. *Knox County Historical Society, Ohio.*

By 1846 Mount Vernon had an imposing town square. It was a town of churches, but the twin spires of St. Paul's Episcopal Church, on the far right, are particularly impressive. That church played a major role in the lives of Jesse and Rebecca Thomas. *Knox County Historical Society, Ohio.*

Jesse Thomas and his friend Henry Curtis accompanied Episcopal bishop Philander Chase on the expedition to identify and buy the tract where Kenyon College was to be situated. Old Kenyon was the first permanent building on the campus. It was built to last, with massive stone walls four feet thick at their base. *Photo by Howard Korn, courtesy of Kenyon College.*

This crude allegorical woodcut, created fourteen years after the Missouri Compromise, demonstrates how, for many, preservation of the Union had become the paramount issue. Ironically, the compromise, which divided the Union, became the exemplar of its unity. *Library of Congress.*

CHAPTER 8

Illinois Statehood

esse and Rebecca Thomas's household had gone through some changes since their arrival in the Illinois Territory. When the War of 1812 had broken out on the frontier, Rebecca's elder son, John Francis Hamtramck Jr., not yet fifteen but aspiring to emulate his father, left home to take up a military career. He wrangled an appointment as a sergeant in the First Infantry under Major Zachary Taylor on an expedition up the Mississippi River and fought in an action in the summer of 1814 against Sac and Fox Indians supported by British batteries. Commended for his bravery in that action, he put in to become an officer, and then, helped no doubt by his name and the support of both his guardian, William Henry Harrison, and his stepfather, he received an appointment to West Point the following year. Both of Rebecca's stepdaughters were married and left home about that time, and, with her elder son gone, only her younger son, Alexander McKenzie Hamtramck, and her daughter Rebecca were left at home.[1]

By 1817, Jesse and Rebecca had grown restless in Kaskaskia, aware that the center of gravity in Illinois was moving northward. Late that year, taking advantage of a new offer to federal officials to acquire additional lands, they decided to move eighty miles north of their original homestead in Randolph County to settle in Cahokia, then the county seat of St. Clair County.[2] Cahokia was an even older settlement than Kaskaskia, with similar deep French roots, and was in the northernmost part of the American Bottom. Like Kaskaskia, Cahokia was built too close to the river, and periodic flooding destined it also to be bypassed by future settlers.

During his association with John Edgar and the Morrisons, Jesse Thomas had already developed an affinity for long-established Illinoisans with French roots. The other Americans who settled around the Thomases in Cahokia also respected the French for their gracious and relaxed lifestyle, many of them speaking the local Creole dialect and following Creole customs. A number of them, like his young friend Elias Kent Kane, married French women. The French society in Illinois was by that time down on its luck, living off the wealth and property it had accumulated in earlier times. It was an egalitarian society, however, bred of an older, more genteel way of life that was already fading and that was essentially different from the rough-edged equality espoused by the recent poor white immigrants from the southern uplands or the working-class immigrants from the Northeast who were to be the two waves of the future in Illinois. It was also a culture with a broad tolerance for slavery.

Though Jesse Thomas had served continuously as a judge since the beginning of the territorial period in Illinois, the position apparently never fully engaged him, and, until he was able to return full time to politics, he continued to dabble in real estate and other businesses. In one of his better-documented ventures, he established in 1817 in Cahokia the first wool-carding machine put into operation in Illinois. Wool carding is the process by which the longer fibers of wool are brushed, straightened, and aligned with wire teeth before being spun into yarn. Since antiquity, wool had been carded by hand, a very time-consuming process. A mechanical method had been developed for the first time in England in 1748 and had been one of the catalysts for the Industrial Revolution. With the introduction of a greater number of sheep into Illinois, many housewives were spending an inordinate amount of time carding wool by hand, and Thomas sensed that a mechanical means of carding would be a good investment and might even influence a few votes by making settlers' lives a little easier.

There were carding machines in the eastern states but none in Illinois, and Thomas determined to set one up in Cahokia, to be powered by the tread of oxen on a large incline wheel in the lower floor of the building. He was unable to find anyone in the territory with any knowledge of the process, but he went ahead anyway, confident that he could find someone to run it. In the spring of 1817, he proceeded by keelboat down the Mississippi and up the Ohio to Pittsburgh, where he purchased the necessary equipment and arranged for its shipment to Cahokia. Lore has it that the equipment was shipped on the steamboat *Zebulon M. Pike*, on the first successful effort to negotiate the Mississippi upriver from its junction with the Ohio, or it may have been shipped by keelboat, which would have been less expensive and possibly more reliable.[3]

On his return trip from Pittsburgh, Thomas stopped off to attend to business in Mount Vernon, Ohio, where he heard of an enterprising seventeen-year-old named Adam Snyder who was said to know something about carding machines. Snyder, the nephew of a former Pennsylvania governor, was working at the time in a general store at a crossroads town southeast of Mount Vernon, where he had come two years earlier from his father's farm in Pennsylvania. Thomas persuaded Snyder to leave his job at the general store and go with him to Illinois to run the new carding mill.

Snyder soon became a Thomas protégé. After successfully launching the carding mill, Snyder went on to study law and, with Thomas's support and assistance, was admitted to the bar and began a successful political career as a state senator, a U.S. representative, and a nominee for governor. His political career began while Jesse Thomas was still at the height of his power, and their friendship was certainly an important factor in Snyder's success. Like Kane, he married a woman of French descent. The Snyder family remained close with the Thomas family thereafter.

In addition to his business forays, Thomas continued to earn a reputation for fairness as a territorial judge, but he never wandered far from the arena of politics. As one of the foremost public servants in the Illinois Territory, with experience as a legislator on both the territorial and national levels and as the only judge to have served during the entire territorial period, he was poised when the movement for Illinois statehood gathered steam. Clearly, he and Ninian Edwards, who had been governor since the territory was formed in 1808, were the two leading men in Illinois politics. Statehood was not a universally accepted goal at the time. Those who benefited from territorial patronage, or from the light hand of a distant government, opposed statehood, claiming that "the population of the territory was in too great a state of ignorance and too much lacerated by party contentions to become independent."[4] Certainly Edwards was unenthusiastic about statehood and the diminution in his power that would come with it. However, both he and Thomas recognized, when the movement was thoroughly underway, that they had better join in if they wished to retain their preeminence after statehood.

Perhaps the most important difference between Thomas and Edwards was that the latter was a born elitist who viewed "the people" as an abstract, homogeneous concept, whereas Thomas, a far more practical individual, saw a world made up of individuals with varying interests. This was Thomas's power, as he could shift with the times in building majorities in favor of his positions, but it was also his downfall, as alliances built from disparate elements were inherently unstable. He had the additional disadvantage of being the leader of a group defined less by its shared political views than by its opposition to Edwards.

The most interesting aspect of the statehood campaign in Illinois was that slavery never became a seriously divisive factor, which is particularly surprising when compared with the process in Missouri two years later. The handling of the issue of slavery was certainly the prime difference in the two statehood initiatives, and Jesse Thomas was largely responsible for the relative calm in Illinois. The lessons he learned in the statehood process, when added to his already thorough knowledge of slavery strategies in the Indiana and Illinois Territories, certainly prepared him for his upcoming role in Washington in the Missouri controversy.

Thomas and Edwards, and the factions slowly coalescing around them, began to stake out positions as the bill to make Illinois into a state worked its way through Congress. On January 16, 1818, Edwards's ally Nathaniel Pope, then serving as Illinois' territorial delegate, presented in the House the petition of the General Assembly of the Illinois Territory, praying that the territory be made a state and that the state, when formed, be admitted into the Union on an equal footing with the original states. The petition was referred to a select committee to which, as was typical, Pope was appointed and made chairman. On January 23, Pope reported out an enabling bill that was read twice and committed to a committee of the whole, where it moldered until Congress began to wrap up its business at the end of the session. It finally passed at the very end of the session with Pope pushing through one last amendment to move the boundary of the new state north from the latitude of the southern tip of Lake Michigan to latitude 42°30′, thus securing for the new state the site of the future city of Chicago and the potential to link the Great Lakes with the Mississippi. This fortunate change would not only assure Illinois' future as a commercial hub but would also set up for Jesse Thomas the Illinois and Michigan Canal project, the great internal improvement project that would be one of his principal objects in the Senate and would align him with Henry Clay in his campaign to make internal improvements the glue holding the country together.

On April 18, 1818, President Monroe signed the act authorizing the Illinois Territory to hold a convention to decide whether to form a state government and write a constitution. The enabling act authorized the election of thirty-three convention delegates from Illinois' fifteen counties. The election of delegates was held over a three-day period beginning on July 6. The delegates chosen reflected the patterns of immigration into the territory with more having Southern roots than Northern. Several had been born in Illinois, and only one was of foreign birth. Like their constituents, the delegates' movements westward had generally been gradual. More than half of them had settled for a time in other western states—primarily Tennessee, Ohio, Indiana, and especially Kentucky—before arriving in Illinois. The delegates seem to have drawn on their experiences in those other places in drafting the constitution of 1818, with significant portions of it being modeled on the constitutions of Kentucky, Ohio, and Indiana. Jesse Thomas was chosen as one of the three delegates to represent St Clair County. His young friend Elias Kent Kane was chosen from Randolph County, and his half brother Michael Jones was a delegate from Gallatin County.

The enabling act's authorization to hold a convention in Illinois was conditioned on the territory having at least forty thousand inhabitants, which was far short of the sixty thousand suggested, but not required, by the Northwest Ordinance. There was another key distinction between the Northwest Ordinance and the Illinois enabling act: the Northwest Ordinance called for the enumeration of free inhabitants, whereas the Illinois enabling act required only a simple count of inhabitants, thus including slaves and indentured servants. This provided yet another reason for Illinoisans to promote slavery. Even reducing the necessary number of inhabitants and loosening definitions may not have been sufficient to meet the population requirement; when the special territorial census was completed, many suspected that it had fallen short of the required number. Proponents of statehood argued that the census had failed to properly account for the immigrants who had been streaming into Illinois during that summer, and accordingly, one of the convention's first actions was to authorize a committee, headed by Kane, to examine the census returns and to "receive and report such other evidence of the actual population of the territory as to them shall seem proper."[5] With this latitude, the committee came up with increased county-by-county totals that conveniently added up to 40,258.

The convention convened in Kaskaskia on August 3, 1818. It is not even known now where in Kaskaskia the delegates met, and, until a lone copy of the journal of the convention was unearthed in 1905, there had not been any record of its proceedings.[6] Jesse Thomas was elected president pro tem and then permanent president. No other candidates were mentioned. He was at his best when participating in, or presiding over, a deliberative body, treating delegates courteously and being conscientiously honorable. He had the kind of Old World bearing that was already fading into the colonial past but also had a pleasant manner that made others want to work with him.[7] Thomas made a short and dignified speech on his election as president, which was the only one reported verbatim in the journal:

> Impressed with the high sense of the honor conferred on me by being called to the chair, and doubting my own abilities to fill the situation with propriety, it is with extreme diffidence that I enter upon the discharge of the duties of the situation thus assigned me: I can only assure you that so far as I possess the capacity nothing shall be wanting on my part to support the dignity of this convention. And whilst I solicit your aid and indulgence on this occasion, suffer me to remark that a spirit of indulgence and harmony amongst ourselves is the surest guarantee to a happy termination of the great work before us.[8]

The enabling act set only two requirements for the new constitution: that it provide for a republican form of government, a requirement carried over from the Virginia act of cession, and that it be not repugnant to the Northwest Ordinance. The requirement of a republican form of government raised interesting questions of definition, which were largely ignored, but the requirement that the constitution be not repugnant to the Northwest Ordinance proved more troublesome when the constitutional convention came up against the Northwest Ordinance's Article VI prohibition on slavery. Thomas and Kane were likely aware that Congress had, in the past, been lenient in interpreting conditions imposed on territories seeking statehood but may also have sensed that Congress was developing a new sensitivity on the issue of slavery. For whatever reason, they decided to handle the issue delicately and thus avoided lighting the match that would lead to conflagration in Missouri's progress to statehood two years later.

Congress's power to oversee state constitutions was unclear. There had been long-standing debates about Congress's authority to regulate territories and set requirements for statehood. The pivotal provision of the U.S. Constitution was Article IV, §3. The two parts of that section vital to the question of slavery were, first, that "new states may be admitted by the Congress into this Union" and, second, that "the Congress shall have power to dispose of and make all needful rules and regulations respecting the territory or other property belonging to the United States; and nothing in this Constitution shall be so construed as to prejudice any claims of the United States, or of any particular state."

The first clause of the section provides that Congress "may" admit new states into the Union. It is permissive and not mandatory, and antislavery advocates argued that Congress therefore had the right to set any reasonable conditions it saw fit, including a ban on slavery, for the admission of a new state. Even equality was not guaranteed in the Constitution—the "equal footing" concept had first been floated for all western lands in Jefferson's proposed Ordinance of 1784 and subsequently in the Northwest Ordinance of 1787, but a consensus could not be found to put that language in the Constitution itself for all future states. In this context, antislavery advocates were, quite logically, convinced that a restriction on the spread of slavery was a reasonable condition. Such a restriction also seemed consistent with the requirement for a republican form of government and with the Declaration of Independence, which was increasingly becoming a linchpin for those who sought to limit the spread of slavery. Slavery supporters, on the other hand, claimed that, since there was no express grant of the right to impose conditions, there could be none, and Congress's choice on statehood could be only up or down—complete equality or continuing territorial status.[9]

The second part of Article IV, §3, grants Congress the power to make all needful rules respecting the territories. Those who wished to restrict slavery again read this section broadly, claiming that it gave Congress the right to prohibit slavery in the territories during the territorial period. This seemed crucial to them because they believed that, if a territory without slavery applied for admission to the Union, its proposed constitution would be unlikely to permit slavery after statehood. Opponents of restriction, on the other hand, had a very limited view of "needful rules," interpreting them strictly to apply only to housekeeping matters such as the administration and sale of public lands. They also argued that the second half of the second part of the section, which provided that "nothing in this Constitution shall be so construed as to prejudice any claims of the United States, or of any particular state," was intended to protect the prerogatives not only of existing states but also of future states and therefore barred conditions on substantive issues like slavery.

It was not even clear that a new state could be required to submit its proposed constitution for review by Congress. This had become a tradition, but there was nothing in Article IV, §3, that required it, and, as was to occur with Missouri, the practice could give opponents in a Congress, or possibly in two different Congresses, a second bite at the apple if their goal was to block statehood. States' rights proponents from slave states, on the other hand, argued that Congress could no more change or amend the constitution of a new state than it could change or amend the constitution of an existing one. And left open in these debates was the crucial question of whether a state could submit to Congress an original constitution without slavery and then, after its admission, amend it to allow slavery.

The parties on both sides of the debate over Article IV, §3, were also thinking ahead to Missouri, where the treaty that brought the territory into the United States might take precedence over the constitutional provision. For example, if a treaty commitment had been made to admit ceded areas as states, that commitment might override what appeared to be the discretionary authority of Congress to admit or not admit states and might limit the authority of Congress to impose conditions on admission. It was argued that just such a commitment in Article III of the Louisiana Treaty did precisely that: "The inhabitants of the ceded territory shall be incorporated in the Union of the United States and admitted as soon as possible according to the principles of the federal Constitution to the enjoyment of all these rights, advantages and immunities of citizens of the United States, and in the mean time they shall be maintained and protected in the free enjoyment of their liberty, property and the Religion which they profess."[10] On the other hand, those opposed to the spread of slavery argued that, even when a treaty required admission of territory as states, Congress could still prohibit slavery if it so chose. After all, France knew when making the treaty that not all American states permitted slavery and could not expect that slavery would be a necessary perquisite of statehood.

The constitutional interpretation of Article IV, §3, had certainly been debated in the cloakrooms and boardinghouses during the ten weeks that the Illinois enabling bill had been awaiting action during the first session of the Fifteenth Congress, but the final decision to impose only minor and uncontroversial conditions obviated the need for any open debate on the constitutional questions. The same would not be the case when Illinois' constitution was later submitted or when the admission of Missouri came up during the second session.

On Wednesday, August 5, the convention delegates determined to appoint a committee of fifteen, one from each county, to frame and report a constitution. By far the most active delegate to the convention, aside from Thomas himself, was his new ally Elias Kent Kane. Thomas, as presiding officer, felt it inappropriate to serve on this committee, but his actual presence was unnecessary as the ubiquitous Kane was on the committee and served as his lieutenant. At twenty-four, Kane was also the youngest delegate, but in spite of his youth and short tenure in Illinois, he had already become influential in territorial affairs. Kane is said to have drafted much of the state constitution in his Kaskaskia office even before the convention opened and by all accounts had the most significant impact of any delegate upon its final form. A week later, on August 12, the committee of fifteen reported back a complete draft quite close, as it turned out, to the final version adopted by the convention, tending to confirm that it had been largely negotiated before the convention began.

If Thomas, Kane, and their allies had carefully dissected all the difficult issues before the delegates convened, none would have occupied their attention more completely than the question of slavery. The tinder was there for the slavery issue to be flammable, but Thomas and Kane were determined to prevent fire from breaking out. Both men probably favored some form of slavery in Illinois but recognized the impracticality of explicitly achieving that goal in a constitution that would presumably be submitted to the U.S. Congress, and, by custom, be voted upon. Thomas and Kane wanted to preserve the possibility of approving slavery in Illinois in the future but, apparently influenced by the language of the enabling act requiring that the new state constitution be "not repugnant" to the Northwest Ordinance, decided they could not submit a constitution openly authorizing slavery. Their strategy seems to have been to achieve as much as they thought possible in the original constitution and to set the stage for a revision of the constitution after statehood. Accordingly, they urged the adoption of a version that prohibited slavery and involuntary servitude but was silent on the existing system of indentured servitude, which could therefore continue in place. Illinois thus bided its time, delaying for five years the attempt to establish slavery in the new state, which would eventually be tried in the constitution crisis of 1823–24. This contrasted dramatically with the more confrontational and incendiary approach taken by Missouri's constitutional convention in 1820.

Two other states had already been formed out of the Northwest Territory, and each had a slavery provision in its constitution. The Illinoisans had to consider both these provisions in drafting their own. The most recent was that of Indiana in 1816, which provided that "there shall be neither slavery nor involuntary servitude in this state, otherwise than for the punishment of crimes, whereof the party shall have been duly convicted. Nor shall any indenture of any negro or mulatto hereafter made, and executed out of the bounds of this state be of any validity within the state." This prohibition was cemented by a further provision barring any amendment that would allow slavery: "But, as the holding any part of the human Creation in slavery, or involuntary servitude, can only originate in usurpation and tyranny, no alteration of this constitution shall ever take place so as to introduce slavery or involuntary servitude in this State, otherwise than for the punishment of crimes, whereof the party shall have been duly convicted."[11]

This sweeping prohibition was antithetical to the flexibility the leaders of the Illinois constitutional convention were trying to achieve in their state and therefore posed a serious problem for them. The distinct difference of philosophy with respect to slavery between Indiana and Illinois, as discussed earlier, can be traced back to the initial split of the Illinois Territory from the Indiana Territory, when some of the antislavery elements in the eastern part of the territory were happy to see proslavery Illinois split off. With Illinois gone, the remainder of Indiana was free to express its strong antislavery sentiments. It must have intrigued Thomas and Kane, however, that the strong anti-amendment provision of the Indiana Constitution seemed to confirm their belief that, in its absence, a state would have the power to amend its constitution.

Fortuitously for Thomas and his allies, the other, and older, precedent was more useful. Ohio's constitution of 1803 was also antislavery but was far less definitive in its denunciation of the institution:

> There shall be neither slavery nor involuntary servitude in this State, otherwise than for the punishment of crimes, whereof the party shall have been duly convicted; nor shall any male person, arrived at the age of twenty-one years, or female person arrived at the age of eighteen years, be held to serve any person as a servant, under the pretense of indenture or otherwise, unless such person shall enter into such indenture while in a state of perfect freedom, and on a condition of a bona fide consideration, received or to be

received, for their service, except as before excepted. Nor shall any indenture of any negro or mulatto, hereafter made and executed out of the State, or if made in the State, where the term of service exceeds one year, be of the least validity, except those given in the case of apprenticeships.[12]

The language "except as before excepted" was the significant phrase, intended to provide a loophole for slave owners who had held their slaves in Ohio since before the renunciation of slavery in the Northwest Ordinance or who had brought their slaves into the territory from another jurisdiction that recognized slaves as property. All these slaves were to be considered as property protected by other provisions of the Northwest Ordinance and therefore as being "before excepted." They would, therefore, be bound to servitude, quite probably for life. This "before excepted" concept was one that the Illinois convention eagerly grasped onto. There was, however, another provision in the Ohio Constitution that caused problems for the Illinois delegates. The Ohio Constitution, like the Indiana Constitution, had a provision prohibiting the future amendment of the constitution "so as to introduce slavery or involuntary servitude into this State."[13] It was the provision on which the Indiana prohibition of amendment was clearly modeled, but, in light of the "except as before excepted" language in Ohio, its effect was somewhat unclear; it was apparently intended only to bar future attempts to import slaves.

These provisions from Ohio and Indiana were the ones to which the Illinois convention could most logically look as it took up the question of slavery. On Friday, August 14, the delegates, after working their way section by section through the other articles of the constitution, finally reached Article VI, the one that dealt with slavery, which was probably not coincidentally numbered the same as the provision on slavery in the Northwest Ordinance. The original version of the slavery article contained just one section:

§1 There shall be neither slavery nor involuntary servitude in this state, otherwise than for the punishment of crimes, whereof the party shall have been duly convicted; nor shall any male person, arrived at the age of —— years, nor female person arrived at the age of —— years, be held to serve any person as servant under pretense of indenture or otherwise, unless such person shall enter into such indenture while in a state of perfect freedom, and on condition of a bona fide consideration, received or to be received for their service, except as before excepted. Nor shall any indenture of any negro or mulatto, hereafter made and executed out of this state, or if made in the state where the term of service exceeds one year, be of the least validity, except those given in the case of apprenticeships.

This initial version was modeled on the Ohio Constitution and, like it, was an artful combination of the old Article VI of the Northwest Ordinance, which purported to ban slavery, and the subsequent indenture laws that had been used to shelter the practice. On that Friday a motion was made to fill in the blanks with the ages of twenty-one and eighteen, the same ages as had been used in the Ohio Constitution, which was an improvement over the existing indenture laws in the Illinois Territory that allowed children born of slaves to be free only on reaching the age of twenty-five. Like New York and Ohio, Illinois opted for a time-based solution to the slavery issue, permitting slavery to go on for some set period of years, rather than a geographical dividing line, as ultimately adopted in the Missouri Compromise.

Further consideration was postponed until the article was taken up for its second reading on Tuesday, August 18. To that point, the delegates had acted in general unanimity and without the need for a roll-call vote on any issue, but on that day they slowed their pace. The first section of Article VI was read, considered, and amended as follows:

§1 Neither slavery nor involuntary servitude shall hereafter be introduced into this state, otherwise than for the punishment of crimes, whereof the party shall have been duly convicted; nor shall any male person arrived at the age of twenty-one years, nor female person arrived at the age of eighteen years, be held to serve any person as a servant under any indenture hereafter made, unless such person shall enter into such indenture while in a state of perfect freedom, and on condition of a bona fide consideration received or to be received for their service, except as before excepted. Nor shall any indenture of any negro or mulatto, hereafter made and executed out of this state, or if made in the state, where the term of service exceeds one year, be of the least validity, except those given in case of apprenticeships.

The change in the opening sentence of the section was particularly significant. By saying that slavery could not "hereafter be introduced," the delegates protected the slavery that already existed in Illinois even more explicitly than they had with the tortuous "except as before excepted" language, which they also left in. Already the delegates were moving away from the language of the Ohio Constitution. Then the removal of the word "pretense" modifying "indenture" was practically an admission that the delegates recognized that the entire indenture framework was in fact a pretense for slavery. Finally, the convention added that the provision applied only to indentures "hereafter made," which underlined the change in the first sentence.

A second section was then proposed to be added to Article VI:

> Nor shall any person bound to labor in any other state, be hired to labor in this state, except within the tract reserved for the salt works near Shawneetown, nor even at that place for a longer period than one year at one time; nor shall it be allowed there, after the year ——; any violation of this article, shall effect the emancipation of such person from his obligation to service.

The Salines were vital to the new state; taxes on the salt produced there were to cover almost a quarter of the state's expenses in the early years.[14] This new section, applying only to the Salines, permitted the importation of slaves from elsewhere to work there, but only for a year at a time. Work in the Salines was considered by many to be the one kind of labor that could not practically be done by any but slave labor. Tellingly, this provision was intended to set a year after which this practice would no longer be allowed even in the Salines, leaving blank the actual year to be determined by the delegates later.

The amendment of the first section was approved by a roll-call vote of 17 to 14, and the addition of the second section was approved without a roll call. Jesse Thomas, as the presiding officer, did not vote on any of these matters, but his lieutenant Elias Kane voted with the majority on both, indicating that this ambiguous compromise version of Article VI was the one Thomas backed. Article VI was then put aside for two days until Thursday, August 20, 1818, at which time the phrase "except as before excepted" in the first section, which had been carried over from the Ohio Constitution, was the focus of attention. The meaning of the phrase was apparently thought to be insufficiently clear, though the obtuseness had been intentional and probably thought desirable by

Thomas, Kane, and their allies. That phrase had been thought the minimum necessary to ensure that slaves previously held under the territory's indenture laws would continue to be so held even after statehood and had the added advantage of being hard to understand. However, the changes already made to §1 had now made the phrase unnecessary. This move to clarity embold-ened the proslavery forces to seek an even more explicit statement protecting preexisting slavery. Accordingly, a motion was made to strike the phrase and substitute a new §3 to the slavery article. The purpose of the new section was to achieve in a separate and more explicit provision what exactly had been intended by the "except as before excepted" language that had been stricken:

> §3 Each and every person who has been bound to service by con-tract or indenture, in virtue of the laws of the Illinois territory heretofore existing, and in conformity with the provisions of the same, without fraud or collusion, shall be held to a specific per-formance of their contracts or indentures; and such negroes, and mulattoes as have been registered in conformity with the aforesaid laws shall serve out the time appointed by said laws: Provided however, that the children hereafter born of such persons, negroes and mulattoes, shall become free; the males at the age of twen-ty-one years, the females at the age of eighteen years. Each and every child born of indentured parents shall be entered with the clerk of the county in which they reside, by their owners within six months after the birth of said child.

The test vote on this new §3 reflected the sentiments of the convention dele-gates. Some ardently wanted a constitution clearly sanctioning slavery, some were as ardently opposed to slavery and wanted a clear prohibition, but the majority, including Thomas and Kane, supported an obfuscatory compromise that preserved the status quo in Illinois and left the issue to be resolved at a later date.

After the "except as before excepted" language had been stricken out on August 20 and before the new §3 was adopted, antislavery delegates made one last effort for a ban on slavery by moving to eliminate the second section in its entirety. In the absence of the "except as before excepted" language in the first section, the scales would have tilted against slavery, but, as noted, other changes in §1 supported a proslavery interpretation. In perhaps the best measure of sentiment at the convention on the issue of slavery, this motion was defeated 21 to 10. The blank in the second section was then filled, setting the year 1825 as the last in which slaves could be imported into Illinois to work the Salines. This choice of year was clearly intended to provide a critical decision point for slavery in Illinois and in fact set the stage for the subsequent conventionist campaign in 1823–24 to amend the state constitution in Illinois to permit slavery. This was the last adjustment to Article VI in the convention, and the article was adopted in that form.

In retrospect it appears the original authors of the Illinois Constitution contemplated from the start that an effort to amend would be made prior to 1825. This hypothesis seems even more likely because Illinois' constitution was the only one of the three drafted in the Old Northwest to that time that lacked a prohibition of future amendment of its slavery provisions. Given that there were three delegates in the convention who had leased saltworks from the government and were committed to the perpetuation of slavery past 1825, including Willis Hargrove, the delegate with the most slaves and the closest associations with the saltworks, it made sense that at least some of the delegates had in mind from the beginning a second constitutional convention after statehood to legalize slavery. Hargrove went on to lead the conventionist movement four years later.

As the convention drew to a close, there were some who claimed that neither the Northwest Ordinance nor Illinois' 1818 constitution were intended to impinge on existing property rights in slaves, and there were others who optimistically believed that the plangent pronouncements of Article VI in each of those two documents were intended as an absolute ban on slavery before and after statehood; but there were apparently many more, like Thomas and Kane, who preferred a more ambiguous outcome, recognizing that any attempt to establish slavery at the time of statehood would be controversial and might lead to rejection of the Illinois Constitution in Washington. The two of them were more interested in statehood than they were in slavery. They also believed that, as a new state, Illinois would have every right to revisit the issue of slavery after statehood, but, for the time being, they both opted to perpetuate the ambivalence of proto-slavery in Illinois. Thomas and Kane were also well aware that any move to make Illinois an overtly slave state was bound to upset the implicit balance in Washington between slave and free states. They were realistic enough to recognize that the best that could be hoped for Illinois was a system of proto-slavery that would make Illinois seem like a Northern state to the undiscerning until such time as the issue could be revisited. They held out inducements to the antislavery delegates as necessary concessions at key points in the debate, such as lowering the ages at which children of slaves would be freed, but only when absolutely required to do so. The lessons Thomas learned in these negotiations over slavery, when added to his already thorough knowledge of previous slavery strategies in the Indiana and Illinois Territories, prepared him for his upcoming role in Washington in the Missouri controversy.

The only other provisions of the Illinois Constitution of particular importance to Thomas and Kane were those dealing with the judiciary, and they too related to the issue of slavery in an unusual provision setting the terms of supreme court judges. Their tenure was to be based on good behavior, except for the original judges, who had set terms expiring in 1824. The setting of this deadline in 1824, when combined with setting the deadline for slavery in the Salines in 1825, seems to confirm that the omnipresent Kane, in conjunction with Thomas, had decided earlier to set the stage for a reconsideration of the constitution in approximately 1824.[15]

CHAPTER 9

First Months in the U.S. Senate

ven though Illinois' constitution had not yet been submitted to Congress and it had not been admitted as a state, its enabling act had authorized it to elect a state government. Accordingly, elections for the new state government were held on September 17, 1818, and on October 5, the newly minted General Assembly met at Kaskaskia in a simple two-story stucco and brick building rented for four dollars a day from Dr. George Fisher, an eminent physician who was also a politician and judge. There were fourteen senators and twenty-nine representatives, and forty of them appeared to open the General Assembly in a low-ceilinged room that also served as Daniel Pope Cook's law office.[1]

The General Assembly took for granted that Congress would admit Illinois as a state and, after two days of ceremonial preliminaries, proceeded to the choice of its first two U.S. senators, making that its first substantive order of business. At that time senators were chosen by their state legislatures, and the General Assembly met for that purpose in a joint session. The legislators naturally focused their attention on the men, almost all Southern and pro-slavery, who had played major roles during the territorial period, and the two most prominent among them were Ninian Edwards and Jesse Thomas. By virtue of his position, many of the legislators were indebted to Edwards; but Thomas also had a number of friends among them, including his half brother Michael Jones, who was representing Gallatin County in the Senate.

The forty assembled legislators may have perceived a need to choose one senator from each of the two nascent parties, but they did not move smoothly to that end. The candidates nominated were Edwards, Thomas, Leonard

White, Michael Jones of Kaskaskia, Joseph Street, and Robert Morrison. White, a former government agent in the Salines and colonel in the militia, was a member of the Edwards amalgam and the most serious candidate after Edwards and Thomas. In the joint session, each legislator voted for two candidates in the first round, with twenty-one votes being required for election. On the initial ballot, Edwards was elected as the first senator with thirty-two votes; White came second with seventeen; Thomas third with fifteen; Jones fourth with ten; and Street and Morrison, with three each, were dropped from the second ballot. On the second ballot, White led with sixteen votes, Thomas was second with fourteen, and Jones third with ten. Jones was dropped on the third ballot, and Thomas, picking up more of his votes than White, was elected 21 to 18.[2]

In the early years of statehood, the Thomas faction held its own against Edwards and his allies. Shadrach Bond Jr. was elected as the state's first governor without opposition. Elias Kent Kane served as the first secretary of state, an office in which his intimate knowledge of the constitution gave him unusual power. Even more important, Thomas's ally John McLean won the election for the first short term as Illinois' sole representative in the U.S. House, although he was defeated a year later by Daniel Pope Cook, who thereafter claimed the office as his own by defeating Kane in 1820, McLean in 1822, and Bond in 1824. These early elections in the new state set the pattern for the two opposing factions, with the Thomas party holding the edge on state offices and the Edwards party, with the exception of Thomas himself, in Washington.

The First General Assembly also addressed the issue of slavery. Once statehood was a fait accompli, Illinoisans evidently felt confident enough to take up the sensitive issue. A serious financial downturn was on the horizon for the entire country, and advocates of slavery came out in the open, arguing that wealthier settlers would not come to the new state if they did not have the right to own slaves. On the day before it adjourned, the General Assembly passed "An act respecting free negroes, mulattoes, servants and slaves," which formally continued Illinois' system of proto-slavery.[3]

Before departing in November 1818 for Washington, Thomas changed his residence yet again, this time from Cahokia to the new town founded by Governor—now Senator—Edwards and bearing his name. Jesse and Rebecca had lived for only a couple of years in Cahokia before making this move farther north to follow the shifting pattern of Illinois population. Edwardsville, at the northern edge of the American Bottom, was the new county seat of Madison County, and Thomas had already made a number of real estate investments there. Though it must have been difficult for him to choke down the idea of living in a town that was enriching his principal political adversary, it was to be his home for the rest of his time in Illinois.

While Thomas was making his last arrangements in Edwardsville, the new Illinois Constitution was sent ahead to Washington, and on Monday, November 16, 1818, the first day of the second session of the Fifteenth Congress, Speaker Henry Clay put it before the House, where it was ordered to lie on the table.[4] That Thursday, as John McLean, Illinois' lone representative in the House, prepared to present his credentials and take his oath of office, a difficulty developed over slavery that foreshadowed the divisions that would bedevil the creation of every territory and state from that time to the Civil War. It began with Clay expressing his hesitation in administering the oath to McLean when Congress had not yet admitted Illinois as a state. He was intimating, for the first time, that the admission of a state might be more than a ministerial act and might involve a serious examination of its constitution and its compliance with its enabling act.

Clay submitted this question of protocol to the House, and a lively discussion ensued. William Henry Harrison, then serving as a representative from Ohio, pointed out that in the past, representatives from new states had been seated before their constitutions had been approved and argued that this precedent should be followed. Timothy Pitkin, Federalist of Connecticut, the first person to speak on the subject who might have been motivated by antislavery motives, urged delay in order to ascertain whether Illinois had the population specified in its enabling act. Those arguing that the constitution must be examined before McLean was seated were victorious. This temporary success would embolden those opposed to the extension of slavery, who, from about this time, were referred to as restrictionists. A few days later they would attempt a bolder initiative, but for the time being, they let Illinois' proposed constitution be referred to a select committee.[5]

On the next day, the select committee reported to the House a resolution declaring the admission of Illinois into the Union, on an equal footing with the original states. John Spencer of New York, however, taking up where Pitkin had left off the day before, inquired whether there was documentation establishing that the state had the requisite population. Richard Anderson, chair of the select committee, said that it had no information beyond what was contained in the preamble to the constitution, which stated that all requisites of the enabling act had been complied with, but that he had himself seen in newspapers evidence sufficient to satisfy him on this question. Following this brief exchange, the resolution was ordered to be engrossed for a third reading, which was usually tantamount to passage.[6]

But when the engrossed bill was read for the third time the following Monday, November 23, and the question was put whether it should pass, James Tallmadge of New York, forty-one-year-old former secretary to New York governor George Clinton and a veteran of the War of 1812, launched the campaign against slavery in the West by issuing a new challenge. Tallmadge, who was later in that same session to propose the famous amendment bearing his name that would have extinguished slavery in Missouri within a generation, attacked the resolution admitting Illinois, first questioning the adequacy of the documentation of the required population but then going beyond that to assert that "the principle of slavery, if not adopted in the constitution, was at least not sufficiently prohibited." He asserted that some prohibition of slavery was required by Article VI of the Northwest Ordinance and that "the sixth article of the constitution of the new State of Illinois, in each of its three sections . . . contravened this stipulation, either in the letter or the spirit." After carefully examining all three sections, he "felt himself constrained to come to the conclusion that they embraced a complete recognition of existing slavery, if not provisions for its future introduction and toleration; particularly in the passage wherein they permit the hiring of slaves, the property of non-residents, for any number of years consecutively." On this basis he urged the rejection of Illinois' constitution, or at least its sixth article.[7]

Tallmadge was very well prepared for his attack. He went on to parse the provision on slavery in the constitution of Indiana, the state most recently admitted from the Northwest Territory, "to show how carefully and scrupulously it had guarded against slavery in any shape, and in the strongest terms reprobated it." He specifically applauded the clause of the Indiana Constitution that forbade any amendment of its slavery provision. This, he said, was what was required for any state seeking admission from the Northwest Territory. Jesse Thomas's friend George Poindexter of Mississippi, who was on the select committee, responded to Tallmadge. Poindexter had worked closely with Thomas in the second session of the Tenth Congress on the twin bills extending the suffrage in both the Indiana and Mississippi Territories and had helped Thomas obtain his appointment as a territorial judge in Illinois.

He appears to have been very well briefed on the intricacies of the Northwest Territory, possibly by Thomas himself. Poindexter purported to agree with the general sentiments of Tallmadge's proposal but criticized his exclusive reliance on the Indiana Constitution. He pointed out that the substance of the Illinois slavery article "was almost literally copied from the constitution of Ohio." As previously discussed, that was not entirely true, but almost so, and Tallmadge was caught flat-footed. Poindexter also claimed that the prohibition of amendments in the Indiana Constitution would be of no force or effect if Indiana were to call a new convention. There was a further animated exchange involving other representatives, including William Henry Harrison, after which the resolution admitting Illinois was passed 117 to 34 and sent to the Senate for concurrence, which was given routinely.[8] But the tocsin had been sounded.

On December 3, 1818, President Monroe signed the resolution declaring the admission of Illinois into the Union. On December 4, the two freshly minted senators from the new state appeared for the first time in the U.S. Senate. They produced their credentials, which were read, the oath prescribed by law was administered, and they took their seats. Their terms then had to be assigned. The Constitution required the Senate to designate classes of senators to ensure that a third of the Senate came up for reelection every two years, and accordingly, the Illinois enabling act had specified that one of the two new senators was to be a class one senator, with a term expiring at the end of the Fifteenth Congress in March 1819 (in other words, in three months), and the other was to be a class three senator, with a term expiring at the end of the Seventeenth Congress in March 1823.[9] It might seem logical that the longer term would be awarded to the senator chosen first by his state legislature, which would have been Edwards, but that was not the tradition in the Senate. Instead, to determine the terms for the two men, Senator Jeremiah Morrow of Ohio moved that the secretary of the Senate put into the ballot box two papers of equal size, numbered one and three, with the understanding that the senator who drew number one was to be inserted in the class of senators whose term of service would expire at the end of that Congress. The numbers were rolled up and put in the box, and Edwards, who at least was given the right to choose first, drew number one and thus the short term.[10]

In the U.S. Senate, Jesse Thomas found himself in his element. He addressed himself diligently to the work before him and made every effort to inform himself fully on the rules and procedures of the Senate. His time as speaker in the Indiana territorial House had made him a knowledgeable and practical legislator, and he was already familiar with the workings of the House of Representatives from his short time as the territorial delegate from Indiana. He also found among the senators many men who had served with him during his brief time in the House ten years before. In the Senate, Thomas made almost no set speeches but instead gave watchful attention to its deliberations, only occasionally nudging his colleagues with insights gained through practical experience and a thorough knowledge of legislative procedure. As a good instinctive politician, he put the interests of his constituents first; but he also had a broad sense of what he believed right, important, and practicable for the entire country, as was soon to be borne out in his role in the impasse over Missouri statehood.

Because they did not join the Senate until the second session of the Fifteenth Congress, neither Thomas nor Edwards received an appointment to one of the twelve standing committees that considered specific issues and drafted legislation. This system of standing committees was then only two years old but was to have a profound impact on Thomas's career in the Senate. Even more important for Thomas than a committee assignment, however, was the early support he was given by William Harris Crawford. Following their first brief acquaintance in Washington during Thomas's term as territorial delegate, they had become friends. In the intervening years, Crawford had launched himself on a meteoric career, becoming president pro tempore of the Senate in 1811, then acting vice president in 1812 when Vice President George Clinton died, and finally minister to France during the entire course of the War of 1812. These early achievements, though impressive, were only the beginning of a career that was to make Crawford one of the most powerful political figures of his era. On his voyage home from France, he received word he had been appointed secretary of war by James Madison. He served well enough in that post that he was a serious contender for the presidency against James Monroe in 1816 but graciously stood aside. By the time he and Thomas renewed their friendship, Crawford was serving as Monroe's secretary of the treasury and was widely considered the Republicans' most likely candidate to succeed Monroe in 1824. It was only natural that Crawford would become Thomas's mentor.

Slavery and public lands were to be the issues most closely identified with Thomas during the first two sessions of the Senate in which he participated, but before those storms broke he was involved behind the scenes in one other matter that was to have important consequences for him personally. General

Andrew Jackson had just completed a successful campaign against the Seminoles in Spanish Florida that went well beyond his instructions from President Monroe and was capped by the execution of two local traders, an Englishman named Ambrister and a Scot named Arbuthnot, who were almost certainly innocent of the charges against them and whose deaths amounted to militarily sanctioned murder. The president, cabinet, and certain members of Congress were outraged at the same time that a large part of the public was excited by Jackson's imperialism.[11]

Both Henry Clay and William Crawford immediately recognized that, on top of his brilliant victory at New Orleans in 1815, Jackson's success in Florida would make him a formidable dark horse adversary in the 1824 contest for the White House. They set out to undermine Jackson through congressional hearings charging, quite accurately, that he had exceeded his orders in Florida and should be censured rather than praised. Clay, as Speaker, could take an active role in this attack, but Crawford, as a member of the cabinet, had to be more circumspect, conducting his campaign through surrogates in Congress. It is logical to assume that Thomas was one of his principal lieutenants in the Senate. A select committee on the Seminole War was appointed in the Senate with a majority of its members being Crawford supporters. The committee's report, when it was released on February 24, 1819, was a low-key, well-reasoned, and balanced indictment that bore all the hallmarks of participation by a broad spectrum of careful draftsmen, possibly including Crawford, Clay, and Thomas in addition to the committee members.[12]

The final report was not submitted to the House until the very end of the Fifteenth Congress. By that time, Jackson had arrived in Washington to lead his own defense. He had already pronounced that these "hellish machinations" were the work of Crawford and Clay, and he was so successful in defending himself that they were forced to recognize that attacking Jackson might prove more dangerous than letting him be.[13] Monroe, for his part, was in a difficult spot. He wanted to criticize Jackson, but he did not want to give back any of the land Jackson had secured by exceeding his orders. Jackson's enemies concluded they were better off using the report as it was rather than risking that Jackson's popularity might lead to a vote exonerating him. Without further ado, the committee report was tabled in the House and allowed to quietly die, and no action was taken in the Senate. But Jackson was never to forget those who lined up against him in the censure campaign. His intense animosity for Thomas in later years is one of the best indicators that Jackson thought Thomas was among those against him. Some of the major figures aligned against Jackson, like Crawford, managed ultimately to reconcile themselves with him, but only because Jackson later felt he needed their political support. Jackson instead focused his lasting vituperation on the supporting players like Thomas.

Although the issue of whether to extend slavery into the newly organized territories and states of the Louisiana Purchase was the one for which Thomas is remembered by history, to contemporaries, and even to him at the time, it was by no means the most important issue he faced. A slew of other issues seemed to be more pressing. The first, and arguably the most important, was the economic downturn that had started in the East several years before and had now developed into a full-blown financial panic. A second critical issue was the insatiable appetite for the public lands that were both a principal source of revenue for the young Republic and the critical fuel for its westward expansion. A third issue was the program of tariffs and internal improvements being pushed by Henry Clay. Clay understood that a protective tariff would be popular in the Northeast, and thus help his campaign for the presidency; it must also have been apparent to him that a higher tariff would take the pressure off public lands as a source of revenue, allowing for a reduction in the cost of land for his supporters on the frontier. A fourth issue of growing importance was the corruption encouraged by the unfettered pursuit of economic advantage following the War of 1812 and the very long period of one-party rule that had allowed it to flourish unchecked. Diverse as these other issues were, they all figured into Thomas's Senate career, and they all became caught up one way or another in the controversy over slavery.

Thomas had also to pay close attention to the political situation in Illinois. There had previously been a large degree of unanimity in Illinois on the desirability of slavery, but the issue had become more contentious as statehood approached. With the infusion of a new wave of immigrants from the Northeast, the climate in the state gradually shifted, and it made sense that one of the two incipient parties, either the one centered on Thomas or the one centered on Edwards, was going to move to a less obviously proslavery stance. As it developed, it was the Edwards party, largely under the influence of Daniel Pope Cook, that chose to tone down its support for slavery. This was ironic given that some of the leaders of that party were far larger slaveholders than any leaders of the Thomas party. Edwards, for example, was known to campaign from a carriage driven by a black slave. The first test for this new antislavery approach came in the statewide election for Illinois' lone representative in the U.S. House in 1819. In the initial special House contest in 1818, John McLean, a Thomas ally and a Southerner with pronounced pro-slavery convictions, had prevailed; but in the regular election in 1819, Cook, the perennial antislavery champion of the Edwards party, took charge of the seat he would hold for three terms. The 1818 election had probably been a fair representation of statewide sentiment at a time when the bulk of the state's population was still in the southern third of the state, bordered on the south and west by slavery; but by 1819 the tide of immigration from the Northeast was already rising and the connection of Illinois to the Northeast, through the Great Lakes, was strengthening.

Daniel Pope Cook became the voice for this new wave of Illinoisans and the most effective adversary of slavery in Illinois. A generation younger than Thomas and Edwards, he played an almost equally important role in the early history of Illinois. He, like Edwards, was related to the Pope family of Kentucky. A number of sources indicate a closer relationship between Daniel Pope Cook and the brothers Nathaniel Pope, secretary and then delegate from the Illinois Territory, and John "One-Arm" Pope, the senator from Kentucky, but the only established blood tie is through Cook's great-great-grandmother Elizabeth Pope, making Daniel a third cousin once removed to the two brothers.

Like the other members of the Pope family, Cook grew up and was educated in Kentucky. From the time of his arrival in Illinois in 1815 at the age of twenty-one, he had been both hard working and precocious. Aside from his thriving law practice, he also became auditor of public accounts and served as a judge of the Western Circuit, where he and Thomas developed an early dislike for each other. He started off in Kaskaskia, running all his various functions out of an office at the end of the frame building also occupied by William Morrison's store. A year later he moved north to Edwardsville, where he not only expanded his fledgling law practice but also went into the newspaper business. He and a partner purchased the moribund *Illinois Herald*, the first paper published in the Illinois Territory, and turned it into a small but well-run weekly called the *Western Intelligencer*.[14]

After this meteoric start in Illinois politics, Cook changed course dramatically, giving up his varied life in Illinois to move to Washington, D.C., where he hoped to secure a leg up from his Pope connections. In 1817 Cook was sent to London to accompany back John Quincy Adams, who had just been appointed to serve as secretary of state under James Monroe. This was an easy plum for One-Arm Pope to dispense because he and Adams had married sisters. On the long return trip, Cook became a friend of the Federalist Adams and was even offered a post in the State Department. Thereafter, despite being a westerner and of necessity a Republican, Cook was imbued with Adams's antislavery sentiments.

Returning to Illinois after his stint in Washington and London, Cook launched intertwined careers as land speculator and politician. Like most of the lawyers in the territory, he found that the bulk of his work came from disputed land titles, and he was savvy enough to buy up some of the better claims and pursue them to a desired legal resolution. Cook was extremely competent as a lawyer, but his real love was politics. He was an ardent supporter of statehood and used his newspaper to influence the territorial legislature, becoming by far the most effective advocate for statehood at a time when others were not particularly eager to change a status quo from which they benefited.

When statehood came, Cook's loss to McLean for a seat in the U.S. House in 1818 was bitter, but on March 5, 1819, the General Assembly elected him as Illinois' first attorney general, a position in which he served only briefly before he defeated McLean in a stunning reversal of the year before. His victory marked a sea change in Illinois politics: for the first time somebody other than an out-and-out Southern sympathizer was in a position of political power. Cook also advanced his political career and strengthened his ties to the Edwards faction by his marriage in 1821 to Edwards's daughter Julia.

Thomas thus knew there was growing antislavery sentiment in Illinois. In this light, the controversy over slavery became a struggle to define the character of the state. Both Thomas and Edwards still believed the sympathies of the state's most powerful citizens were with the aristocratic South. To varying degrees they appear to have been convinced that the viability of the region was dependent on slavery. With the arrival of the Panic of 1819, their conviction moved from the ideological to the practical. Future governor Thomas Ford, looking back on that time, captured the sense of anxiety that pervaded the first years of statehood:

> About this time . . . a tide of immigrants was pouring into Missouri through Illinois, from Virginia and Kentucky. In the fall of the year, every great road was crowded and full of them, all bound to Missouri, with their money, and long trains of teams and negroes. These were the most wealthy and best-educated immigrants from

the slave states. Many of our people who had land and farms to sell, looked upon the good fortune of Missouri with envy; whilst the lordly immigrant, as he passed along with his money and droves of negroes, took a malicious pleasure in increasing it, by pretending to regret the short-sighted policy of Illinois, which excluded him from settlement amongst us; and from purchasing the lands of our people. In this mode, a desire to make Illinois a slave State, became quite prevalent.[15]

Jesse Thomas came to Washington with Illinois' debate over slavery fresh in his mind. If proslavery advocates at the state convention had a tacit understanding that the slavery issue would be revisited in the first years of statehood, it would have been very helpful to slavery advocates to have Missouri admitted as a slave state, thus perpetuating the slavery cordon that already existed along the short border with Kentucky to the south and the longer border with the Missouri Territory to the west. In addition, Jesse Thomas was interested in Missouri not only for its potential effect on Illinois but also for its immediate effect on the welfare and future of his older brother, Richard, who lived in Missouri and continued as a leading light in the conservative political elite that was fighting for control in Missouri.

Missouri's was not the first application for statehood from the lands of the Louisiana Purchase—Louisiana had already been admitted as a slave state in 1812—but it was the first from the northern part of the purchase, from lands on the same latitude as states that Northerners considered to be their heartland. Since a chunk of Louisiana was on the eastern bank of the Mississippi, Missouri was also the first state to be made up entirely of land on the western bank of the great river. All recognized that what was done there with respect to slavery could provide a template for the rest of the trans-Mississippi West. When Thomas took his seat in the Senate, the majority of members of Congress probably assumed that Missouri would join the Union as a slave state. Slavery had been practiced there for a century during the French and Spanish periods, and during the period of American control the rate of increase in the slave population had matched that of the white population, making the proportion of slaves relatively constant at about 20 percent.[16] The capital investment in slavery, accordingly, had grown dramatically, and Missouri slaveholders were understandably concerned that the American government might seek to deprive them of their property. The first petition to abolish slavery in Missouri had been presented in Congress in 1804, and there had been a steady drumbeat since. The fears of the proslavery faction seemed confirmed when the area of the Louisiana Purchase north of the present state of Louisiana, known as the Louisiana District, was, as discussed earlier, put briefly under the authority of the Indiana Territory, making it subject to the strictures of Article VI of the Northwest Ordinance. This arrangement was universally detested in Missouri.

As a result, Congress had hurriedly passed a third act on March 3, 1805, which created the Missouri Territory and made it no longer subject to the Northwest Ordinance. The act contained no prohibition on slavery, and from then on during Missouri's territorial period, the institution continued to flourish with the tacit approval of the American government. Fifteen years later, in the debates during the Missouri controversy, a number of anti-restrictionists pointed out that it seemed a bit behind times to now attempt to impose restrictions. However, despite a recognized momentum to admit Missouri as a slave state, there was a significant, and growing, minority of Northern representatives who thought that Congress should impose restrictions in order to prevent the further spread of slavery west of the Mississippi.

In response, proslavery elements argued the already shopworn notion of diffusion, claiming that, if the institution of slavery were allowed to spread into new areas, slaves would be a smaller proportion of the population everywhere and slavery would gradually disappear. They argued diffusion as a necessity, positing that if slaves were strictly contained in the Southern states that then permitted slavery, they might eventually become a majority and overwhelm their owners. The diffusionists flocked to the banners of Henry Clay, Speaker of the House, and James Barbour, president pro tem of the Senate, who, as leaders of the American Colonization Society, argued for repatriation of American slaves to Africa. Tough-minded observers understood, however, that it was unlikely there would ever be the money or will to make the repatriation program a reality. In the end, diffusion and the closely related idea of colonization became no more than tortured rationalizations for the South's inability to address the institution of slavery.[17]

The political dynamic in the Senate when Illinois' senators arrived in Washington that December was almost evenly balanced. At the time there were eight states (Virginia, North Carolina, South Carolina, Georgia, Kentucky, Tennessee, Mississippi, and Louisiana) that were indisputably Southern and proslavery. Ranged on the other side were seven (New Hampshire, Vermont,

Massachusetts, Connecticut, Rhode Island, New York, and New Jersey) that were reliably Northern and antislavery. Then there were the mid-Atlantic swing states (Pennsylvania, Delaware, and Maryland), which had in the past gone both ways on many sectional issues but which tended to go two to one on slavery (Maryland and Delaware supporting it and Pennsylvania opposed). Last, there were the three new states admitted from the Northwest Territory, which were in theory free states but had latent or, at least in the case of Illinois, not-so-latent Southern sympathies. When the votes came on the extension of slavery, these states also split two to one (with Ohio and Indiana voting against and Illinois for). As it turned out, then, it was Illinois that tipped the balance in the Senate in favor of the anti-restrictionists, despite the fact it was generally regarded as a Northern state. The next state maneuvering to be admitted to the Union was Alabama, which would bring to nine the number of states admitted beyond the original thirteen: Vermont, the three from the Northwest Territory, and five from south of the Ohio River. The House was an entirely different proposition because the Northern states were far more populous, and there were thus many more restrictionist congressmen.[18]

In the Missouri debate that erupted soon after Jesse Thomas joined the Senate, there were ideologues, either for or against slavery, so committed to their positions that they could brook no compromise. In their view, whether pro- or antislavery, there was a clear answer to the questions before them that should apply uniformly throughout the land. These purists often made up their minds first about the issue of slavery and then marshaled their constitutional and other arguments to support their preconceived conclusions. Neither group could countenance any separation of the country between slave and free. Ranged in the middle between the two extremes were moderates, some more favorable to slavery and some less. The moderates had their principles on the slavery question but were willing to compromise them as the price for preserving the Union. They could even contemplate rules related to slavery that might apply differently in different sections of the country, including the possibility of a geographical dividing line between slave and free. Jesse Thomas was squarely in the middle, probably at that point in his life still slightly proslavery but comfortable working with antislavery moderates to fashion a compromise.

Both extremists and moderates honestly believed, or found it useful to assert, that the issue of slavery in Missouri was controlled by constitutional principles. Although these principles were raised at different times and in different contexts by the various participants in the Missouri controversy, they are continuous threads weaving their way through the Fifteenth and Sixteenth Congresses. As in the debate over the admission of Illinois, the most important constitutional questions addressed by both sides related to the powers of Congress to regulate territories and admit new states. The ideologues on either fringe once again made of the constitutional issues what they wished, and in such sweeping terms as to suggest that the passions of their pro- or antislavery beliefs influenced their opinions of the Constitution rather than vice versa. Nonetheless, there were interesting and even learned discussions on the meaning of Article IV, §3, the constitutional provision on territories and states, that expanded the debate begun in the Fifteenth Congress.

Once again Congress rehashed the history of states previously admitted to the Union and conditions that had or had not been imposed upon them, going back to the conditions Virginia had placed on its cession of the land that later became the Northwest Territory. Congress debated the various meanings that could be attached to a state's admission to the Union on an "equal footing with the original states," the language used in the Northwest Ordinance, and the absence of that same language from the subsequently negotiated Article IV, §3, of the U.S. Constitution. Most senators and representatives were willing to concede that, under the second clause of Article IV, §3, Congress could set rules on slavery in territories (as it had done in the Northwest Territory), but of those willing to accept that proposition a significant number denied that Congress had the right to set such rules after that territory became a state. They reasoned that such a limitation would be incompatible with the notion of "equal footing" since no such limitation had been placed on any state admitted earlier. Thus was framed one of the earliest expressions of the doctrine of states' rights. For their part, those who opposed slavery argued that the constitutional provision on the admission of new states (contained in the first clause of Article IV, §3) was framed as permissive and not mandatory and therefore implied that Congress had the right to set conditions on the admission of new states. They went on to argue that Congress had the right to accept or reject constitutions of new states as an extension of this permissive power.

With the exception of the state of Louisiana, however, all prior admissions had fallen into two general categories that were not entirely applicable in considering Missouri. Either admissions had occurred from the Northwest Territory, where they were subject to the cessions that made up that territory and then to the Northwest Ordinance of 1787, or they were carve-outs from existing states by acts of their legislatures that typically imposed conditions (for example, Kentucky, Tennessee, Mississippi, and Alabama). Recognition by Congress of conditions laid down by states that were ceding part of their territory was quite different from Congress itself imposing conditions on newly acquired territories. The Louisiana Purchase marked the first time the federal government had acquired property from a foreign power. Missouri, therefore, was most like Louisiana, which had been admitted in 1812 with some very mild conditions. Both Louisiana and Missouri had had well-established slaveholding cultures before acquisition by the United States. Most significant, both were subject to Article III of the Louisiana Purchase Treaty of 1803, which appeared to require Congress to respect the property rights of the prior residents of the purchased areas, including their property rights in their slaves, and to admit new states from the purchase as soon as possible. Proslavery advocates argued that the treaty had negated the permissive language in the first clause of Article IV, §3, and required the early admission of Missouri. Restrictionists, on the other hand, relied on the requirement in the treaty that the inhabitants be admitted "according to the principles of the federal Constitution," which they believed were inconsistent with slavery. The treaty language aside, there was the practical problem that the Louisiana Purchase had been made with revenues raised from the South as well as from the North. It may have been a bargain, but, nonetheless, the two sections of the country participated in it and arguably had legitimate claims that their values be reflected in it.

The partisans locked horns even about the intent of the Constitutional Convention in setting the procedure for the admission of new states. Restrictionists pointed out that earlier drafts of Article IV, §3, had called for a vote of two-thirds of the members present from each branch of Congress to consent to the admission of new states. Although the language was later changed, they argued that the original proposal showed a general intent that a bare majority should not suffice. These constitutional debates had been under seal, but after a long debate they were unsealed.[19] Supporters of slavery, however, also took comfort from another part of the unsealed minutes that provided that "if the admission be consented to, the new states shall be admitted on the same terms with the original States." This language, the equivalent of the "equal footing" language in the Ordinance of 1787, was a telling argument against the imposition of conditions.

In addition to delving back into the deliberations of the Constitutional Convention concerning the vote required to admit new states, restrictionists also wanted to examine the convention's intent with respect to Article 1, §9, which provided that "the migration or importation of such persons as any of the states now existing shall think proper to admit, shall not be prohibited by the Congress prior to the year one thousand eight hundred and eight, but a tax or duty may be imposed on such importation, not exceeding ten dollars for each person." As with the Constitutional Convention's other tortuous compromise on slavery, the so-called three-fifths rule that so embittered the North, the distasteful words "slave" or "slavery" were not used. In both instances, the desire to avoid using those words resulted in circumlocutions that fueled debate in 1820.

Although most believed that the Constitution's migration or importation clause became a dead letter in 1807 when Congress passed the act prohibiting the further importation of slaves into the United States, it reemerged in 1820 in the form of an argument over Congress's authority to regulate the "migration or importation" of slaves from existing states into new territories and states. According to restrictionists, if Congress had to be prohibited from legislating on the migration or importation of slaves before 1808, it must, in the absence of that provision, have had the power to do so. Therefore, any time after the prohibition was lifted in 1808, Congress could exercise that power, and it was proper for it to do so to regulate the internal slave trade in Missouri. Opponents of restriction, on the other hand, argued that the clause was meant to apply only to persons coming from abroad and was not meant to apply to the movement of persons within the United States. They also pointed out that the constitutional provision on the slave trade applied only to "any of the states now existing," that is, in their view, to the original thirteen states. Now it was the anti-restrictionists who wanted to delve into the historical files to prove that the convention had not intended to regulate the movement of slaves between states or territories, and they succeeded in having this part of the secret files also made public. Constitutionally, if not morally, the anti-restrictionists got the better of these arguments.

Regardless of conflicting views on whether Congress had the right to impose conditions on statehood or pass on the acceptability of new state constitutions, the question floating beneath all these debates, whether spoken or unspoken, was the power of the states to later change whatever arrangement on slavery was negotiated in their original constitutions. Clearly, if the state constitution addressed slavery, whether pro or con, that formulation could be changed only by constitutional amendment in the state, which, as shall be seen, was a challenging prospect, calling for a vote of more than a simple majority in both houses of the state legislature and sometimes involving two successive legislatures or a popular vote. If, on the other hand, a state constitution were silent on the subject of slavery, the state's practices could usually be changed by simple majorities in its legislature. Whatever the mechanism for amendment, however, most recognized that a state constitution could be changed after statehood to permit slavery.

Furthermore, besides these arguments over the constitutional provision governing territories and states, the Northwest Ordinance, the Louisiana Purchase Treaty, and the various compromises on slavery contained in the original Constitution, the proslavery faction argued, most fundamentally, that any emancipation program, whether outright or gradual, would involve the taking of property, which could be done only with due process of law and, logically, with compensation. This was the principle upon which the proslavery faction ultimately relied, and it was a difficult one for the restrictionists to refute.

There were a number of ways short of outright prohibition that the slavery issue could have been compromised in the Missouri bill, if the extremists on both sides of the political divide had wished to do so. In Louisiana, there had been a condition imposed that no slave could be brought into the state unless accompanied by an owner who was settling there.[20] Although not much of a restriction, it at least set a precedent for conditions. A more effective option would be to permit slaves already in the state to remain in servitude while prohibiting the importation of any additional slaves. Likewise, if instead Congress wished to focus on emancipation, it could make the process gradual, with the children of slaves born after the date of the act to be free at a certain age. A combination of these methods had been adopted in New York's emancipation legislation, with which James Tallmadge was familiar; he now advocated applying them in Missouri. These were the same methods used in the slavery article of the Illinois Constitution, which Jesse Thomas now backed away from for fear of losing Southern support. All of these measures would have led to the ending of slavery over time without the drawing of a geographical line. All of them might have been possible if tried twenty years before when the importance of slavery was declining, and all of them would have been more statesmanlike solutions, with less intentional ambiguity, and with more potential to avert the tragedy of the Civil War. Unfortunately, the only remaining compromise option, and the one that became the central thread of the final solution, was the devising of a geographical line to separate slave and nonslave states. The exact delimiting of the line would be a matter of painful negotiation, but, by its very nature, Congress could keep fiddling with the line until it found one that would garner the largest number of votes, which, with any luck, would be enough for passage of an overall compromise.

It was the custom for the House to take up statehood applications before the Senate since such requests were usually transmitted to Washington by the territorial delegate, who sat in the House. The first petition for Missouri statehood had been a privately sponsored one made in 1817 that John Scott, Missouri's territorial delegate, did not present in the House until March 16, 1818, nine months before Thomas's arrival in Washington. Scott, married to John Rice Jones's daughter Harriet, was to play an important part in the controversy and in the early history of Missouri. Henry Clay, the Speaker of the House, referred the petition to a carefully chosen select committee composed of Scott, George Robertson of Kentucky, George Poindexter of Mississippi, William Hendricks of Indiana, Arthur Livermore of New Hampshire, Elijah Hunt Mills of Massachusetts, and Henry Baldwin of Pennsylvania. The select committee worked on the matter for the next three weeks and, on April 3, reported out a routine bill that would have enabled Missouri to organize as a state. The bill made no mention of slavery. Clay, recognizing that the slavery issue was going to have to be addressed, had the bill committed to a committee of the whole. He, as Speaker, controlled when the bill would be taken up, and he relegated it to a holding pattern, awaiting a propitious time to proceed.[21]

Other members of the House also recognized that slavery, heretofore not a controversial subject in statehood applications, would henceforth be bitterly divisive. Some members were, even at that early date, testing the parameters of debate and trying out possible compromises. On April 4, the day after the select committee reported out its Missouri bill, Arthur Livermore, one of its members, demonstrated why he had been an apt pick for the committee. Livermore, a Republican from New England, where most of his neighbors were Federalists, was used to going his own way. Though a staunch opponent of slavery, he was throughout the next several years an even stronger proponent of compromise, a stance that would cost him his seat in the Seventeenth Congress. Livermore made his first move toward compromise by proposing a constitutional amendment prohibiting slavery in states thereafter admitted. What some have viewed as a radical antislavery proposal really was not at the time. Though not made explicit, the timing of Livermore's proposal and his role on the select committee suggest that his constitutional amendment was meant to be considered in tandem with the Missouri enabling bill reported the day before; that is, it was not intended to apply to Louisiana or Missouri but only to the balance of the area west of the Mississippi. Because Livermore's constitutional initiative would have required a two-thirds vote in both houses of Congress and the approval of three-quarters of the states, it was a dead letter in the form in which he proposed it. The *House Journal* was succinct about the proposal's fate: "It was determined in the negative"—no yeas and nays, no division, no chance.[22] But Livermore had made his first attempt to find common ground and was to keep trying.

The first session of the Fifteenth Congress ended soon afterward, near the end of April 1818, with the Missouri enabling act still in limbo. By the time the Fifteenth Congress reassembled for its second session in November, Illinois had written its constitution and submitted the final product to Congress as required by its enabling act. It had also elected its U.S. senators, who were thrown into the middle of the swirling debate over slavery in the West. Although James Tallmadge's attempt to block the admission of Illinois had failed, thirty-four Northern votes had lined up on his side and were now ready for a much harder fight over Missouri. With the pro-Southern Illinois legislators in their seats, Clay prepared to take up Missouri statehood but still delayed another two weeks before reigniting the controversy on December 18 by presenting another petition from Missouri's territorial legislature asking leave to adopt a constitution and form a state government. Clay had the petition referred to the committee of the whole and, over the next few weeks, orchestrated the referral of numerous other petitions pro and con to the same destination.[23]

It was not, however, until February 13, 1819, that Clay gave John Scott the green light to move the House to take up enabling bills for both Missouri and Alabama.[24] Bringing forward two potential slave states at the same time appears in retrospect unwise, but perhaps Clay thought they would be viewed as essentially similar and Alabama would thus actually help Missouri to be admitted. The Senate had already approved an enabling bill for Alabama without restriction as to slavery, thus providing additional impetus for the approval of Missouri's bill.[25] At that point there were (in theory, counting Illinois as nonslave) eleven nonslave and ten slave states, so the shibboleth of requiring exactly equal numbers of slave and nonslave states had not yet implanted itself in the American political consciousness. It did not seem far-fetched to go from a Union with one extra nonslave state to one with one extra slave state.

When Clay gave Scott the signal to proceed on February 13, the House took up Missouri before Alabama. The committee of the whole discussed various possible amendments to the Missouri enabling bill, with many congressmen speaking. In the course of the afternoon, James Tallmadge first raised the possibility of an amendment to substantially limit slavery in Missouri by prohibiting the importation of slaves into the new state (what later became the non-importation provision of his amendment) and providing for the emancipation of all children born to slaves when they reached the age of twenty-five (his gradual emancipation provision). In making his amendment, Tallmadge was certainly cooperating with John W. Taylor, the recognized leader of the New York delegation in the House, which tended to go its own way, being more committed to New York's governor, DeWitt Clinton, than to any other segment of the Republican Party. In fact, Tallmadge probably agreed to serve as a stalking horse for Taylor because he had already determined to leave Congress at the end of the session to run for the New York senate, and Taylor was trying to maintain some neutrality on the issue in hopes of being an ultimate peacemaker.

This bifurcated amendment gave rise to a debate described as "interesting and pretty wide" in which Arthur Livermore and others supported Tallmadge. Because of the conflagration it set off, Tallmadge's amendment is usually viewed as radical, but in the context of the far-ranging search for a compromise then going on in Congress, even his amendment contained elements of conciliation. February 13 was a Saturday, and to give House members a chance to consider Tallmadge's amendment, the committee of the whole rose before a vote could be taken, and the House adjourned for the weekend to regroup. Tallmadge's antislavery initiative had been unexpected and had turned on its head the assumption that Missouri would be easily admitted as a slave state. John Scott, Missouri's territorial delegate, had not even been present and learned that trouble was brewing only "at a late period, at second hand, through the medium of a foreigner, the Portuguese ambassador."[26]

When the House reconvened on Monday, February 15, its chemistry had fundamentally shifted in favor of Tallmadge and his allies. Taylor, who was to succeed Clay as Speaker in the second session of the Sixteenth Congress, entered the fray at Tallmadge's side. An antislavery pragmatist, Taylor hinted at a national dividing line between slave and free running the entire length of the country. The makings of such a line were at hand. In a long speech that day, Taylor touched briefly on both the Ohio River and the border between

Pennsylvania and Maryland as being components of a possible line.[27] The latter section of that line, now familiarly known as the Mason-Dixon Line, had not previously been used as a line of demarcation between slave and free but had begun to take on that significance as gradual emancipation occurred north of the line.

"Mason and Dixon's Line" had been surveyed between 1763 and 1767 to settle colonial border disputes between Maryland and Pennsylvania, but Taylor's was one of the first references to it in the context of slavery.[28] It had not been, and even then was not, a clear demarcation between slave and free in the border states, although it was slowly becoming so. Perhaps the real reason that it emerged as the eastern leg of the proposed line was that its western end connected so conveniently to the eastern end of the Ohio River, which had been implicitly recognized as a dividing line in the Northwest Ordinance. These two connected lines, the Mason-Dixon Line and the Ohio River, were in the back of the minds of all who were weighing the idea of a geographical dividing line as the basis for compromise, and interest now focused on what the next westward leg of the line might be. A logical choice, and the one ultimately taken, was to extend the new leg west from the approximate point where the Ohio joins the Mississippi along the 36°30′ parallel of latitude.

Discussion of a dividing line went no further at that early stage in the Missouri debate, but it was to remain a leitmotif. More than a year later, Representative James Stevens of Connecticut would revert to the subject, saying prophetically of a compromise based upon a geographical line, "I am in favor of a compromise, but have strong objections to that now under consideration . . . I greatly fear it would tend to perpetuate the evil we seek to remedy. The south line of Pennsylvania State and the Ohio waters now form the boundary line between the two parties. If you continue that line by the 36°30′ of north latitude, to the Pacific Ocean, I fear it will not prove a pacific measure. This would be to place on your records a perpetual rallying place for party."[29]

After Taylor made his very effective speech on February 15, 1819, supporting Tallmadge, the House committee of the whole decided by a vote of 79 to 67 to incorporate the Tallmadge amendment in its bill. The next day, Tuesday, February 16, the House considered the bill as reported out by the committee of the whole. Despite the fact that the full House had participated in the committee of the whole the day before, the rules of the House permitted the House itself to consider the same motions that had been made and defeated in the committee of the whole. Accordingly, another effort was made on

Tuesday to strike out the Tallmadge amendment on the floor of the House. John Scott was now back in the House to defend the interests of Missouri. He did so strongly, saying he would thank Taylor to "condescend to tell him what precise line of latitude suited his conscience, his humanity or his political views." Scott concluded a lengthy speech with the implicit threat that Missouri would go its own way as an independent entity if it could not be admitted with slavery intact.[30]

Tallmadge rose to make an equally impassioned defense of his initiative. Referring to comments previously made by Representative Thomas Cobb of Georgia, Tallmadge remarked that Cobb,

> in addition to other expressions of great warmth, has said, "that, if we persist, the union will be dissolved;" and, with a look fixed on me, has told us, "we have kindled a fire which all the waters of the ocean cannot put out, which seas of blood can only extinguish."
>
> Sir, language of this sort has no effect on me; my purpose is fixed, it is interwoven with my existence, its durability is limited with my life, it is a great and glorious cause, setting bounds to a slavery the most cruel and debasing the world ever witnessed; it is the freedom of man; it is the cause of unredeemed and unregenerated human beings.
>
> Sir, if a dissolution of the Union must take place, let it be so! If civil war, which gentlemen so much threaten, must come, I can only say, let it come![31]

February 16 may have marked the extreme of violent debate in the House, possibly because the slavery issue caught everyone unaware, and no one had yet quite focused on the possible consequences of the radical statements they were making.

Because the entire House had voted on these same questions the day before, the effort to revisit those votes on the floor of the House appeared doomed to failure, but Clay and other leaders devised the strategy, to which they often returned, of dividing Tallmadge's amendment into separate sections. If these separate slices could be properly structured, House leaders might be able to cobble together different majorities for some or all of what they wanted. This was a truly unusual and troubling strategy, implying that Congress might actually pass a bill that a majority of its members would oppose if the bill were presented to them as a single unit. Certainly some parts of the legislation considered in this piecemeal fashion might have been presented as separate bills meriting separate votes, but in most cases, the subject matter was so intertwined that it logically should have been considered in a single bill, and Clay's critics were entirely right in asserting that such a bill should be voted on as a stand-alone measure and not broken up for votes on its constituent parts. However, if this principle had been followed in the Fifteenth and Sixteenth Congresses, there would have been no compromise on Missouri.

On February 16, Clay required first a vote on non-importation and then, subsequently, a vote on the gradual emancipation of children born to slaves in Missouri after statehood. Clay apparently believed that he and his allies would fail to block non-importation but just might defeat gradual emancipation. The latter was more vulnerable because of constitutional concerns that gradual emancipation would be viewed as the taking of property and, perhaps more important emotionally, because of a generalized fear that freed slaves would pose a danger in communities in the South and West. Although months later the strategy of dividing the question was to succeed brilliantly in ending the Missouri controversy, it failed in its first application. The non-importation clause was voted on first and upheld by a vote of 87 to 76. The vote on the gradual emancipation clause, though closer at 82 to 78, still, to Clay's disappointment, came out in favor of upholding Tallmadge's proposal.[32] There was still hope, however, that, if the same division of the question could be tried in the Senate and succeed, the very close vote on the second provision in the House might be reversed and a compromise achieved after all.

The next day, Wednesday, February 17, 1819, was to prove one of the most important in the debates over slavery west of the Mississippi. Having already passed an enabling bill for Missouri on Tuesday, the House on Wednesday resolved itself into a committee of the whole to consider a bill to create the Arkansas Territory out of the southern part of the Missouri Territory. The Arkansas Territory was to be carved off preparatory to Missouri becoming a state and was to consist of what are now the states of Arkansas and Oklahoma. Again the issue was raised of what to do about slavery. The issue in Arkansas was different in two fundamental ways, one involving constitutional principle and the other involving political expediency. The constitutional consideration was that the second clause of Article IV, §3, clearly gave Congress more authority to set conditions in creating and administering territories than it had with respect to the admission of states under the first clause. In other words,

Congress was legitimately in the business of running territories, whereas its involvement in the affairs of new states was questionable. Accordingly, Congress should have had more power to restrict slavery in the territory of Arkansas than it had in the state of Missouri. On the other hand, the practical consideration was that Arkansas was farther south than Missouri and, like Louisiana, clearly within the perceived orbit of the slave states. Expediency, therefore, favored slavery in Arkansas. John Taylor, relying on Congress's power to regulate territories, immediately moved to amend the Arkansas bill by inserting a provision similar to Tallmadge's amendment to the Missouri bill. The motion gave rise to "a wide and long-continued debate, covering part of the ground previously occupied by this subject, but differing in part, as the present proposition was to impose a consideration on a Territorial government, instead of, as in the former case, to enjoin the adoption of the principle in the constitution of a State, and as applied to a more southern Territory."[33]

The heat that had accompanied the Missouri debate carried over to Arkansas, as Taylor launched barbs at Henry Clay in his speech supporting his amendment:

> He has charged us with being under the influence of negrophobia. Sir, he mistook the mark. I thank God that the disease mentioned by that gentleman, is unknown to my constituents; and it is because I wish to exclude it from Arkansas, that I moved this amendment. But, sir, the excitement which this motion has produced, too clearly shows that the negrophobia does unhappily prevail in another section of this country; that it haunts its subjects in their dreams, and disturbs their waking hours. You, sir, have lately seen its influence on one honorable gentleman [Edward Colston, of Virginia], who considered the appearance of a black face in the gallery, pending yesterday's discussion, of sufficient importance to justify a grave address to the Committee, and an animated philippic upon the impropriety of this debate.[34]

After Taylor sat down, Clay, wishing to recognize an able orator to answer Taylor's ardor, turned to Louis McLane of Delaware, who was throughout the crisis a moderating influence in favor of compromise. McLane was just beginning his second term in the House but was already marked as a political figure with a brilliant future. He was also a key swing vote, a Federalist from a state with both slave and abolitionist elements. Last, he was an ally of Jesse Thomas's mentor William Crawford. McLane had qualms about putting any conditions on statehood. He was also one of the early proponents of the concept of a dividing line between slave and free if it could be imposed on territories only and not made a condition for the admission of any state. McLane indicated that he

> would unite with gentlemen in any course within the pale of the Constitution, for the gradual abolition of slavery in the United States. Beyond this, the oath he had taken as a member of the House, forbade him to go. The fixing of a line on the west of the Mississippi, north of which slavery should not be tolerated, had always been with him a favorite policy, and he hoped the day was not distant when upon principles of fair compromise it might constitutionally be effected. He was apprehensive however, that the present premature attempt, and the feelings it had elicited, would interpose new and almost insuperable obstacles to the attainment of the end.

In other words, he thought the concept of a dividing line had promise but had to be properly nurtured. At the conclusion of his lengthy remarks, McLane returned to the theme of compromise:

> At the same time, I do not mean to abandon the policy to which I alluded in the commencement of my remarks. I think it but fair that both sections of the Union should be accommodated on this subject, with regard to which so much feeling has been manifested. The same great motives of policy which reconciled and harmonized the jarring and discordant elements of our system originally, and which enabled the framers of our happy Constitution to compromise the different interests which then prevailed upon this and other subjects, if properly cherished by us, will enable us to achieve similar objects. If we meet upon principles of reciprocity, we cannot fail to do justice to all. It has already been avowed by gentlemen on this floor, from the South and the West, that they will agree upon a line which shall divide the slaveholding from the non-slaveholding States. It is this proposition I am anxious

to effect; but I wish to effect it by some compact which shall be binding upon all parties, and all subsequent Legislatures; which cannot be changed, and will not fluctuate with the diversity of feeling and of sentiment to which this Empire in its march must be destined.[35]

McLane does not identify the gentlemen from the South and West who had avowed agreement on a dividing line, but it seems certain that they included Jesse Thomas and others from the West and the South acting for William Crawford in the Congress.[36] Note that in this formulation McLane describes "a line which shall divide the slaveholding from the non-slaveholding States." This was a slip, and he was later clear that his line was meant to apply only to territories.

It is important to note that McLane was searching for something more than an ordinary law, something that would be "binding upon all parties, and all subsequent Legislatures," and that therefore could not be easily amended or repealed. What he imagined instead was a compact, based on legal principles of contract and subject to amendment only by joint agreement of the parties. Who the "parties" might be presents some difficulty since presumably he meant something more than a simple majority vote in the Senate and House. The concept of a compact had been employed before in the Northwest Ordinance, which "ordained and declared, that the following articles [including Article VI prohibiting slavery] shall be considered as articles of compact between the original States and the people and States in the said Territory, and forever remain unalterable, unless by common consent." Here the parties providing common consent are clearer—they are, on one side, the federal government and, on the other, the people and states composing the territory. Thirty-five years later the North tried to argue that the Missouri Compromise had been just such a "sacred pledge" and was not subject to repeal.[37] The attraction of McLane and the later abolitionists to the concept of a compact was its suggestion of permanence. If the concept had been included in the language of the Missouri Compromise, its repeal in 1854 would have been more difficult.

Taylor's initiative to impose the Tallmadge amendment on the Arkansas Territory was supported by Tallmadge, Livermore, and others of their allies and opposed by Clay and a number of other anti-restrictionists, including Henry Storrs of New York, who was to make significant compromise proposals of his own, and Charles Kinsey of New Jersey, who was to serve on the conference committee that shaped the final compromise. Kinsey and Henry Baldwin of Pennsylvania, both of whom ultimately supported the compromise, did so because of their concern about tariffs, and they hoped that, by voting with the anti-restrictionists, they could pick up some Southern votes in favor of high tariffs that primarily benefited Northerners. Throughout the debate, they were concerned that a bitter, drawn-out controversy over slavery might prevent their tariff bill from even being considered.[38]

Several members spoke more than once, and the debate was maintained "with much animation" until nearly four o'clock when Taylor's motion was finally voted upon. Again, as with the Tallmadge amendment, the motion was divided into two parts that were voted on separately; but, for this more southerly territory, geography trumped constitutional principle, and the House voted down non-importation 80 to 68 and gradual emancipation without even recording the yeas and nays. Despite having that day already considered statehood for Missouri and territorial status for Arkansas, the House committee of the whole at the end of the day turned to Alabama statehood as well.[39] The committee completed work on both the Arkansas and Alabama bills and reported both to the House before adjourning close to five o'clock, thus bringing to a close a very long day of intense negotiations over slavery on the frontier.

The Senate received that same day the formal notification from the clerk of the House that the Missouri enabling bill had passed, with the Tallmadge amendment attached, and the senators no doubt also learned through the grapevine of Clay's tactic of voting separately on the two parts of the amendment in the hope of defeating at least one of them and of how close the vote had been on gradual emancipation. The House bill was referred to the same select committee that had been established on December 11, 1818, to address the issue of Alabama statehood. The committee was headed by Charles Tait, of Georgia, a moderate Southerner who later supported the Missouri Compromise. Missouri was now in play in the Fifteenth Congress and, from this point on, would be dealt with concurrently in both houses.

The next day, Thursday, February 18, the House again turned its attention to Arkansas, proceeding to consider the bill that had been reported out of the committee of the whole the day before. As with the House's enabling bill for Missouri, an effort was made to do in the full House what had failed in the committee of the whole, and Taylor again moved to add the two parts of the Tallmadge amendment, as he had done the day before in the committee of the whole. This time the tactic almost succeeded, because a number of Taylor's opponents of the day before were absent. Non-importation still lost, albeit by the very narrow margin of 71 to 70, but gradual emancipation, which had been a closer issue than non-importation the day before, was now victorious, 75 to 73. That success, however, was short-lived, as Lewis Williams, of North Carolina, immediately moved to reconsider the vote just taken. Although opposed to gradual emancipation, Williams had believed the measure might pass and chose to vote with the majority for the purpose of availing himself of the House rule allowing a member who had voted for a proposition to move its reconsideration, which he promptly did. In fact, if Williams had voted as he was inclined the first time, the vote would have been 74–74, leaving Clay to break the tie by voting against. Because votes were cast in alphabetical order, there were only two House members to vote after Williams, but he must have been unsure of their votes, or perhaps he was just following a pre-agreed-upon strategy without realizing that immediate victory was within his grasp. As Williams made his motion for reconsideration, members were being urgently called back into the House, and by the time a vote was taken, eight more members were on the floor, four adding their votes in favor of gradual emancipation and four against. There was further intense procedural jockeying as evening approached, and eventually the bill was tabled until noon the next day. The House then took up the Alabama enabling bill the Senate had approved a month earlier. There were some ineffectual attempts to add amendments aimed at limiting slavery, but in the end the House abandoned its own bill and concurred with the Senate's.[40]

The next day, Friday, the House again returned to the Arkansas question, and George Robertson of Kentucky moved to take up the motion of the day before to reconsider the gradual emancipation amendment that had been added to the Arkansas bill. The vote was an 88 to 88 tie, with all but nine of the members voting. Henry Clay, as Speaker, was called on to break the tie and of course voted against the amendment. Had the vote gone the other way, gradual emancipation might have gained a toehold in a southerly territory and slowed the expansion of slavery west of the Mississippi. The House passage of the Arkansas bill, 89 to 87, was almost anticlimactic.[41]

With a hard-fought consensus in the House in favor of slavery in Arkansas and against it in Missouri, Ezekiel Whitman, a Federalist from the Maine District of Massachusetts, perceived a possible dividing line along the southern border of the future state of Missouri and suggested this as a practical solution to the problem of slavery west of the Mississippi:

Gentlemen abhor sectional lines of demarcation between the different descriptions of population in the Union, and so do I. When they can be avoided, I would avoid them. But we have them in relation to this subject already. The line is distinctly marked. It is, I confess, one of our misfortunes. But, sir, it is unavoidable. We have heretofore found it necessary and proper to observe it in forming States north of the Ohio, without admitting, and south of the Ohio with, the admission of slaves. Having so begun, we must continue on. And in doing so, we must, as in the case of every other legislative act, exercise a sound discretion, and do that which shall best comport with the demands of the different and varying interests of the different portions of the Union.[42]

As a vote neared on the Arkansas bill, John Taylor for the third time introduced a non-importation amendment. He must have known that he lacked the votes to pass this amendment but perhaps hoped the tally would be close enough to encourage further compromise. He did in fact lose 90 to 86 but immediately went on to propose his own version of the line proposed by Representative Whitman to divide slave from free in all the areas west of the Mississippi. After first stating that he thought it important that some line be designated beyond which slavery should not be permitted, Taylor proposed adding a sweeping geographical prohibition to the bill: "That neither slavery nor involuntary servitude shall hereafter be introduced into any part of the Territories of the United States, lying north of 36 degrees and 30 minutes of north latitude." Taylor thus reintroduced the concept of a line he had first hinted at on February 15. It was a concept that was to resurface, in one form or another, many times during the Missouri controversy, and it formed part of the final resolution. It is possible that Jesse Thomas immediately recognized the utility of Taylor's line. Aside from the attraction of using a line first proposed by an opponent, he undoubtedly focused on the fact that the 36°30' line was also the western extension of the southern borders of both Virginia and Kentucky, both of which were slave states, and, therefore, there could be no definite prohibition against making Missouri a third exception to the general rule of no slavery north of that line.[43]

It is important to note, both here and in the debates that followed in the House and Senate, that some of the dividing lines that were proposed between slave and free applied only to the Louisiana Purchase, while others, by their terms, would have applied to lands farther west that were still under the control of Spain but seemingly destined to become part of the United States. Sometimes these differences may have been inadvertent, but more often they reflected different assessments of the likelihood of picking up necessary support for a compromise or of resolving in advance problems that could otherwise be expected to cause bitterness and rivalry in the future. Taylor, for his part, apparently consciously chose a line that ran to the Pacific, though he was wise enough not to make the assertion explicit.

In those proposals that were specifically limited to the Louisiana Purchase, the uncertainty surrounding the definition of the western extent of the purchase added a further complication. Its western boundary had been left undefined since the time of the purchase in 1803, at which time American representatives had agreed to receive on behalf of the United States "the Colony or Province of Louisiana with the same extent that it now has in the hand of Spain, and that it had when France possessed it," but, since Spain had controlled the largely unexplored territory on both sides of its western boundary before ceding Louisiana to France, no one had paid much attention to where the boundary might actually be located.[44] At the time the Missouri controversy was raging, sixteen years later, John Quincy Adams, secretary of state, was negotiating what came to be called the Adams-Onis Treaty with Spain, which had as one of its principal purposes the settlement of the western boundary of the Louisiana Purchase. Because of the weak position of Spain in these negotiations, it appeared likely that Adams would prove successful in pushing the boundary as far west as possible, thus including in American territory an area considerably greater than Jefferson could reasonably have expected in 1803.

The Adams-Onis Treaty was finally concluded in February 1819, opening vast new areas to American expansion. In addition to giving East and West Florida to the United States, the treaty also resolved the western boundary of the Louisiana Purchase by easing back on American claims to Texas in return for a very generous definition of the more northerly part of the purchase. The treaty thus curtailed the area acquired from France south of the 36°30′ line and expanded it north of the line. The treaty set the western boundary of the Louisiana Purchase starting at the mouth of the Sabine River in the Gulf of Mexico, then running north along the Sabine, then west along the Red River, then north along the 100th meridian to the Arkansas River, which it followed west to its source in the Rockies, then north to 42° north latitude, then west

The Missouri Compromise

The Treaty of 1818 with Britain and the Adams-Onis Treaty of 1819 with Spain together finally resolved the full extent of the Louisiana Purchase. Secretary of State John Quincy Adams, from Massachusetts and strongly against slavery, gave up claims to Texas and other areas in the Southwest in return for a wide swath of territory north of the 36°30' line, which was established a few months later by the Missouri Compromise.

to the Pacific Ocean. The treaty was approved by the Senate on February 22, 1819, but it was not finally ratified by the Spanish government until after the Missouri controversy was over. Nonetheless, the negotiated boundary line was very much in the minds of senators and representatives as they debated various compromises.

In the course of the day on February 19, other lines were proposed. Arthur Livermore conceived Taylor's proposal "to be made in the true spirit of compromise, which ought to be met," but suggested a different line that was not specified in the *House Journal* or the *Annals of Congress* but was, given Livermore's sentiments, presumably farther south. To counter that initiative, William Henry Harrison proposed a line running due west from where the

Des Moines River flows into the Mississippi, but only to the western edge of
the Louisiana Purchase. Under Harrison's proposal the land to the north of
his line would become a part of the Michigan Territory and therefore subject
to Article VI of the Northwest Ordinance. This Article VI solution may have
occurred to Harrison because of the brief time in 1804–5 when the northern
part of the Louisiana Purchase was made part of the Indiana Territory, and
Harrison, as governor, was responsible for applying Article VI there. Harrison
was very explicit that this was what he intended: "And the laws now in force
in the [Michigan] Territory as well as the ordinance of Congress prohibiting
slavery or involuntary servitude in said Territory of Michigan, shall be in
force in that part of the Missouri Territory lying north of the said east and
west line." Harrison likely made the decision to introduce Article VI into
the debate because he was aware of its very useful ambiguity and of all the
proto-slavery measures that had flourished under its aegis.[45]

Purists from the North and the South objected to this discussion of a
line of demarcation. Ideologues on both sides of the debate opposed any line
on the logical grounds that if a practice were deemed unconstitutional or
otherwise illegal in one part of the country, it should be so everywhere. The
debate grew bitter as Southerners accused Northerners of trying to foment a
slave rebellion. Salma Hale of New Hampshire, who was soon to leave the
House, wrote that "it was a painful scene & I hope a similar discussion will
never again take place in our walls."[46] After several more brisk exchanges,
Taylor decided to withdraw his amendment, stating that "he perceived from
the debate, as well as from conversation, that it was not probable any line
would be agreed on by the House, or any compromise of opinion be effected."
Perhaps he recognized even then that it would be easier to rally House members to a line that was first proposed and approved by the Senate. Taylor and
his allies thus conceded slavery in the Arkansas Territory, and the Arkansas
bill moved on to the Senate.

The focus now shifted to the Senate, where on the following Monday,
February 22, Tait's committee reported out the Missouri enabling bill as passed
by the House, but with an amendment to strike the Tallmadge amendment.
The next day, Tait reported out the Arkansas bill just as it had been passed
in the House, and on Wednesday, he moved that the Missouri enabling bill
be put off until Friday. The debate did not in fact resume until Saturday,
when an attempt to put off the Arkansas bill to March 5 was voted down.
Pro-restriction senators then tried to attach to the Arkansas bill the two parts

of the Tallmadge amendment that the House had narrowly failed to adopt. The Senate, adopting the tactic Clay had used in the House, proceeded to vote separately on the two parts of the Tallmadge amendment, as applied to Arkansas, voting down the gradual emancipation provision 31 to 7 and the non-importation provision 22 to 16, with Thomas and Edwards in the majority both times.[47]

With time now growing short in the Fifteenth Congress, the Senate resumed consideration of the Missouri enabling bill on Monday, March 1. James Burrill Jr., of Rhode Island, who would prove to be Thomas's most important ally among the Federalists, was opposed to slavery but willing to compromise in the interest of preserving the Union. Burrill now led a doomed effort to restore Tallmadge's proposals, but the 19 to 14 vote was a clear signal of the size of the Senate majority opposed to restriction. The bill was then passed on a voice vote, and the secretary of the Senate was instructed to notify the House that it had refused to accede to the amendments that the House had proposed. On Tuesday, March 2, the House took up the Missouri bill as sent back from the Senate to decide whether to accept the stripping out of the Tallmadge amendment. After a vigorous debate, Tallmadge himself, sensing that many of his supporters were tempted to go along with the Senate and admit Missouri, moved the indefinite postponement of the bill, perhaps in the belief that the Sixteenth Congress might contain more opponents of slavery than the Fifteenth. His motion was voted down, and the House went on to consider the bill, agreeing easily with most of the Senate amendments but leaving the Tallmadge amendment to last. Finally, on this penultimate day of the Fifteenth Congress, the question was voted on, and the House chose to stand by Tallmadge's proposals by the narrow vote of 78 to 76. It is hard to imagine, but if one vote had changed in the House at the close of the Fifteenth Congress, Clay would have been called on to resolve the tie and would have voted against the Tallmadge amendment, opening the way for Missouri's admission as a state and avoiding the tumult that instead enveloped the Sixteenth Congress. By the narrowest of margins, compromise had slipped the grasp of the legislators, and as time went by, it would prove increasingly elusive.[48]

CHAPTER 10

Maneuvering for Position

A t the close of the Fifteenth Congress in the spring of 1819, the country at large, with the exception of Missouri and Illinois, did not feel the same intensity about Missouri as did the ardent partisans in Congress. In fact, that spring and early summer, ordinary citizens on the Eastern Seaboard were more concerned about the gathering financial panic and the declining state of the economy. There were, however, two centers of activity in the East that were to affect the landscape when the Missouri debate resumed in the fall. The first was in Massachusetts, where early that summer the Federalist legislature passed an act by which the predominantly Republican district of Maine, up until then a part of Massachusetts, could become a separate state, thus putting another potential state into play in the negotiations that ensued. Because of congressional dawdling on prior attempts at separation, the act stipulated that Maine must obtain the approval of the U.S. Congress by March 4 of the following year, a deadline that proved later to be critically important in the Missouri controversy.

The other locus of activity during that summer was the middle states of Pennsylvania, New Jersey, and New York, where antislavery emotion concerning Missouri was starting to build. Elias Boudinot, a philanthropist and a Federalist, presided over the first large antislavery gathering, held in Burlington County, New Jersey, on August 30. This marked the beginning of a resurgence of Federalist leadership in the antislavery cause. The Burlington meetings were followed by mass gatherings in New York City, where followers of DeWitt Clinton joined Federalists in the crusade. The involvement of Federalists, Clintonians, and others gave rise to the conviction among

Southern Republicans, and particularly President Monroe, that the entire effort was being organized not so much to stop the spread of slavery as to split the Republican Party into Southern and Northern wings, with the Federalists positioning themselves to absorb the latter. The success of the Federalists in the fall elections lent credence to Monroe's fears, though, as shall be seen, there is also evidence that Monroe and the proslavery moderates used the bugbear of a Federalist plot to good effect to gain the grudging support of a few key Southern moderates and the ultimate acquiescence of many Southern radicals. It was ironic, but essential to the Union, that at least some Southerners proved in the end to be more worried about Federalists than they were about the principle of unrestricted slavery in the West.[1]

When the Sixteenth Congress convened on December 6, slavery on the frontier was once again in the forefront, even as more practical-minded legislators pushed Congress to turn its attention to the deepening economic crisis. The slavery issue first arose when the proposed constitution of the state of Alabama was presented on December 8, initially in the Senate and then in the House. The Senate passed the joint resolution in perfunctory fashion and rushed it over to the House, where some antislavery members tried to delay consideration. The House, however, decided to follow suit and push through the resolution that day, thus taking Alabama off the table as a potential bargaining chip in the upcoming statehood negotiations that now involved only Missouri and Maine.[2] The anti-restrictionists' fear had been that Alabama might be paired with Maine to maintain the approximate balance between slave and nonslave states, leaving them without a bargaining chip to pair with Missouri. Though the House for its various reasons chose to push Alabama through, anti-restrictionists could not fail to notice that some of their adversaries were prepared to oppose the extension of slavery even in a clearly Southern state.

With Alabama's admission, there was parity between slave and free, with eleven states in each camp. In this calculus, Illinois was considered a free state despite its indenture statutes and its two Southern-leaning senators. Parity was to be the new model for the future, and now that Alabama was off the table, the only potential states left in play were Missouri and Maine, one logically a slave state and the other nonslave. Anti-restrictionists advocated pairing the two of them, hoping to use the March 4, 1820, deadline for the admission of Maine as leverage to speed statehood for Missouri. This initiative, seeking statehood in tandem for Maine and

Missouri, was formally renewed in the House the very day that Alabama became part of the Union, although in the House's typically haphazard fashion, the statehood applications for the two of them were handled in separate committees.

James Tallmadge had chosen not to run for reelection to the Sixteenth Congress, but John W. Taylor, his New York colleague, now picked up his banner. Taylor led an active and independent group of DeWitt Clinton supporters in the New York delegation that included individuals like Henry Storrs and James Strong who were still adamant on the issue of restriction. The group worked together for a compromise with an antislavery slant, but Taylor's initiatives were also colored by his ongoing behind-the-scenes campaign to garner the Southern votes necessary to succeed Henry Clay as Speaker of the House (which he was to do in November of 1820). On the same day that Congress passed the act authorizing the admission of Alabama and that statehood petitions for Maine and Missouri were refiled from the Fifteenth Congress, Strong gave notice that he planned to submit a bill the following day to prohibit the further extension of slavery within the "Territories of the United States." The next day, slavery-related issues continued their rapid progress with John Scott of the special committee on the admission of Missouri reporting a bill "authorizing the people of the Territory of Missouri to form a constitution and State government, and for the admission of such State into the Union on an equal footing with the original States." The bill, the same as the one filed in the prior Congress and likewise silent on the subject of slavery, was read twice and committed to a committee of the whole, where it would be endlessly debated.[3]

Initial consideration of Scott's bill was delayed for a few days, however, to afford time for another effort at compromise, this one carefully organized by Taylor. Taylor took more time with this compromise initiative than he had with his effort the previous spring. He knew that he was walking a narrow line in his attempts to be conciliatory with his Southern colleagues, which did not sit well with his restrictionist allies. Salma Hale, who had just left the House, wrote Taylor from New Hampshire that "I am not, I allow, where I can take a view of the whole ground, but here I see no necessity for a compromise. If we are firm for two years, changes of sentiment, & a new apportionment of representatives [following the census of 1820], will I feel confident give us the victory." Taylor thought otherwise, however, and unveiled his new initiative on Tuesday, December 14:

All who love our country, and consider the Union of these States as the ark of its safety, must ever view with deep regret sectional interests agitating our national councils. [Taylor] could not himself, nor would he ask others, to make a sacrifice of principle to expediency. He could never sanction the existence of slavery where it could be excluded consistently with the Constitution and public faith. But it ought not to be forgotten that the American family is composed of many members; if their interests are various, they mutually must be respected; if their prejudices are strong, they must be treated with forbearance. He did not know whether conciliation were practicable, but he considered the attainment worthy of an effort. He was desirous that the question should be settled in that spirit of amity and brotherly love which carried us through the perils of a Revolution, and produced the adoption of our Federal Constitution.

Taylor went on to propose the formation of a committee "to inquire into the expediency of prohibiting by law the introduction of slaves into the territories of the United States west of the Mississippi" and the postponement of the Missouri bill until that committee completed its work.[4]

On careful reading, Taylor's proposal prohibited only the future introduction of slaves west of the Mississippi and had no application to the slaves already there. Likewise, his proposal was limited only to the territories of the United States and did not purport to apply after statehood. Since it was put forward after the bill authorizing Missouri's admission as a state was already before the House, it might not have applied to Missouri at all, depending on the order in which bills were approved. These elements had all been present in Tallmadge's non-importation provision, and it made sense for Taylor to follow this branch of Tallmadge's amendment because, of the two parts Tallmadge had put forward, this one had fared better in both House (winning) and Senate (losing). Taylor surely understood the implications of his proposal, since he restated it in the same terms two weeks later. In this light, Taylor's initiative could be viewed as a genuine effort at compromise under which Missouri (and possibly Arkansas) might come in as slave states and slavery would be barred in the rest of the western territories only until statehood. George Strother of Virginia, a member of the select committee on Missouri statehood, proposed, however, that Taylor's proposition should lie on the table till the next day, to give time for reflection. The obvious intent was to permit an informal canvas on whether such a compromise was possible. Taylor assented to this course, and the House adjourned.[5]

In the Senate the next day, Jonathan Roberts of Pennsylvania presented a petition from an abolition meeting in Philadelphia to prohibit the admission of any new state that did not forbid the further introduction of slavery.[6] Roberts's petition, like Taylor's motion, depending on the order in which bills were considered, might have only prohibited the further introduction of slavery after the unconditional admission of Missouri. It is also noteworthy that the petition, like Taylor's proposal, dropped the gradual emancipation provision of Tallmadge's amendment, thus agreeing to a situation in which, although no new slaves could be imported into the state, slaves already in the state and their progeny would continue to be held as chattel. Although they recognized that such a law was unlikely to pass, these were important concessions from opponents of slavery.

Meanwhile, later that day in the House, Taylor renewed his motion and said that he hoped to delay other discussion of the issue, which he feared would become divisive, until his committee had completed its work. Following appointment of the committee, Taylor moved to postpone consideration of the Missouri bill until the first Monday in February 1820. This long delay would put considerable pressure on the House, because at that point it would have only a month to resolve the controversy before the expiration of the deadline for the admission of Maine. From this point on, anti-restrictionists would stall in hopes that an enabling act for Missouri could not be successfully negotiated in time to make the deadline. William Lowndes, lieutenant in the House for John C. Calhoun, did not object to postponement but thought the proposed delay too long. The pragmatic Arthur Livermore wanted a long delay so other business could be finished first (and so Congress might be forced by the March 4 deadline to admit Maine before taking final action on Missouri). Scott opposed a long delay and displayed a degree of truculence that reflected the growing frustration of his fellow Missourians: "If, on the other hand, the bill ultimately was lost, it was equally necessary that the people should be soon apprized of its failure, that they might have time to act for themselves, and frame a form of government, which he was convinced they would do, without waiting to again apply to Congress for the mere means of organization." Livermore also argued that, since Taylor's committee was constituted only to consider territories, it was irrelevant to the formation of new states, thus signaling he recognized that Taylor's proposed compromise was based on the possibility of different treatment for territories and states. After further discussion, the Missouri bill was postponed to January 10, a little more than three weeks off.[7] In fact, because of unforeseen complications in the Senate, the House would not take up the subject of Missouri again for six weeks.

All this maneuvering over slavery in the West occurred even before the Senate had had an opportunity to organize itself into committees, which was typically its first task at the start of a new Congress. When, on Thursday, December 16, the Senate finally took the time to appoint its standing committees, there was a startling development for Jesse Thomas, who was elected to the Committee on Public Lands. Committee members were elected by their fellow senators by secret ballot, the five receiving the highest number of votes for each committee being chosen and the one with the highest number becoming chairman. After a total Senate experience of only three months in the prior session, Thomas received the third most votes in the polling for this very important committee. Within a month, Thomas was chairman of the committee, replacing Thomas Williams of Mississippi, a supporter of Andrew Jackson. When a standing committee was formed on February 8, 1820, to deal with roads and canals, Thomas was also appointed to that committee. Before the creation of the Committee on Roads and Canals, there were only twelve standing committees in the Senate, usually with five members each, so, with forty-four senators and many senior senators holding multiple assignments, new senators were not even assured a committee appointment. Thus it was that Thomas was catapulted into a very powerful position both in the Senate and in Illinois.[8]

The most plausible explanation for Thomas's rapid advancement is the support he had from William Harris Crawford. Crawford was, after James Monroe, arguably the most commanding figure on a political stage crowded with outstanding men. His family had come to Georgia from Virginia, and his strong support in Virginia, long the cradle of presidents, gave Crawford a great advantage in the impending 1824 race that was already bubbling in 1820. He thought that now, after allowing Monroe two uncontested terms, Monroe would support him fully, even though his states' rights politics sometimes ran counter to Monroe's nationalism. When instead Monroe maintained strict neutrality, relations between the two men grew frosty, and Crawford geared up his campaign against Secretary of War John C. Calhoun and Secretary of State John Quincy Adams, his principal challengers for the great prize of the presidency in 1824. The long line of Virginians who had dominated the presidency seemed certain to be coming to an end, and for the first time the frontier would be a major factor in a national election. Reflecting this new reality, Henry Clay of Kentucky, the Speaker of the House and the first great western politician, became the fourth major figure to join in the quest. Crawford, however, was still viewed as the strongest of the contenders.

It was, in fact, typical for western senators to predominate on the Public Lands Committee; but Thomas's early elevation to that office clearly depended on the influence of Crawford, who had many friends in the Senate and was Thomas's principal mentor from his first arrival there. Certainly, Thomas had qualities that impressed Crawford and others and suited him to deal with both public lands issues and the question of slavery west of the Mississippi: his skill as a legal draftsman; his ability to parse legislation and shepherd laws through the legislative process; his position as a Southern-leaning senator from a nominally Northern state; and, last, but not least, his ambivalent views on slavery, which gave him some credibility with both sides. However precisely it occurred, Thomas's role as an emerging leader was an impressive accomplishment for a freshman senator.

Jesse Thomas used his new position on the Committee on Public Lands to advance his interests and to block his adversaries. For example, less than a month after his appointment, he shepherded through the Senate motions that the Public Lands Committee look into establishing additional land offices in Illinois and resolving issues related to preemption in the state. Two weeks later, he made sure that, when Ninian Edwards presented to the Senate the resolutions of the Illinois legislature urging the extension of the National Road into Illinois, the matter was referred to the Public Lands Committee, where Thomas, and not Edwards, would receive the credit for any progress made.[9]

In the opening days of the new Congress, various petitions, memorials, and bills relating to Maine and Missouri were presented in the House by both sides, but nothing substantive was done in the House or Senate while discussions continued behind the scenes. Finally, on December 21, John Holmes, from the District of Maine, serving on the House select committee addressing statehood for Maine, reported a bill for its admission, reflecting growing concern about the looming March 4 deadline. John Floyd of Virginia moved that Holmes's bill be made the order of the day for the second Monday of January and be committed to the same committee of the whole as the bill for admitting Missouri. Floyd's initiative was intended to make sure that the subjects of Maine and Missouri would come up on the same day that Taylor's compromise committee was slated to report. There clearly were still a number of people hoping that Taylor's attempt at compromise would succeed. Holmes, however, concerned about the approaching deadline, successfully opposed Floyd's motion, and the Maine bill was made the order of the day for the next day.[10]

The next day, however, Holmes's hopes were disappointed—his bill was relegated to a later date and did not come up again until two days after Taylor, on December 28, pulled the plug on the compromise committee he had set up fourteen days before. The committee's mandate still had two weeks to run, but Taylor admitted defeat early, saying that "the committee had found that, after a free interchange of opinions, they could not, consistently with their ideas of public duty, come to any conclusion, or agree to any report which could promise to unite to any degree the conflicting views of the House on this question."[11] After the House agreed to discharge his committee, Taylor gave notice that he intended to present for future discussion a resolution "prohibiting the further admission of slaves into the Territories of the United States west of the river Mississippi." As in his earlier articulation of this same proposition, a key word was "further"—that is, would his proposition affect slaves already in the Louisiana Purchase?

It is also intriguing to ponder whether the capitalization of the word "Territories" matters. The discussion of capitalization in this and other speeches published in the *Annals of Congress* assumes that the speaker supplied the reporter with a copy of his speech, with his preferred capitalization, or was at least permitted to edit the reporter's notes and make sure his speech was properly reproduced. Otherwise, the choice to capitalize or not would be up to the reporter and would have no significance for the reader. There is a greater likelihood that a reporter would check the wording and capitalization of a motion with the proposer. Although capitalization was quite informal at the time, it does appear that many speakers did make conscious choices on capitalization that were, for the most part, accurately reflected in the written record. When Taylor first stated his resolution on December 14, he used a small *t*, but when he restated it on December 28, he used a capital *T*, suggesting that Congress would not assert authority to regulate importation of slaves until unorganized territory was actually organized in the first stage of territorial government. The latter interpretation would broaden the window for slave owners to import slaves.

On the next day, Wednesday, December 29, William Smith of South Carolina rose in the Senate to present a memorial from the Missouri territorial General Assembly praying for admission as a separate and independent state. The memorial was read and referred to the Judiciary Committee, which was the first time a matter relating to Missouri had been referred to that committee. Subsequent petitions on Maine were also referred to that committee, and from then on it would be the committee charged with trying to formulate a uniform policy on territories and states. The Committee on the Judiciary was dominated by Southerners and was certain to favor proslavery solutions.

Debate had been postponed while Taylor's behind-the-scenes negotiations progressed, with both senators and representatives hesitant to engage in oratory that would harden positions and make compromise more difficult. Once Taylor abandoned his initiative, however, speeches flowed forth, vastly complicating the chances for a successful compromise. It was becoming clearer by the day that almost every member of Congress was going to want to go on the record, some of them at great length, on the subject of slavery in Missouri. Even the weather seemed to reflect the rising tension in Congress. It had already been a particularly rigorous winter, but a blizzard commenced the night of December 29 and continued with increasing violence into the night of the following day.[12] As the storm raged outside, the House resolved itself into a committee of the whole to consider the bill reported out by the select committee on the admission of Maine. There was some bickering over the number of current Massachusetts representatives to be taken from Massachusetts and given to Maine, but John Holmes moved to strip that provision out of the bill so that the statehood issue would not become bogged down.[13]

The motion to report the Maine bill to the House for final action was met head-on by Henry Clay, who declared that he was not yet prepared to allow a vote. He said that he was not opposed to the admission of Maine but that, before the House acted, he wished to know how far the restrictionists would be able to assert their will on Missouri. In other words, he wanted the admission of Missouri on acceptable terms to be a condition to the admission of Maine. He also pointed out that in 1791 the admission of Kentucky had been delayed eighteen months until Vermont was ready for statehood and that the two states, one from the Northeast and one from the West, had then been connected together in the same act. Clay concluded "with that frankness which perhaps too much belonged to his character" that he would oppose the separate admission of Maine, evidently enjoying the rich irony of restrictionists, who wished to impose conditions on the admission of Missouri, now being put in the position of objecting to the propriety of placing conditions on the admission of Maine. Holmes grew frustrated over Clay's effort to link Maine and Missouri, pointing out that several unsuccessful attempts had already been made to separate Maine from Massachusetts over the past twenty years and the current effort, so far advanced as it was, must be successful before the March 4 deadline. Holmes went on to say that he hoped that the doctrine proposed by the advocates of restriction in Missouri did not extend quite as far as Clay had intimated, to which Clay retorted, in an audible undertone, "Yes, it did!"[14]

Although there was still a relaxed and occasionally good-humored tone to the discussion over the next few weeks, this stormy day marked the beginning of the fiery and continuous debates that raged in the House during January and February 1820 leading up to the final adoption of the Missouri Compromise on March 3. Numerous representatives weighed in on that first day of debate, including, notably, some like Samuel Foote of Connecticut and Henry Storrs of New York, who had labored from the very beginning to try to fashion a compromise. Foote's actions are of particular interest because he was likely acting in concert with John Quincy Adams in the House throughout the controversy.[15] Underlying all these discussions was the issue of time, which seemed to be running against the supporters of slavery, in the short run because the deadline imposed by Massachusetts on statehood for Maine dictated prompt and fair action and in the long run because, with the 1820 census, the North's burgeoning population would give it ironclad control of the House. By Friday, the snowstorm had abated, but it continued very cold. The Potomac was frozen below Alexandria, and the snow had "swirled into piles like haycocks." The blizzard of petitions and memorials also continued in the House. Finally, however, the separate Maine bill was ordered to be engrossed and read a third time on the following Monday, at which time it was passed and promptly submitted to the upper house for its concurrence.[16]

The Senate, however, was not in a cooperative frame of mind. James Barbour of Virginia, president of the Senate and a close ally of President Monroe, was banking on being able to link the admission of the two states and then use the March 4 deadline to squeeze Missouri through. When the House bill came over that Monday, Barbour signaled that he planned to make a motion that the Maine bill be recommitted to the Committee on the Judiciary with instructions to amend it to make Missouri statehood a condition for Maine statehood and to authorize the admission of Missouri "upon an equal footing with the original States in all respects whatever." Equal footing, of course, was the seminal language from the Northwest Ordinance used as code here for "without restriction on slavery." There is no record of Barbour making his motion, but he must have done so and it must have carried, for, on Thursday, January 6, William Smith, the chairman of the Senate Judiciary Committee, reported out the House bill on Maine with the Missouri bill, without any restriction on slavery, as an amendment. William Pinkney of Maryland, just seated to replace a senator who had died, moved that discussion be postponed for a week because of the magnitude of the questions raised, and his motion was carried.[17]

An unsettled calm enveloped the capital as all sensed that the crisis was nearing. Several of the participants at this time raised the bugbear of a Federalist conspiracy supposedly masterminded by Rufus King, that party's unofficial leader, to take up the antislavery banner in order to split Northern from Southern Republicans. John Holmes was typical in his description of the rumored plot: "But, is it not probable that there are some jugglers behind the screen who are playing a deeper game—who are combining to rally under this standard, as the last resort, the forlorn hope of an expiring party?"[18] It is ironic that at that juncture politics was considered a "deeper game" than slavery, particularly since, as discussed earlier, it is unlikely any such plot existed except possibly in the minds of Monroe and his allies, who wished to use it to convince wavering Southern Republicans to support a compromise. The interplay of the supposed Federalist plot and the Missouri controversy would play out on parallel tracks over the next month in Richmond, the home of the most virulent haters of Federalists, and in Washington, where Monroe was trying to shape a coalition in favor of compromise. In the end, it turned out that the Republicans had much more to fear from sincere antislavery partisans in their own party than they did from Federalists or renegade Clintonian Republicans.

In the last month of 1819 and the first few months of 1820, the interplay between Washington and Richmond proved to be critical, mainly because Monroe was maneuvering to secure the Republican nomination for the 1820 presidential election. During this period, Monroe's son-in-law and secretary, George Hay, served as his political representative in Virginia. On December 24, Hay wrote Monroe warning of a possible insurrection of Virginia Republicans and suggesting that Monroe's support in his own state was in danger unless he stood firm against restriction of any kind in Missouri. During those few weeks, Monroe collaborated with Hay in writing carefully crafted articles for the *Richmond Enquirer* intended to arouse fears of the Federalists while protecting Monroe from attack and still leaving open the possibility of compromise. Meanwhile, back in Washington, Monroe was marshaling every available resource to gain the necessary votes to win passage of the compromise. He conferred privately with John Quincy Adams, indicating that he thought some compromise possible, and he enlisted the aid of the ubiquitous Nicholas Biddle, the powerful president of the First National Bank who routinely used economic suasion to achieve political ends.[19]

On January 10, Monroe wrote Hay that it seemed probable that a western extension of the northern boundary of Missouri might be used as a dividing line between slave and free territories.[20] It is no surprise that Monroe was aware of the possibility of a compromise based on a dividing line, as the subject had arisen in the previous Congress, but the fact that he brought it up at that juncture indicates that he was probably intimately involved with congressional leaders in discussing a compromise formula, possibly not acting directly but rather through his cabinet officers, principally Crawford, Calhoun, and Adams.

On Friday, January 14, the Senate resumed consideration of the Maine bill with Barbour's amendment making the admission of Missouri a condition to admission of Maine. Jonathan Roberts, of Pennsylvania, led an attempt to have the bill recommitted to the Judiciary Committee with instructions to separate Maine from Missouri and to restore to the Missouri bill the restriction on slavery it had had when it came over from the House (that is, both provisions of the Tallmadge amendment). After a very lengthy debate, Roberts's proposal was voted down 25 to 18. That was a significant vote because it signaled that there was a safe majority in the Senate opposed to restriction in Missouri. On the following Monday, with the Missouri crisis entering its seventh week in that session, Jesse Thomas quietly initiated his effort at compromise. He did so by giving notice in the Senate that he planned the next day to ask leave to bring in a freestanding bill "to prohibit the introduction of slavery into the territories of the United States North and West of the contemplated state of Missouri." Up to that time Congress had been working on a House bill authorizing Missouri statehood, with the Tallmadge amendment attached, which had been passed in the House and referred to the Senate for its consideration (the House Missouri bill), and a Senate bill authorizing Maine statehood with Barbour's amendment making admission of Missouri a condition to admission

of Maine, which was still in the Senate (the Maine-Missouri bill). Thomas
initially chose not to attach his initiative to either bill.[21]

A little later that morning, debate recommenced on the Maine-Missouri
bill, at which point Thomas's fellow senator Ninian Edwards "offered an
amendment, having in view the principle of compromise (by exclusion of
slavery from the other territories of the United States)," but subsequently
withdrew it to give an opportunity for Jonathan Roberts to make an alternative
motion based on non-importation of slaves into Missouri.[22] It is interesting
that Edwards made a motion so closely paralleling Thomas's earlier proposal
and then so quickly withdrew it. It is also interesting that he launched his
initiative as an amendment to the Maine-Missouri bill rather than as a freestanding bill as Thomas had done, showing a certain lack of sensitivity to
legislative strategy. Thomas's bill would ultimately become an amendment
to the Maine-Missouri bill, but Thomas must have recognized that it would
have a better chance of acceptance initially if it were freestanding and not
a condition to the admission of a state, which would weigh it down with
unnecessary baggage. In any event, Edwards's move indicates that he may
have been aware of the discussions leading up to Thomas's bill and somehow
wanted to snatch the initiative from his more careful and deliberate colleague.

For his part, Roberts, who had been blocked the previous Friday in his
attempt to reattach both elements of the Tallmadge amendment to the
Maine-Missouri bill, apparently thought he might be more successful trying
on Monday for half a loaf and sought to reattach just the non-importation
provision. Roberts, like Thomas, was a Crawford ally, even though he came
from a restrictionist state, and it appears that he cooperated with Thomas
and Crawford to set the stage for compromise. Hence the moves and coun-
termoves of Thomas and Roberts were probably carefully worked out behind
the scenes. The vote the prior Friday indicated that Roberts's new endeavor
would ultimately be unsuccessful, but it nonetheless became the focus of debate
for the next two weeks, culminating in Senator Barbour's three-hour speech
on January 31 and February 1. The outcome in the Senate was never really in
doubt, though, and the many intervening speeches were simply a matter of
various senators demanding the opportunity to showcase their oratorical skills
and to put their views on the record. The opening of the floodgates of rhetoric
and recrimination, however, made compromise that much more difficult.

On Tuesday, January 18, as promised the previous day, Jesse Thomas asked
and obtained leave to bring in a freestanding bill to prohibit the introduction

of slavery into the territories of the United States west and north of the contemplated state of Missouri, which was read and passed to the second reading.[23] Unlike Edwards's proposal of the day before, Thomas's bill had been carefully crafted and written out for submission to the Senate. In this first version of his compromise, Thomas proposed to achieve his purpose by providing that Article VI of the Northwest Ordinance would apply to all the territory belonging to the United States west of the Mississippi other than the present-day states of Missouri, Arkansas, and Louisiana. He evidently hoped to exploit the limitations and ambiguities of Article VI, with which he had worked so long and skillfully in the Indiana and Illinois Territories, to create the possibility of proto-slavery if that proved necessary for compromise.

The definition of the area covered by Thomas's bill was itself a masterpiece of draftsmanship, because he wanted his bill to describe a line separating slave and free territory, running from the Gulf of Mexico to the Canadian border and back south again, without mentioning the proposed state of Missouri. He feared any mention of Missouri would cause his initiative to lose its status as a freestanding bill and result in it being swept up as an amendment to the Maine-Missouri bill. Likewise, since he wanted to exclude as much territory to the north and west as would ultimately be determined to belong to the United States when the western and northern boundaries of the Louisiana Purchase were finally determined, he had to keep those boundaries fluid until the Adams-Onis Treaty and the Treaty of 1818 were ratified. This initial effort by Thomas was much more generous to the restrictionists than his final effort a month later. Like Taylor's initiative of several weeks before, Thomas's proposal did not affect preexisting slavery and applied only during the territorial period.

The next day was filled with more speeches, one of them a rambling discourse by Ninian Edwards, who had taken umbrage at a remark made the previous Friday that he felt impugned him as being unfaithful to the supposedly nonslaveholding western state he represented. Edwards now declaimed at length his distaste for slavery and his faith in diffusion as a remedy for it. Fortunately, just as he was turning to his constitutional arguments against restriction, which promised to be especially ponderous, he claimed to have developed a sore throat and sat down.[24] By contrast, Jesse Thomas was one of the few senators who never made a set speech on the Missouri controversy yet achieved much more by working quietly and efficiently behind the scenes.

On Thursday, the Senate continued to debate the Maine bill and the amendments to it proposed by Barbour and Roberts. It was not until Friday,

January 21, that Thomas again brought up his freestanding bill, and then it was only to move that it be referred to a select committee, to consist of five members, to consider and report thereon. By vote of their fellow senators, Thomas, along with the Federalist James Burrill of Rhode Island; Richard Johnson, Republican of Kentucky; William Palmer, Republican of Vermont; and James Pleasants, Republican of Virginia, were appointed to the committee. Thomas is listed first in the *Senate Journal* and presumably was the chair of this committee.[25]

Later that Friday, the Senate resumed consideration of the Maine bill together with the amendments proposed thereto. Senator William Pinkney of Maryland commenced his famous but ostentatious speech in favor of slavery, which lasted for three hours that day and two more hours on Monday; the speech was not reproduced in the *Annals of Congress* but by all accounts epitomized the kind of provocative rhetoric that Thomas was trying so hard to avoid. John Taylor wrote his wife over the intervening weekend that "the business of the session progresses slowly & I expect it will be continued until a late day in the Spring. The question of slavery in Missouri has been under debate in the Senate for the last week & excites immense interest. There has nothing been like it since the declaration of war."[26]

Following the completion of Pinkney's speech on Monday, Harrison Gray Otis said he wished to reply but not until the following day since the Senate would have "little relish for the plain fare which he could offer" after "the intellectual banquet which they had just enjoyed." Meanwhile, in the House that Monday, Henry Clay announced that the admission of Missouri was to be the first order of the day, and John Taylor immediately moved that consideration of the bill be postponed for a week to give the Senate a chance to decide on the amendment Roberts had proposed. Taylor was apparently still hopeful of a compromise and wanted the Senate to propose one in the hope that the House might be more willing to accept it than one of its own devising that risked defeat in the Senate. But Taylor's motion to postpone eventually lost 88 to 87, and the divisive debate roared on.[27]

On Tuesday, January 25, in the Senate, Otis responded to Pinkney in a speech covering eighteen pages in the *Annals*. Otis was a Federalist from Massachusetts who had voted against restriction in the Fifteenth Congress but then, under the influence of Federalist leader Rufus King, became a restrictionist in the Sixteenth. Otis started his speech by noting that the Ordinance of 1787, which was "justly styled the immortal ordinance," imposed conditions on the admission of new states. Specifically, he viewed Article VI as "a perpetual canon against involuntary servitude" and not as a condition that could be abrogated after statehood. Furthermore, the ordinance had been accepted by the state of Virginia when it confirmed its cession and had been considered a binding compact guiding the creation of all subsequent states.[28] This interpretation of Article VI was markedly different from that of Thomas and others, like Pinkney, who asserted that Article VI could in fact be abrogated after statehood.

On that same day, the House, on the motion of Missouri's delegate John Scott, resolved itself into a committee of the whole on the Missouri bill. The committee of the whole continued the next day, and Henry Storrs of New York stepped forward as the new champion of compromise based on a dividing line. He proposed curtailing the proposed state of Missouri by making the Missouri River its northern boundary "with the view of drawing a line on which those in favor of, and those opposed to the slave restriction, might compromise their views." His original concept was that the Missouri River might provide the boundary between slave and free in the West in the same way that the Ohio River had in the East. Vote counting on Storrs's proposal continued in the cloakrooms and overnight in the boardinghouses where representatives lived, and by the next morning Storrs apparently became convinced that not only would supporters of Missouri statehood be put off by the radical reduction in the size of the new state he had proposed but also supporters of restriction would think he was giving away too much. The Missouri River, after all, turns in a more northerly direction west of the proposed new state, and, under Storrs's original formulation, what later became Kansas, Nebraska, Colorado, and Wyoming would have been open to slavery. Storrs, no doubt, had been tempted to go in that direction because settlement of those states seemed in 1820 to be, at best, a very distant possibility. For whatever reason, Storrs rose on Wednesday, withdrew the amendment that he had offered the previous day, and proposed in its place a line along the 38th degree of north latitude extending west of Missouri. This proposal would give Missouri back its northern tier and let it come in as a slave state but would then draw an east-west line starting about halfway up Missouri's western boundary and extending in theory to the Pacific, which would be the boundary between slave and free in territories thereafter. By the end of the day, Storrs's second motion had also been voted down. John Taylor then temporarily abandoned the effort to devise an acceptable dividing line and reverted to his earlier position by proposing the imposition of the non-importation provision of the Tallmadge amendment on the new state of Missouri.[29]

Some of the state legislatures had attempted to bind their representatives in Congress to take particular positions on the slavery issue. New York's legislature, for example, had instructed its delegation to vote for restriction in Missouri. John Taylor, however, as leader of that delegation had followed his own conscience, as had his colleagues. Henry Meigs, for instance, said that he found himself in a peculiar situation because he had been instructed by his legislature to vote for restriction in Missouri but could not "in conscience or judgment, consent to impose this restriction upon Missouri." His Federalist colleague from New York, Henry Storrs, apparently felt even less bound by the instruction from the New York legislature.[30] The debate was gradually growing rancorous. Henry Clay had written a few days before that "the Missouri question engrosses the whole thoughts of the members, and constitutes almost the only topic of conversation. It is a most unhappy question, awakening sectional feelings, and exasperating them to the highest degree. The words, civil war, and disunion, are uttered almost without emotion." In the Senate the ostensible subject of the continuing debate was the Maine bill with Barbour's amendment to it making the admission of Missouri a condition to the admission of Maine and Roberts's forbidding further importation of slaves into Missouri. In fact, however, the debate was becoming more and more a free-ranging attack on, or defense of, slavery. It had started with Pinkney's speech on January 21 and was to last almost two weeks. As Otis followed Pinkney and William Smith of South Carolina followed Otis, the discussion grew more heated as the climate outside again grew forbidding. On the night of January 26 there was another snowstorm in Washington, but the debate roared on with Senators Benjamin Ruggles and William Trimble, both from Ohio, and then David Morril from New Hampshire, taking up the cudgel against Barbour's amendment, and finally with Barbour himself ending with a three-hour peroration on January 31 and February 1. Then, finally, Roberts's amendment was definitively voted down 27 to 16.[31]

Meanwhile in the House, despite the failures of both Taylor and Storrs, the possibility of compromise was still alive, if only barely. Its next proponent was Samuel Foote of Connecticut, a firm ally of John Quincy Adams then serving his first term in Congress, who may even have been acting for Adams in hopes of negotiating a compromise that Adams, like each of the other 1824 presidential aspirants, dearly wanted in order to preserve the Union over which he hoped to preside. On Thursday, January 27, Foote moved the postponement of further debate on the Missouri bill to the following Thursday.

> His object was in the meantime to consider, in the hope of its adoption, a proposition for the prohibition of the further introduction of slavery west of the Mississippi. Should such a measure be adopted, the Territories in that quarter would be placed on the same footing as the Ordinance of 1787 had placed the Northwest Territory. The question now agitated in Congress might then, perhaps, be left to the good sense of the people of the States to be formed out of that Territory; and, should any question present itself on the subject of the admission of slavery into any such state, it might be left for the proper tribunal, the Supreme Court, to determine it.[32]

Though his motion to delay was voted down, Foote's proposal had several interesting antecedents and suggestions for the future. First, it respected the distinction between congressional authority over territories, as opposed to states, which was becoming central to the debate. Foote was apparently willing to concede that the people of the states to be formed would have the right after statehood to decide for themselves the question of slavery. Second, it relied upon the Northwest Ordinance and the ambiguities inherent in it, as had both Harrison and Thomas. Third, by setting up the Supreme Court as the ultimate arbitrator, Foote acknowledged that the Northwest Ordinance contained ambiguities that, in the interests of compromising the controversy, were better left to subsequent resolution by the Supreme Court. Most intriguingly, Foote's proposal closely paralleled the various versions of the amendment Jesse Thomas was soon to make in the Senate and indicates that the two may have already been conferring.

The postponement proposed by Foote was opposed on the ground that it would only serve to delay "the interchange of opinions on the question now fairly before the House, which, whatever else was done, would certainly take place, and could not be prevented."[33] Foote's proposal was defeated, and the House again resolved itself into a committee of the whole to consider Taylor's motion to amend the bill by imposing a restriction on slavery. Taylor himself took the floor with a speech he described later in a letter to his wife:

> We have been several days engaged in a desultory discussion
> of various amendments to the Missouri bill. The main
> question was taken up yesterday on my amendment to
> prevent the extension of slavery & to require a prohibition
> against it to be inscribed in the constitution as a condition
> of its admission into the Union of States. . . . I have reason
> to believe that my exertions in the cause of freedom were
> altogether satisfactory to the opponents of slavery in that
> territory—the debate will continue several weeks—No
> question has ever excited so deep interests in Congress—It is
> quite doubtful what will be its issue—[34]

The next day, Friday, January 28, Representative John Holmes from the District of Maine spoke about two hours, concluding remarks he had begun the day before. Desperate to push through statehood for Maine, Holmes argued against Taylor's sweeping amendment. Epic speeches continued in both the House and the Senate, many of them lasting upward of four hours and extending from one day to the next over the next five weeks.

At this critical juncture, there is no evidence that Clay and Thomas were in communication. As Thomas organized himself for his second push to compromise the Missouri question, his most likely allies were his mentor William Crawford and his supporters, like James Barbour and Louis McLane, who were already deeply involved in the effort to shape a compromise. Ninian Edwards's son, in his biography of his father written fifty years after the fact, claimed that the elder Edwards "had a very important agency in bringing about the compromise which resulted in terminating the controversy in regard to the admission of Missouri into the Union. Although the proviso which passed was proposed by Jesse B. Thomas . . . it was the result of a conference of public men, before whom it was introduced by Senator Edwards in the form in which [it] finally passed." This account, not verified elsewhere and implying a high degree of cooperation between Edwards and his enemies in the Crawford camp, does not seem plausible. More likely Edwards was kept abreast of developments through Richard Johnson of Kentucky, who had been appointed to the committee considering the first version of Thomas's freestanding bill. Johnson, future vice president under Martin Van Buren, had been a friend of Edwards's in Kentucky and was a fellow supporter of John C. Calhoun, and he and his brother James were among the Kentuckians who had invested in the Bank of Edwardsville.[35]

In the Senate, the defeat of the Roberts non-importation amendment had never been in doubt despite the tour de force of political eloquence that had gone on for the previous two weeks, but Barbour, Thomas, and the others who were trying to mold the debate in the Senate understood that the combatants on both sides of the issue had needed this public brawl to wear themselves down to a point where they might be receptive to the kind of compromise their quieter colleagues were trying to shape. Finally, the stage seemed set for Thomas to relaunch the initiative he had first suggested on January 18. Characteristically, he did not press his own claim but rather, in the Senate session on February 2, stepped aside yet again, this time in favor of James Burrill Jr., Federalist of Rhode Island, who had served on the select committee to consider Thomas's original freestanding bill prohibiting the introduction of slavery into the territories north and west of Missouri. Although Thomas had chaired that select committee, he now allowed Burrill to propose an interesting amendment to the Maine-Missouri bill meant to amplify what was meant by the requirement that Missouri's constitution be "republican, and not repugnant to the Constitution of the United States." The requirement in the Northwest Ordinance that new states have a republican form of government was the one condition on the admission of new states that all could agree on, and it was for this reason that the requirement had been included in the Missouri amendment to the Maine bill. In an apparently innocuous and totally uncontroversial way, Burrill now sought to expand on what was meant by a republican form of government by reference to the first three articles of the Northwest Ordinance. The three articles set forth the universally accepted tenets of freedom of religion, habeas corpus and various other due process rights, and access to education, all of which were unassailable aspects of republican government.[36] In the context of Thomas's earlier and later initiatives, however, it is clear what Thomas and Burrill had in mind—once Congress accepted that Articles I through III of the Northwest Ordinance were necessary parts of the definition of a republican form of government, it was a short leap to include the other articles as well, especially the pivotal Article VI. After a speech of considerable length in support of his motion, Burrill agreed to postpone further debate to the next day.

Burrill, as a New Englander, was probably not as conversant with the Northwest Ordinance's Article VI and its potential to satisfy both sides in the slavery debate as were frontiersmen like William Henry Harrison and Jesse Thomas, so Burrill's approach almost certainly originated with men like them who had lived under the Northwest Ordinance. It appeared to be a sound course, though, and Thomas and his allies now seemed well launched on an approach to compromise that again would rely ultimately on Article VI of the Ordinance. Their path, however, was to be indirect and destined to have turns and counterturns before finally garnering the votes necessary for passage.

As the Senate inched tentatively toward compromise, President Monroe watched anxiously from the sidelines, unable to intervene directly. In that earlier period of the Republic, a president attempting overtly to influence congressional politics would have been considered to be acting improperly. So far in the debate there had been little direct evidence of Monroe's involvement in the negotiations, but it is clear from this point on that he was communicating behind the scenes with the principals in Congress, as were his cabinet officers. On Wednesday, February 2, the day Burrill was making his proposal in the Senate, James Barbour conferred with Monroe about the advisability of his initiative to tie Missouri to Maine. He suspected the combined Maine-Missouri bill could never pass in the House and was rethinking the entire strategy. He now thought the South's agreement to first separately admit Maine might be viewed as an act of conciliation and induce the North to then agree to the admission of Missouri. The president concurred and approved proceeding to implement the strategy, provided Barbour could line up other Southern senators to support the plan.[37]

However, before Barbour could move forward with his gesture of conciliation on February 3, events overtook him. Overnight and during the day on the third, Burrill, Thomas, Barbour, and others must have conferred because, in the Senate that day, as the last order of business, Burrill withdrew his amendment "for the purpose of allowing a different amendment to be offered," and Thomas finally took the stage, rising to propose the second version of his compromise proposal, this one an amendment to the Maine-Missouri bill rather than a freestanding bill:

> And be it further enacted, That in all that tract of country ceded by France to the United States, under the name of Louisiana, which lies north of thirty-six degrees and thirty minutes north latitude, excepting only such part thereof, as is included within the limits of the State contemplated by this act, there shall be neither slavery nor involuntary servitude otherwise than in the punishment of crimes whereof the party shall have been duly convicted; Provided always, That any person escaping into the same, from whom labor

or service is lawfully claimed in any State or Territory of the United
States, such fugitive may be lawfully reclaimed and conveyed to
the person claiming his or her labor or service as aforesaid.[38]

Because of the way that Burrill withdrew his amendment in favor of Thomas's,
it would have been reasonable to expect that Thomas's would cover some of
the same ground as the one it replaced. Instead, this new version of Thomas's
amendment made no mention whatsoever of the Northwest Ordinance. Yet
appearances would again prove deceiving and events would show that the
Northwest Ordinance, and specifically its Article VI, had always remained
very much in Thomas's mind and that all the various versions of his compromise were based upon it.

   It is notable also that, in this second version of his proposal, Thomas, as a
skilled negotiator, transformed for his own purposes the notion of the 36°30′
line first introduced by antislavery moderate John Taylor in the House debate
on Arkansas in the previous Congress. It is also interesting to compare the
line set forth in this new version of Thomas's amendment with the carefully
crafted, and basically similar, line in his original freestanding bill. Its new
version had a similar effect but defined the line in a way that made it unnecessary to anticipate the exact boundaries of the future state of Missouri and
left open to slavery a considerably larger area, including any other areas south
of 36°30′ that Secretary of State John Quincy Adams might be able to wrest
from Spain in his ongoing negotiations.

   His amendment having been read, Thomas moved that further consideration of the subject be postponed to the following Monday, evidently with
the wish that a consensus could be cobbled together on his proposal over
the weekend. This first step toward compromise in the Senate was of great
importance. To that point the House had struggled unsuccessfully to agree
on a formula for compromise that could elicit the support of a majority. From
the initial effort by Tallmadge, leadership had shifted from him to Taylor to
Harrison to Storrs and finally to Foote, but it had become clear that the House
could not settle on a formula until it had a better idea of what compromise
the Senate might commit itself to. In this light, the first halting steps toward
compromise in the Senate were of critical importance. Barbour liked this
initial effort sufficiently to postpone the initiative he had discussed with the
president and to keep Maine and Missouri connected for the time being,
thus ensuring inaction until Thomas's concept could be more fully developed
and supported.

While the Senate let Thomas's amendment gestate, the House on Friday, February 4, again addressed the subject of a dividing line when Benjamin Hardin of Kentucky, cousin of Thomas's Illinois colleague Jeptha Hardin, took the floor to speak against restriction. He, like Foote, argued the need to compromise the question to prevent having Missouri set itself up as an independent country. Most significant, Hardin alluded to Thomas's proposal, made formally in the Senate the day before, although he altered it slightly to have the dividing line run west from a point on Missouri's western boundary (not specifying whether that point might be Missouri's southwestern corner, as Thomas proposed; or its northwestern corner, approximately as Harrison had proposed; or the center, as Storrs had proposed). It is significant that Hardin's line, unlike Thomas's, ran all the way to the Pacific and therefore had implications beyond the Louisiana Purchase. He also appeared to contemplate that the prohibition would be permanent, applying not only to territories but also to the states formed from them. Nonetheless, it seems the House was generally cognizant of what was going on in the Senate, and arguments over Thomas's initiative were to roil debate in both House and Senate from that point on.

After Hardin concluded his remarks, Daniel Pope Cook rose to address the committee of the whole: "Missouri and Illinois are separated only by the intervention of the Mississippi river. Their immediate adjacency, therefore, gives rise to a particular interest, superadded to the common interest felt by the people of Illinois. Thus situated, I feel it my bounden duty to give [Taylor's] amendment my support."[39] Cook then attempted a kind of rhetorical jujitsu by claiming that proponents of Thomas's concept, by specifying in the enabling bill that the state of Missouri would have the right to determine the issue of slavery for itself, was implicitly recognizing that Congress had authority to determine the question and that Congress could therefore equally well choose to withhold its permission. Likewise, Cook asserted that Congress had a right to require that a new state restrict slavery at the time of statehood in a way that would be binding after statehood.

Here William Lowndes, Calhoun's lieutenant in the House, smiled and shook his head, and Cook continued, "An honorable gentleman shakes his head, who has favored this proposition, and I am thereby left to understand that such is not the nature of the proposition. Then, away with your compromise. Let Missouri in, and the predominance of slave influence is settled, and the whole country will be overrun with it. Indeed, I am opposed to any compromise on the subject."[40]

CHAPTER 11

The Missouri Compromise: The Final Struggle

This was truly the bleak midwinter of negotiations over Missouri; by early February 1820 there had been snow on the ground for five weeks. John Taylor wrote his wife on Friday, the fourth, that "the Missouri debate continues to occupy the attention of both houses of Congress. We see no end to it yet. It may probably require two or three weeks to bring it to a close—The issue of the question is considered quite doubtful." On that same Friday, Henry Meigs of New York, showing how fractured congressional thinking had become, had chased chimeras in a speech to the House as hardheaded negotiations continued behind the scenes in the Senate. Meigs's preamble and resolution were decidedly fantastical:

> Whereas slavery in the United States is an evil of great and increasing magnitude; one which merits the greatest efforts of this nation to remedy: Therefore,
>
> Resolved, That a committee be appointed to inquire into the expediency of devoting the public lands as a fund for the purpose of,
>
> 1st. Employing a naval force competent to the annihilation of the slave trade;
>
> 2dly. The emancipation of slaves in the United States; and
>
> 3dly. Colonizing them in such a way as shall be conducive to their comfort and happiness, in Africa, their mother country.

When the Senate again openly took up the Missouri question as the last order of business on Monday, February 7, the field had shifted yet again. Jesse

Thomas, for the purpose of "modifying or introducing it in another shape," withdrew the amendment that he had offered the previous Thursday, and discussion was promptly postponed to the next day.[1]

In the House that Monday, Louis McLane took the floor. McLane was in a difficult position as he had been instructed by the Delaware legislature to oppose any extension of slavery but was personally convinced that was the wrong course. McLane, certainly in close communication with William Harris Crawford, Thomas, and other moderates, was critical of those extremists "wholly unable to allay or direct" the spirit of discord they unleashed in the land and went on to briefly and accurately describe Thomas's proposal:

> But if, consulting the present state of things, gentlemen will yield something to a spirit of harmony and mutual interests, we may now put this unpleasant subject to sleep forever. The people of Missouri will enter the Union with their rights unimpaired, and their feeling undisturbed; devoted to your institutions, and inspired with full confidence in your justice and generosity. The territorial soil will then be unpolluted with slavery. Its introduction in regard to that being prohibited, much the largest portion of the Western world will be peopled by a population unfriendly to slavery; and when they come to frame their state constitutions, preparatory to their future admission into the Union, they will voluntarily form them in conformity with their habits and principles. For, I desire to be understood as denying the authority of Congress to make any regulation for a Territory, which can be binding upon the people against their consent, when they come to make their constitution, and after their admission into the Union. I sanctify no irrevocable ordinances; but their Territorial regulations will accomplish the object, by creating a population whose interests it will be voluntarily to adopt the restriction. In this way, too, Missouri will be seated in the midst of non-slaveholding States, and the force of public sentiment will soon lead to the emancipation of her present slave population.[2]

McLane by this time had given up his notion of a compact binding for all time and now thoroughly understood the distinction between territories and states.

Having withdrawn his first amendment on Monday and promised a new one for the next day, Thomas and his allies were still wrestling with new wording on Tuesday. His new version in fact did not see the light of day for eight more days, being put on hold while the president dealt with potential insurrection in the Virginia presidential nominating caucus scheduled to meet the evening of February 9 in Richmond. Virginia politics were controlled at the time by the Richmond Junto, the extremely conservative faction led by newspaper editor Thomas Richie, and it was William Crawford rather than Monroe who was closest to the junto. Monroe's nationalist politics had angered conservative Southerners, and he had to deal with the very real possibility that the junto, and therefore his native state, would not support his reelection in 1820. The idea of a compromise was such anathema to the junto that it would have been foolhardy for Monroe to make public his support for Thomas's formula or anything like it until he had safely weathered the nominating caucus; yet his support was going to be essential if the compromise was to have any chance of passing, which explains why all negotiations went underground until the Virginia caucus finally decided on February 9 to support Monroe's reelection. It was not until that point that the president could safely launch his campaign to support a compromise in Missouri.[3]

On Tuesday, February 8, Monroe had written George Hay, who was still in Richmond endeavoring to protect the president's back, that he was convinced the restrictionists were prepared to split the Union at the Alleghenies if they did not prevail.[4] This may have been primarily for Hay's use in bucking up Monroe's wavering supporters in the Richmond Junto, but it also reflected Monroe's worst fears. That day and the next Monroe undertook serious lobbying on the Missouri question, but still behind the scenes because of the impending presidential caucus. On the ninth, Monroe met with Representative Mark Hill of Maine, who was later to prove one of the critical Northern votes in favor of compromise. The members of the Massachusetts congressional delegation from Maine were natural targets of Monroe's arm-twisting, and with the Virginia caucus behind him, Monroe went to work on them. Monroe also began to signal to others his support for Thomas's initiative.[5]

In the House on Wednesday, February 9, Samuel Foote, the antislavery moderate from Connecticut who was an ultimate supporter of the compromise, introduced a motion "that there shall be neither slavery nor involuntary servitude in any of the territories of the United States" but somewhat lamely provided that this language "not be construed to alter the condition or civil rights of any person now held to service or labor in the said territories." In an

effort to reach a compromise, Foote also refused to require that constitutions
of new states prohibit slavery, resolving instead "that it be, and it is hereby,
recommended to the inhabitants of the several territories of the United States,
that, for the purpose of effectually preventing the further extension of slavery, each territory, when authorized by Congress to form a constitution and
State government, shall, by express provision in their constitution, prohibit
involuntary servitude or slavery, otherwise than in the punishment of crimes."[6]
Foote's proposal was a generous offer by a Northerner since the Senate had
already voted on February 2, by a majority of almost two-thirds, to allow in
Missouri without restriction, and, if that measure was approved by the House
before Foote's freestanding resolution was acted upon, then his motion would
apply only to states admitted subsequently.

On Thursday and Friday of that week, despite pleas for more time for
negotiations, the Senate, under steady pressure from the down-easters in
the Massachusetts congressional delegation, resumed consideration of the
Maine-Missouri bill in hopes of acting in time to meet the March 4 deadline set by the Massachusetts legislature. Judging deference to the House
to be the best policy at this point, both Thomas and James Barbour framed
Thomas's proposal as an amendment to the House's bill, which was essentially the same as the Senate's with both parts of the Tallmadge amendment
tacked on. Finally, on Wednesday, February 16, after more speechifying, the
Senate voted 23–21 in favor of Barbour's proposal to make the admission of
Missouri a condition for the admission of Maine. The Senate then returned
to substantive discussion of a formula to compromise the issue of slavery
west of the Mississippi. After some debate, and again at the end of the day's
session, Jesse Thomas rose to offer a third version of the concept he had first
introduced as a freestanding bill on January 18, withdrawn from the floor
on January 21 by referring to a select committee, reintroduced as an amendment to the Maine-Missouri bill on February 3, and withdrawn again on
February 7. During the entire period from the time it was first proposed,
it had been the subject of continuous behind-the-scenes discussions, and
it now appeared to be the compromise concept on which the Senate, the
president, and their allies in the House were pinning their hopes. The new
version of his amendment, hashed out by Thomas and his allies over the nine
days since he withdrew his last version, seemed on the surface to be quite
different from its predecessor but, upon closer examination, was very close
to it in ultimate effect:

And be it further enacted, That the sixth article of compact of the ordinance of Congress, passed on the thirteenth day of July, one thousand seven hundred and eighty seven, for the government of the territory of the United States north-west of the river Ohio, shall, to all intents and purposes, be, and hereby is, deemed and held applicable to, and shall have full force and effect in and over, all that tract of country ceded by France to the United States, under the name of Louisiana, which lies north of thirty-six degrees and thirty minutes north latitude, excepting only such part thereof as is included within the limits of the state contemplated by this act.[7]

The new version had been crafted to dovetail with James Burrill's earlier effort to apply Articles I through III of the Northwest Ordinance directly to Missouri, which is evidence that something like this third version of Thomas's amendment had been discussed at the time Burrill made his earlier motion. Out of deference to the resuscitation of his concept, Burrill was placed in the chair to preside over the committee of the whole's discussion of the new motion.

It is interesting to compare the second and third versions because, different though they seem, they do inform each other and show the way Thomas's mind was working. Thomas's use of Article VI in the new version of his amendment echoed not only Burrill's proposal but also the one made a year earlier by William Henry Harrison when he also framed a compromise measure in terms of Article VI of the Northwest Ordinance. Although he experimented briefly with a new approach in his second version, Thomas was essentially only trying to do the same thing as Harrison and Burrill but in a different way. The new approach offered the potential benefit of picking up the support of Harrison and his followers but was just as successful in achieving the same critical obfuscation as was the second version. The use of Article VI in the new version of his compromise permitted Thomas to achieve the particular kind of ambiguity on the subject of slavery he had created with such consummate skill earlier in his career. It proved as useful in the Missouri controversy as it had earlier in the Old Northwest when it allowed Illinois and the other territories formed north of the Ohio to carry on with their particular kind of proto-slavery and keep alive the possibility of a full restoration of slavery at a later date. In the current crisis, Thomas used Article VI to suggest to restrictionists that a prohibition of slavery during the territorial period might carry over to statehood while at the same time reassuring anti-restrictionists behind the scenes that a new state would be free to change its rules on slavery after admission to the Union. An intriguing aspect of his skill as a wordsmith comes in the simple opening phrase "the sixth article of compact" where he uses the word "compact" to convey to restrictionists just the reassuring sense of permanence he thought necessary to attract their support.

There followed a flurry of attempts to amend this third version of Thomas's concept. Probably to increase leverage in upcoming negotiations with the House, James Barbour first moved to amend Thomas's amendment by striking out the proposed 36°30' line and substituting 40° instead, making the proposal very close to the one Harrison had unsuccessfully floated in the House during the debate on forming the Arkansas Territory. Interestingly, Ninian Edwards opposed Barbour's motion, indicating that at least on this matter he and Thomas were allies. After a short discussion, Barbour's motion was voted down with only three or four senators rising in favor of it, thus evidencing that the Senate was serious about trying to find a formula that the House would support. John Eaton of Tennessee then offered, as a substitute for Thomas's amendment, a provision setting the same geographical limits for the prohibition of slavery but providing specifically that the prohibition would apply only "while said portion of country remains a Territory." A substitution was ruled out of order, and Eaton withdrew his motion, but it was not renewed in more procedurally acceptable form because all immediately recognized that removing the intentional ambiguity from Thomas's proposal would doom it to defeat. William Trimble also put forward an amendment that was outside the range of compromise acceptable to the House and was voted down.[8]

Thomas had put forward the third version of his amendment as one of the last items of business on the day it was proposed, a habit that Thomas almost invariably followed in order to allow for informal discussion of his proposals overnight. The three alternatives to it were voted down before the Senate adjourned for the night to consider in cloakrooms and over dinner whether this third version of Thomas's proposal might attract enough votes to pass. The answer, apparently, was that it would not, and when the matter was taken up again at the end of the next day's session, Thomas must have stunned his fellow senators by abruptly withdrawing the third version of his proposal before it could be debated any further. Thomas had apparently become convinced that the wholesale importation of Article VI's ambiguity into the Missouri controversy would not work and that a more subtle effort to incorporate its underlying concepts would be necessary. As a practical politician, he immediately abandoned his third version and put forward his fourth and final attempt, reverting to a very slightly modified version of his second attempt:

> And be it further enacted, That, in all that territory ceded by France to the United States, under the name of Louisiana, which lies north of thirty-six degrees and thirty minutes north latitude, excepting only such part thereof as is included within the limits of the state contemplated by this act, slavery and involuntary servitude, otherwise than in the punishment of crimes whereof the party shall have been duly convicted, shall be and is hereby forever prohibited; Provided, always, That any person escaping into the same, from whom labor or service is lawfully claimed in any State or Territory of the United States, such fugitive may be lawfully reclaimed and conveyed to the person claiming his or her labor or service as aforesaid.[9]

In both versions of Thomas's concept that were on the floor that Thursday, the third and then the fourth, Thomas showed his instinct for legislative ambiguity. Even though the main actors in the drama understood the ambiguity, it allowed them to plausibly maintain that they had not given way on any matter of principle. It was his purpose under either version, as it had been in earlier iterations, to paper over regional differences on slavery rather than force definitive statements that could not gain a majority in Congress. His legerdemain with all four versions of his proposal raises questions about what he was trying to achieve with the various changes and what specific interests he was trying to woo. He and James Burrill, the antislavery moderate whose support was essential, clearly could not decide whether to make explicit reference to Article VI of the Northwest Ordinance. It is even possible that Thomas may have decided that it was important to float his third version, which put back in the specific reference to Article VI, as a red herring to set up his final version. Or he may have felt the need to tweak his second version in very subtle ways and thought he could do so more easily, and with less attention being paid to his changes, by suggesting a quite different third amendment, then pulling it and substituting the tweaked fourth version.

So what were these final tweaks, and what did they seek to achieve? Aside from the remarkably rapid resuscitation of the second version of Thomas's proposal, the most intriguing aspects of the fourth and final version are the two seemingly slight, but in fact major, differences from the second. First, in describing the area in which the prohibition on slavery would apply, Thomas now used the phrase "that territory ceded by France to the United States" in place of "that tract of country ceded by France to the United States," which had been used in the first two versions. "Territory" can be used in a general way to describe a large area of land or in a specific way to describe a precursor form of government to statehood. Generally, but not always, a lowercase *t* is used for the former and a capital *T* for the latter. Throughout the negotiations, Thomas sought to exploit the ambiguity of the word, often covering his tracks through conscious use of lowercase or capital letters. In his second version, he had used a small *t* in stating that the Northwest Ordinance applied to "the territory . . . northwest of the river Ohio." As mentioned earlier, capitalization or the lack thereof in the *Annals of Congress* may have been purely accidental, but, also as mentioned earlier, it is much more likely that a reporter would check the wording of a formal motion with the proposer. Furthermore, the substitution of "territory" for "tract of country" seems very conscious, and, in that context, using a small *t* seems a way of disguising what he had done, allowing anti-restrictionists to interpret his amendment as applying only during the territorial period and restrictionists as applying generally to that geographic area before and after statehood. Thomas was seeking to incorporate in his amendment the same ambiguity about the scope of his slavery prohibition that had clothed Article VI of the Northwest Ordinance in his early days in the Old Northwest, that is, whether it would apply after statehood. Even though others, notably Henry Storrs on January 26,[10] had used capital *T* "Territories" in their formulations of compromise, Jesse Thomas knew that restrictionists would balk at a capital *T* formulation, particularly in language known to come from him, which they would immediately interpret as indicating Thomas's determination to prohibit slavery only during the territorial period. He opted instead for a small *t* and a dose of ambiguity. Proslavery states' rights senators looking for a rationale on which they could justify voting for the amendment now settled on the word "territory," agreeing that, yes, slavery would be prohibited as long as a territory remained a territory but not necessarily after it became a state.

There are telltale signs that Southern politicians always relied upon a distinction between pre- and post-statehood limitations on slavery and were willing to allow prohibitions on slavery during the territorial period or even at the time of statehood provided that the new state would then be free to adopt slavery at some later date. What Missouri feared, as expressed by Thomas Hart Benton, was a prohibition "to be placed upon her as a condition of her admission into the Union, and to be binding upon her afterwards"[11]—in other words, a compact as binding as the one for which Louis McLane had originally hoped and as permanent as the one for which Harrison Gray Otis argued. To avoid this sort of definiteness, proslavery proponents never wanted to make the distinction between territory and state explicit for fear of precipitating an equally explicit response from their opponents. Thomas's language kept that question in limbo.

The second change from the earlier versions of Thomas's proposal is the mandate that, in the described area, slavery and involuntary servitude "shall be and is hereby forever prohibited," which adds a satisfying sense of permanence to the prohibition but which arguably has exactly the same effect as the earlier language. So, once again, Thomas giveth at the same time as he taketh away, suggesting to restrictionists, by his second change, that the prohibition would apply "forever" at the same time that he suggested to anti-restrictionists, by his first change, that it would apply only during the territorial period. Thus we see Thomas tinkering with both sides of the intentional ambiguity of his proposal, subtly changing what was on offer for both anti-restrictionists and restrictionists. Sometimes in the waning hours of negotiation, such small changes, even if essentially meaningless, offer parties a path to agreement.

On Wednesday, February 16, it was agreed to take the question on the fourth and final version of the Thomas amendment as a part of the Senate bill uniting Maine and Missouri, but the Senate again adjourned before the vote was taken, once more giving an opportunity for informal discussions and arm-twisting over dinner and breakfast. On Thursday, after some other amendments necessary to make the different parts of the bill conform to each other, the question was taken on ordering the bill, as amended, to be engrossed and read a third time, and this critical motion carried by a vote of 24 to 20 in favor. Finally, on Friday, February 18, Jesse Thomas's amendment carried 34 to 10, an impressive vote of confidence for this long-running and disciplined effort at compromise. The bill was completed and renamed "An act for the admission of the State of Maine into the Union, and to enable the people of the Missouri Territory to form a constitution and State government, and for the admission of such State into the Union, on an equal footing with the original States; and to prohibit slavery in certain Territories." Even the seemingly innocuous change of title was freighted with meaning. The small *t* of Thomas's amendment became a capital *T* in the act's title, thus strengthening the argument that the prohibition was intended to apply only during the territorial period. The bill, with its new title, was then passed, and a message was sent to the House that the Senate had passed the House's Missouri bill with amendments and requested the concurrence of the House.[12] Passage in the Senate had been relatively easy, but what Thomas and his allies had been searching for so assiduously was a formula that would be acceptable to a majority in the House, and that was where attention now shifted.[13]

From a tactical point of view, Thomas's proposal was intended to make the Senate's decision to make admission of Missouri a condition to admission of Maine more palatable to Northern representatives. Since the combination by the Senate of the two states into one bill was clearly a Southern measure, the leaders of the fight in the House, particularly Henry Clay and Louis McLane, welcomed Thomas's proposal as a sweetener for the North. However, the House was still enmeshed in its debate over its own version of the Missouri bill and did not turn to the Senate's amendments until the next day, Saturday, February 19. It was a sign of increasing tension that both houses of Congress began resorting to Saturday sessions as the deadline for Maine statehood approached and other items requiring action before the upcoming end of the session piled up.

When the House took up its Maine bill as referred back by the Senate, John Taylor, carrying the restrictionist torch, moved immediately that the House disagree with the amendments imposed by the Senate. John Scott, Missouri's delegate, recognized that a vote at that time would reject the Senate's amendments and moved that the matter be referred to the committee of the whole that was then considering the House's Missouri bill. On these and a flurry of other motions, there was "a long and animated discussion." John Holmes, of the Maine district of Massachusetts, hoped the amendments would not be committed because, "if they were, it would be some time before they could be acted on, as there were, he believed, at least thirty speeches yet to be delivered on the restrictive proposition now before the Committee; and, until that proposition was decided, the Committee of the Whole would not take up the amendments of the Senate; in the mean time, the period allowed by law of Massachusetts . . . for the consent of Congress to the admission of Maine would arrive, and all that had been done would be lost."[14]

Some in the House hoped to separate the Senate's amendments to the Missouri bill into two parts, first the admission of Missouri with slavery and then the Thomas compromise amendment. The two were clearly not meant by the Senate to be separated nor did it make logical sense to do so, but Henry Clay's new stratagem of voting separately on separate parts of integral bills was temporarily popular, and many representatives wished to follow it with regard to the Senate amendments. There were some, however, who wished to avoid a course that seemed certain to wipe out the Thomas amendment, by then considered by many as the last, best chance at compromise. One of them was George Strother, of Virginia, who remarked that he did not want to rush a vote on the Senate's amendments because the "amendments contained new features, which required reflection; that proposing a compromise, for instance. These questions the House could not be prepared to decide at once, because its attention had been exclusively taken up in considering the restrictive question. It was not proper that the House should be driven into the instant decision of questions of such immense magnitude." Arthur Livermore of New Hampshire was another who favored a slower approach; he "strongly disapproved of the connexion [*sic*] of the bills as they came from the Senate; but he saw something in the amendments which seemed likely to put an end to the disagreeable subject which now occupied the House. He wished the subjects separated, and then some course might be adopted similar to the compromise proposed by the Senate, and the matter ended happily and harmoniously."

Many of those sympathetic to the Thomas compromise were vehemently opposed to making Missouri a condition of Maine. Arthur Livermore was typical of these, as was Henry Storrs, who observed "that it was well known that no man was more in favor of a compromise of the unhappy subject than himself; but even this he would not agree to on compulsion . . . the object of the connexion [*sic*] was to coerce this House, by operating on those members particularly interested in the admission of Maine into the Union. This course he thought was disapproved by the House, and the proper way to show it was by a prompt, a very prompt, rejection of the amendments." This strong opposition to the linking of Missouri and Maine was clearly an issue that had to be resolved before a final compromise could be reached.

Louis McLane was the last of many speakers on the subject that Saturday. He was likewise offended by linking Missouri and Maine but also held out hope for Thomas's amendment. The tone of the remarks by Strother, Livermore, Storrs, and McLane indicates that they all had been involved on the House side in working out the details of the Thomas amendment, and it is likely that they had already laid down as a condition that Maine must be separated from Missouri in the final compromise.[15] Likewise, it is telling that McLane, in his characterization of the compromise, describes it as prohibiting "the introduction of slavery into the Territories," complete with a capital *T.* If McLane were given a chance to review the rendition of his remarks, the capital *T* would clearly reflect his understanding that the prohibition would not necessarily apply after statehood. Following this debate, the question was taken on committing the Senate amendments to the committee of the whole, and it was voted down 107 to 70. A motion was then made to lay the amendments on the table, and print them, so that the House might at least see what it was being called on to decide. That motion was initially voted down 96 to 77, but, before the House could actually vote on the Senate amendments, it reconsidered the matter and approved by a large majority a motion to print the Senate amendments and put off further discussion to the following Tuesday, February 22.

When Tuesday arrived, the House was unable to come to a vote on whether to reject the Senate's bill, and with it the Thomas amendment, out of hand or whether to commit it to a committee of the whole for further discussion. John Randolph of Virginia delivered a two-hour tirade against the Senate's amendments from the point of view of Southern fire-eaters who brooked no restriction on slavery whatsoever; he was followed by John Rhea of Tennessee, who had a similar mission but was cut short by adjournment. Before the House convened on Wednesday, February 23, John Taylor wrote his wife that "there have been made in the House of Representatives alone between 30 & 40 speeches & nearly as many more in the Senate. The tide of speaking is still rising & it is difficult to anticipate when it will ebb." Taylor described his frustrated hope of the day before that the House would reject the Senate's amendments to the Missouri bill and send it back to the Senate.[16]

When the House finally did vote later that Tuesday on the Senate's amendments to the Maine bill, it did so, under Clay's guidance, in three parts. First, the representatives voted to disagree with the portion of the bill linking admission of Maine to that of Missouri, by a vote of 93 to 72. "The question was then taken on disagreeing to the residue of the amendments of the Senate, with the exception of that which embraces what is familiarly called the compromise amendment," and representatives likewise voted to disagree with these other amendments by a vote of 102 to 68. Finally, the House voted on Thomas's compromise provision and voted it down, 159 to 18. Thus the House rejected all the amendments the Senate had made to the House's original

Maine bill but showed its varying degrees of disagreement. The House then again resolved itself into a committee of the whole to resume work on its own version of a Missouri bill.[17]

News of the House rejection of the Senate amendments to the Maine bill was carried over by the House clerk on Wednesday, February 23, and it was then up to the Senate the following day to decide if it would recede from the amendments it had earlier made to the House bill or whether it would stick to its guns. James Burrill made a motion that the Senate recede from its earlier amendments. Nathaniel Macon of North Carolina immediately called for a division of the question, so that the question of prohibiting "the further introduction of slavery into the Territories of the United States" would be considered separately from the provisions for the admission of Missouri, in the hope of gathering different majorities for the two separate parts. It was a very close issue as to whether the two parts of the question could properly be considered separately—logically Congress could prohibit the further introduction of slavery in the territories and not admit Missouri, but the fact was that the former was not going to occur without the latter. The hour was growing late, however, and the matter was tabled.[18]

The next day, Friday, February 25, the Senate again took up Burrill's motion "to recede from the amendments of the Senate, which embrace provisions for the admission of Missouri, and for excluding slaves from the Territories," using the capital *T* formulation as on the day before. As previously, the discussion turned to "a point of order respecting the division of this question . . . so as to separate the question respecting Missouri from that respecting the Territories." Burrill contended that the whole amendment was a unit, the second part depending on the first, and should therefore as a matter of logic be indivisible. Rather than decide the question himself, the presiding officer availed himself of a rule of the Senate that a point of order could be submitted to the decision of the Senate, and a wide-ranging debate followed. The question apparently became more difficult as the discussion continued, and it was at length determined, on the third trial, that the further consideration of the subject be postponed to the next day.[19]

While the Senate wrestled with what to do about the amendments it had made to the House's Maine bill, the House continued to try to fashion its own Missouri bill. Mark Hill, from that part of Massachusetts that hoped to become Maine, rose and said "he did not now wish to consume the time of the House upon a subject, the progress of which seemed to be stamped with all the marks of eternity," but rather to move that the committee of the whole be discharged so that the House could finally come to a vote. William Lowndes, John Calhoun's lieutenant in the House, said that, "if the gentleman from Massachusetts insisted on this motion being put, he would cheerfully vote in favor [of] it; yet, if he would consent to withdraw his motion for the present, to give two or three gentlemen more an opportunity to speak today, he thought it might be a saving of time, and the motion could be renewed again, if necessary, to-morrow morning, which would then, he thought, receive a decided support."[20] Hill acquiesced and withdrew his motion, and the House debate went on. Henry Meigs of New York spoke for a considerable time against restriction in a speech that was not reproduced in the *Annals of Congress* but would be interesting since Meigs was a Crawford ally preparing to vote contrary to the instructions of his state legislature.

At the end of the day, Samuel Smith, of Maryland, rose to make another effort to cut off the House debate on its Missouri bill. He noted that a large number of his constituents had expressed opinions at variance with his own and some might presume he intended to deliver his reasons for the vote he was about to cast but that all he really desired was for the debate to come to an end and a vote to be taken. He believed that "the public business was suffering by the protraction of the debate; the members are weary of it; everyone's opinion was made up on it; and he was unwilling to consume the time of the Committee by any remarks on the question. He therefore forebore [*sic*], and he hoped the question would be taken."[21] No such luck, however, and the clamorous debate and intense parliamentary maneuvering continued into the late afternoon. Finally the question was taken on Taylor's proposed restriction prohibiting the further admission of slaves into the territories west of the Mississippi and agreed to, by a wide margin. Taylor then moved that the committee rise, as he presumed it was not prepared to go into the various details of the bill that evening, several of which were important, and would lead to many other questions. The motion was opposed by John Scott and an array of anti-restrictionists but finally prevailed, and about five o'clock the House adjourned.

On Saturday, February 26, the Senate again did battle on dividing the question into two parts—first, making the admission of Missouri a condition for the admission of Maine, and second, the Thomas compromise. It was the hope of the antislavery forces that, if the Senate voted separately on these questions, it would negative the idea of holding Maine hostage for the admission of Missouri and then would vote down the compromise amendment because, in the absence of statehood for Missouri, it would be unworkable. The parliamentary wrangle over the division of the question proved to be intractable, and the Senate, after a number of speeches, adjourned for the day without deciding it. John Quincy Adams later wrote of this period that "it was said that in the hottest paroxcysm [*sic*] of the Missouri Question in the Senate, James Barbour, one of the Virginia senators, was going round to all the Free State members, and proposing to them to call a convention of the States, to dissolve the Union, and agree upon the terms of separation, and the mode of disposing of the public debt, and of the Lands, and make other necessary arrangements of disunion."[22]

In the House no one seemed certain how to bring to a close the seemingly endless debate in the committee of the whole on the subject of Missouri. As an alternative way of proceeding, Henry Storrs moved to amend the House bill by inserting verbatim the Thomas proposal in the version then on the floor. By this time the third and fourth versions of Thomas's amendment had been put forward in the Senate, and it is interesting that Storrs was not fully up to speed with them, but at least this is clear evidence that he had been in contact with the Thomas group earlier.[23] The House, however, could still not push the matter out of the committee of the whole and was forced to adjourn.

On Monday, February 28, decisions on Missouri in both the House and the Senate could be put off no longer. Strenuous efforts had been made to shape compromises in both houses, and, though it was very unclear whether majorities could be gathered to support any of them, it was at least clear that whatever support there was for compromise would at some point begin to slip away. Accordingly, the leaderships in both houses decided that a test of strength must be made. On the parliamentary question raised the previous Friday, the Senate finally resolved by a vote of 22 to 17 that it could consider separately the matter of making admission of Missouri a condition for the admission of Maine and the matter of the Thomas compromise. The strategy behind divisibility in the Senate appears different than it was in the House since there seemed to be clear support in the Senate to uphold its original determinations on both matters. Perhaps the Senate foresaw that there would be separate votes later in the House and wanted to go on record as having majorities for each separate part. In any event, the votes went as expected, 23 to 21 on requiring the admission of Missouri as a condition for the admission of Maine and 33 to 11 on the Thomas compromise. The Senate clerk immediately carried over to the House notice that the Senate had insisted on its original amendments.

Meanwhile, as the Missouri issue was coming to a climax and the session was drawing to a close, there were other vital issues distracting members of Congress. In order to address the economic crisis on the western frontier, the Senate felt compelled to turn its attention to the public lands bill that had been proposed by the Public Lands Committee, of which Jesse Thomas was chairman. That matter was in many ways more crucial to Thomas than the admission of Missouri and certainly required equally close attention. Aside from slavery west of the Mississippi and public lands, the House was also at that point consumed by the question of whether to censure General Andrew Jackson for exceeding his orders in the Seminole War—a matter in which Thomas and Crawford were sharply critical of Jackson.

The House, like the Senate, was torn on whether to continue to seek common ground or simply to insist on its earlier positions. When the message was received that the Senate had refused to reconsider its amendments to the House Maine bill, the House was debating possible amendments to its own Missouri bill. Clay and other leaders in the House realized that the final shape of those amendments would be a very good indicator of sentiment in the House on any possible compromise of the Missouri issue. It was especially the moderates like William Lowndes who wanted the House to finalize its Missouri bill and submit it to the Senate before deciding whether to insist on its disagreement with the Senate amendments to the Maine bill or even on whether to have a conference. What he and others apparently hoped was that the House might somehow be persuaded to reconcile the issue on its own initiative by including something like the Thomas compromise in the House's bill on Missouri. These moderates lost out, however, to the hotheads who wanted a vote on insisting on the disagreement of the House to the Senate amendments and wanted that vote again divided into two parts: the admission of Missouri as a condition for the admission of Maine and the Thomas compromise. The House again voted to insist on its disagreement with both parts. The vote to disagree with the Thomas compromise was an astounding 160 to 14, but Lowndes, in explaining his vote against the compromise in these circumstances, showed the distorting effect of separating the question: "Although he [Lowndes] should always be ready to vote for such a proposition, substantially, when presented to him, combined with the free admission of Missouri; yet, as the amendment relative to Missouri had been disagreed to, it would be useless to retain this amendment in connextion [*sic*] with the Maine bill alone, and, as he should therefore now vote against retaining it, he wished his motive to be understood."[24] So the House insisted on its disagreement to the whole of the Senate's amendments to the Maine bill, and the clerk was directed to so inform the Senate.

The Senate was about to adjourn that Monday when the clerk of the House presented himself at the door with this unyielding message. By that time the House had twice considered the Senate amendments and twice rejected them out of hand, signaling that impasse was near. Jesse Thomas, though, had apparently anticipated that this might occur and immediately rose to move that a conference committee be appointed to confer with a similar committee from the House in an effort to resolve these differences. A debate followed, "characterized by some vehemence and warm feeling" between those who wanted simply to adhere to the Senate's previously stated position opposing restriction and those, like Thomas, who wanted to make one last effort at compromise. James Barbour spoke in favor of the conference, as did a number of others. Others spoke just as warmly in favor of adhering to the bill previously passed, which would foreclose a conference. Thomas's remarks were not preserved, but in the end his side prevailed—a motion to defer the question of a conference was voted down, and Thomas's motion requesting a conference, though opposed by a few, was approved by a voice vote without even dividing or recording yeas and nays.

The Senate then balloted for the so-called managers who would make up the conference committee from the Senate, and Senators Thomas, Pinkney, and Barbour were duly elected. Thomas received the most votes and, according to Senate practice at the time, became chairman of the Senate conference committee. It is remarkable that the Senate elected a newcomer from a recently admitted frontier state, who at that time had less than six months' actual experience in the Senate, as the leader of its three-man delegation to decide this momentous and divisive issue.[25] The issue had been brewing in Congress long before his arrival and had proved to that point totally intractable. His selection was in part recognition of the fact that Illinois had recently been through the same process of achieving statehood that Missouri now faced and, though now counted among the nonslave states, was the part of the country most like its neighbor Missouri in being north of 36°30' and largely Southern in culture. His prior experience with House procedure as a territorial delegate may also have been a factor. Although these tactical considerations were certainly important, Thomas's selection was also a tribute to his personal qualities of leadership and reasoned compromise. Also, as at other times in his career, the fact that he had largely kept his views to himself gave him flexibility and room to maneuver.

The Senate immediately sent its clerk to the House with the request for a conference and the names of the Senate managers. The House was just returning its attention to its Missouri bill when the request for a conference arrived. Having already dealt with the Senate amendments to the Maine bill earlier in the day, the House did not want to take up the matter again and put the request aside as it continued to deal with its Missouri bill. That decision made sense if there was still hope of coming to some consensus that could guide further negotiations between the House and Senate. The debate, however, was becoming a free-for-all with both supporters and opponents of restriction speaking against Thomas's concept.

The following day, Tuesday, February 29, the Senate took no action on Maine or Missouri, presumably with the hope that the House would agree to a conference that could address these matters more effectively. The House did eventually address the Senate's request for a conference, and, somewhat surprisingly, Clay managed to gain its approval for that approach. He then proceeded to exercise one of his most important prerogatives by appointing as managers for the House John Holmes, John Taylor, William Lowndes, Charles Kinsey of New Jersey, and James Parker, who like Holmes was from the Maine district of Massachusetts. The latter two were to pay a heavy price for their support of compromise by losing their House seats in the next election.

Although recognizing that Missouri was now relegated to the conference committee, the House chose to continue working on its Missouri bill in the apparent hope that it might provide a roadmap for the work of the conference committee. When the subject of restriction came up, Henry Storrs again proposed an amendment he had put forward earlier to make the restriction hortatory rather than mandatory.[26] This was one of the few other possible paths to compromise, and a number of Southerners supported it, though John Randolph and other hotheads opposed even this watered-down version of the restriction. In speeches lasting well into the afternoon, at least nine representatives spoke for and against Storrs's proposal before it was voted down 94 to 86. In another stab at compromise, John Scott offered an amendment "having for its object, in substance, to prevent the operation of the restriction either on the slaves now in Missouri or on their increase," which was supported by

John Campbell of Ohio. This approach also had some promise as a compromise but was withdrawn at the suggestion of several of Scott's friends who apparently recognized that they might attain this goal without any explicit statement to that effect and that to seek to make the point explicit risked a determination to the contrary. They could also have decided that proslavery Missourians might negotiate even better terms in the conference committee. With these two attempts to soften the antislavery restriction off the table, the House proceeded to concur in the restrictive amendment, as adopted in the committee of the whole, by a vote of 94 to 86. John Taylor then renewed a motion, which he had made unsuccessfully in the committee of the whole, to amend the last section of the bill to make explicit that Missouri's constitution must be approved by Congress before Missouri could be admitted into the Union as a state. This, of course, had long been the practice, but defenders of states' rights argued that prior states had submitted their constitutions as a matter of courtesy and not because it was required. Taylor's motion lost again, by yeas and nays, 125 to 49.

On the following day, March 1, the Senate again took no action on Maine or Missouri. In the House, business was briefly held up by the death of David Walker of Kentucky, who had been ailing during the last days of the Missouri debate. Walker was said to have told his friends to carry him to the Capitol if he was still alive when the vote was taken on the House Missouri bill in order that his last breath might be given in behalf of Missouri. John Randolph moved to adjourn to noon the next day so that members could attend Walker's funeral, which was agreed to, but, when he then moved to make the adjournment effective immediately, in an evident effort to slow down final action on the House's Missouri bill, the House refused him. Accordingly, the House's version of the Missouri bill was read the third time, but before the vote could be taken, Randolph again rose and spoke more than three hours against the bill. When he concluded, the bill was passed by yeas and nays, 91 to 82, and sent on to the Senate for concurrence, at which point the House adjourned.[27]

While the House was putting the finishing touches on its Missouri bill, the conference committee that Thomas and his colleagues had worked so long and diligently to convene met twice that Wednesday, March 1, the first time during the day and then again, apparently on short notice, that night, presumably after the House had adjourned.[28] In 1820 only the north and south wings of the Capitol had been reconstructed following the British burning of Washington, so there was no formal conference chamber; the committee thus likely met in some makeshift space in the Capitol or at a member's lodging. In their second meeting, which definitely occurred somewhere other than the Capitol, all the managers, with the exception of John Taylor, agreed upon a report in three interdependent parts. In its first part, the conference committee recommended that the Senate recede from its amendments to the House's Maine bill, which meant that the Senate would abandon making the admission of Missouri a condition for the admission of Maine. In its second part, however, the conference recommended that both houses address the bill admitting Missouri passed that afternoon in the House and agree to delete its provision prohibiting slavery in Missouri, thus permitting the admission of Missouri without restriction. And in its third and final part, the committee recommended that the final version of the Thomas amendment, with a few unimportant changes of wording and punctuation, be added to the House Missouri bill. Though substantively unimportant, it was symbolically astute to use the House Missouri bill in shaping the compromise as the House was the chamber making the largest concessions and deserved what deference it could be given.

The proposed compromise then had to be submitted to the two chambers for their consideration, which occurred the following morning, Thursday, March 2. Both chambers would have to agree to the same bill in order to submit it to the president. The Senate leadership was well aware that the conference committee had agreed upon a report, but it made the conscious choice to await House action. Accordingly, it went about various housecleaning chores related to the session then coming to an end. Midmorning a message arrived from the House with the Missouri bill the lower chamber had passed the evening before. On the motion of James Barbour, it was taken up immediately, read a first and second time, and forthwith referred to the committee of the whole. By this time, Jesse Thomas had informally communicated the three brief recommendations of the conference committee, and the Senate proceeded to do to the House's bill exactly what the conference committee had resolved the evening before, with Barbour moving to strike out the restriction of slavery in Missouri and Thomas moving to insert his compromise provision. Both motions were approved, and the bill was reported to the full Senate, where its title was amended by adding the words "and to prohibit slavery in certain territories," with "territories" spelled this time with a small *t*. The bill, with its amendments, was then read a third time, passed, and sent to the House of Representatives.[29]

Clay, who had been delaying House action on the conference committee report, immediately turned the attention of that chamber to the Missouri question. John Holmes, as a citizen of the District of Maine, was particularly eager to proceed and made a motion to lay the message from the Senate on the table long enough to give him an opportunity to make the report from the House conference committee, which he did by reading the same report that Thomas had carried back to the Senate, containing the same three short recommendations. The choice of Holmes to be the spokesman for the House managers was an obvious bid for the support of the Massachusetts delegates who were eager for the admission of Maine but still opposed the admission of Missouri as a slave state, even with the Thomas amendment. A restrictionist immediately moved to print the report, an apparent ploy to delay the vote beyond the deadline set by Massachusetts for Maine to achieve its statehood that was now only a day away. In a similar vein, John Taylor questioned the propriety of proceeding to act on the conference report in the House before the Senate had pledged that it would act on the first recommendation by approving the unconditional admission of Maine; William Lowndes forcefully opposed him, again arguing that the Senate would certainly recede from its earlier position, as unanimously recommended by its managers, when it took up the matter.

A long debate ensued, continuing about three hours and ending only with the withdrawal of the motion to print the report, signaling that both sides were ready to stop the debate and decide the matter one way or the other. The House finally turned to the substance of the conference committee report, and, as had certainly been previously planned, Speaker Clay determined to have the House vote separately on each of its three recommendations. Once again the question arose as to whether such a division of the issues was logically proper since, in effect, all three parts had to pass in order for the whole to endure. If the first part passed and the second or third were voted down, the first would then certainly be reconsidered and itself voted down. Clay, however, believed that different majorities would be possible for the parts considered separately, and that proved to be the case. The contest on each recommendation was fierce, starting with the removal of the slavery restriction in the proposed state of Missouri. This had been the second recommendation of the conference committee but the first that Clay chose to put before the House. William Lowndes, Calhoun's ally, spoke first, urging "with great earnestness the propriety of a decision which would restore tranquility to the country— which was demanded by every consideration of discretion, of moderation, of wisdom, and of virtue." More speeches followed before the matter came to a vote. And then, in what was surely the most important vote of the Missouri controversy, the House accepted the recommendation to admit Missouri without any restriction on slavery by a vote of 90 to 87. This vote was even closer than it appeared. John Randolph, who opposed the measure, voted for it in order to be in a position to invoke the House rule that a member voting with the majority could move to reconsider at the next day's session. He evidently believed that overnight he could find or change the one vote necessary to alter the outcome. If Randolph had instead voted his true conviction on March 2, the vote would have been 89 to 88. Thus did the House, under the careful coaxing and generalship of Henry Clay, ultimately jettison both parts of the Tallmadge amendment it had fought for more than a year to preserve.[30]

The House then voted on the third recommendation of the conference committee, the so-called Thomas amendment. John Taylor proposed the same change to Thomas's amendment in the House that William Trimble had put forward in the Senate. Taylor's amendment was voted down and the House finally voted affirmatively on the Thomas amendment—yeas 134, nays 42. Only then did the House act quickly and decisively on the first of the conference committee's recommendations, the unconditional admission of Maine. The House also concurred in the change in the bill's title, which had been agreed to in the Senate, although the account of this change of title in the *Annals of Congress* for the House spells "territories" with a capital *T*, whereas the same change in title, when made earlier in the Senate, had spelled it with a small *t*. The statute as actually signed by the president spelled the word with a small *t*, the version that was more favorable to the restrictionists.[31]

The tactic of voting separately on the three parts of the compromise was, and has remained, controversial. Clay and his allies had presciently worked out the strategic order in which the three parts were considered. The parliamentary maneuver of dividing the question was well recognized and had been used earlier in the Missouri controversy but was proper only when the separate parts of the question were logically independent and some might succeed while others failed. That was not the case with the Missouri Compromise, where all three parts would ultimately stand or fall together. The choice of this approach was particularly controversial when applied to the final iteration of a piece of legislation as important as the Missouri Compromise. In this instance, the approach clearly led to the approval of interdependent pieces of legislation that would not have been approved if voted on as a unit. In the case of the second and third recommendations, the different parts were components of the same bill, which made the approach even more controversial. And, of course, changing the order in which the three different parts of the conference report were considered was Clay's final act of manipulation. It is unclear whether Thomas himself had a role in devising Clay's strategy, but the structure of the conference report, with its separate recommendations, suggests that he at least contemplated dividing the question. In any event, the *Richmond Enquirer* reflected the feelings of many in complaining that the question had been carried "by a sort of parliamentary coup de main" and "had been palmed upon the nation, without having fairly the consent of its representatives."[32] It was this heavy-handed legerdemain, so typical of Clay, that kept the Missouri Compromise from being an authentic compromise, in which both sides agreed to make sacrifices for the common good.

A sense of exhaustion and relief overtook the capital that evening. There was a feeling on the morning of Friday, March 3, that the crisis was over, at least for now. But even the weather suggested that the sense of calm would not last long. After a stretch of mildness at the end of February, John Taylor wrote his wife that morning that "we now have the rigor of winter again without the snow. . . . When I rose my ink was frozen solid on a table near the fireplace. The lilacs which in our garden had leaved [*sic*] out last month, are now cropt of their verdure & the leaves break like thin ice." As to the compromise, he wrote that "the report of the joint committee was last night confirmed in the House & Missouri is admitted without restriction, but slavery is forever prohibited in all the Continent north and west of Missouri. We have gained all that was possible, if not all that was desired. . . . What we have gained is an ample recompense for all the time & labour it has cost us." But there were portents as well of the difficulties that would be born out of the compromise—notably Taylor's use of the word "forever" in his description of the compromise, showing that he and his allies continued to interpret the compromise as applying after statehood.[33]

In the Senate that morning of March 3, Jesse Thomas rose to make the formal report for the Senate managers in the conference committee, reading from the report written in his own hand, which was identical with the one Holmes had read in the House the day before.[34] As the Senate had acted the day before on the contents of the report, this was strictly a formality, but before Thomas could bring the Maine bill to a vote, he or one of his colleagues discovered a clerical glitch in the bill—the version then before them was left over from the year before and had provided that Maine would become a state "from and after the fifteenth day of March next." Thomas could address this problem only by calling for a second short conference with the House, so the Senate appointed the same managers for this second conference and sent off a message to the House describing the problem and its proposed solution.

The delay to address this clerical slip nearly proved disastrous in the House, which still had more excitement to offer. That morning, John Randolph, having voted with the majority the day before in order to avail himself of the rule that a member who voted with the majority on a bill had a right to move for reconsideration the next day, clearly intended to move for a reconsideration of the vote that had removed the slavery restriction from Missouri. He, of course, did not truly want the restriction restored, but he knew that, if it were put back into place, the entire edifice of the compromise would come tumbling down. Clay, however, was more than Randolph's equal as a parliamentarian and had the added advantage of being in the chair. He declared Randolph's motion out of order until the ordinary business of the morning, as prescribed by the rules of the House, should be disposed of. Randolph appealed this decision to the House, as he was permitted to do, but his colleagues upheld the Speaker. The House then proceeded with its ordinary business, receiving and referring petitions, but Randolph became suspicious that the Speaker was trying to avoid a reconsideration of the vote by sending the bill on to the Senate before Randolph could make his motion. So, when petitions were called for from the members from Virginia, Randolph moved that the House retain the Missouri bill in its possession until such time as he could, according to the rules of the House, make a motion to reconsider the previous day's vote. Clay declared this motion too out of order, for the same reason. Clay clearly wanted to get the House bill on its way to the Senate before Randolph could call for a new vote, but he did not want to do so until the Senate had acted on the conference report and agreed to the admission of Maine without condition.[35]

It was at this point that the anxiously awaited messenger arrived from the Senate, but, instead of informing the House that the Senate had acted to implement the conference report, he was there to ask for a further conference to address the ministerial glitch just discovered in the Maine bill. Clay must have had a sinking feeling that he would be unable to put Randolph off much longer, but he quickly appointed Holmes, Hill, and Taylor as managers for the House and urged them to act quickly. Randolph meanwhile rose to propose that the bill be indefinitely postponed, talking at great length and causing Arthur Livermore to call him to order for deviating from the question. Clay ruled that Randolph was not out of order, probably because he wanted Randolph to pursue this ancillary subject for as long as possible; Randolph, immediately suspicious, withdrew his motion.[36]

During a short interlude in which the Senate dealt with other business and the presentation of petitions continued in the House, the conferees met and quickly agreed to change the wording in the Maine bill. After only a few minutes, Thomas was back on the Senate floor reporting in a brief and matter-of-fact way that the first conference had recommended the actions set forth in his earlier report and that the second conference had proposed substituting the new wording making the act effective that March. The Senate approved the reports of both conference committees. That done, a messenger could finally be dispatched to the House with the news that the Senate had accepted both reports and satisfactorily resolved the Maine bill. Clay immediately sent the amended Missouri bill to the Senate, and, by the time Randolph again got the floor, Clay could inform him that reconsideration was no longer in order because the bill had already been dispatched to the other chamber. Ordinarily volcanic at the slightest provocation, Randolph was now apoplectic, probably rightfully so since he had so clearly expressed his intent to move for reconsideration and was just as clearly entitled to do so. Hesitant to strike back at Clay directly, Randolph moved that the clerk be censured for violating the rules of the House by taking the bill to the Senate, but the other members of the House, grateful to be rid of the Missouri problem that had plagued them for so long, refused him by a vote of 71 to 61. As John Holmes remarked later, "One hour before & one hour after, we should have lost the vote."[37]

Much of the compromise was an exercise in symbolic deference without substance. The Senate finally agreed to vote on the House's bill even though, as amended, it was the equivalent of the Senate bill. The Senate would, as well, give up the symbolic linking of Missouri to Maine, but only on the understanding that both states would be admitted. Congress had done its work and produced a workable compromise that was supported by narrow majorities in both houses. It passed just before the March 4 deadline set by the legislature of Massachusetts, though that deadline had, at the last minute, been extended to avoid forcing Massachusetts's representatives to capitulate on the question of slavery in Missouri.

As a result of the extension, President Monroe had time to consider the bill before signing it. Now the fate of the compromise, and of the Union, was in the hands of the president and the executive branch, as represented by his cabinet. The cabinet, containing as it did three presidential aspirants who very much wanted to govern the whole country and not just their particular part of it, very naturally wanted to support their nationalist president who had the same priority. The three contenders—Crawford, Calhoun, and Adams—had been actively represented by their lieutenants in the congressional debate, most notably, respectively, by Thomas, Lowndes, and Foote. But now it was up to them in their own persons, representing the national government, to pass on the soundness of the compromise.

As soon as congressional action was complete on Friday, Monroe summoned his cabinet for a meeting. It was the first time that he had spoken openly with Adams about the slavery issue west of the Mississippi, although he had presumably been in closer contact with Crawford and Calhoun, whose views were more in sympathy with his own. Monroe now wanted his cabinet to give the compromise its unified and unanimous support, for the sake of posterity but also to provide Monroe cover with the Richmond Junto. He posed two questions: whether it was constitutional to prohibit slavery in a territory and whether such a prohibition would be binding on future states formed north of 36°30′. The answers he sought to these two questions were yes and no, respectively, and he very much wanted unanimity. Tellingly, the second of these questions, phrased as it was, called for an unequivocal answer, at least in the privacy of the president's cabinet, to Thomas's theory that the scope of his amendment was strictly limited to the territorial period. Thomas's mentor William Crawford was present at this cabinet meeting and had a tense exchange with Adams on the subject. Unfortunately, as matters then stood, Adams indicated he would have trouble delivering his no to the second question.[38]

The president was dismayed by this altercation, but Calhoun proposed a way out of the dilemma by reformulating the second question to ask whether the section of the Thomas amendment containing the word "forever" was in conflict with the Constitution. Once again, intentional ambiguity came to the rescue, as·the Southern members of the cabinet could answer the reformulated question in the negative in the belief that forever applied only to the territorial period, and Adams, the lone Northern voice in the cabinet, could do so also, but in the diametrically opposite belief that forever was meant to extend beyond territoriality into statehood. The meeting concluded, and, on Sunday, the president decided to seek from his cabinet formal written responses to the two questions, with the second restated as Calhoun had suggested.[39]

The next day, Monday, March 6, Monroe received back the unanimous opinions he had so earnestly desired. Adams, typically, wished to be the last to deliver his and did so in person at the White House after the opinions of the others were already there: "I took to the president's my answers to his two Constitutional questions, and he desired me to have them deposited in the [State] Department, together with those of the other members of the administration. They differed only as they assigned their reasons for thinking the eighth section of the Missouri Bill consistent with the Constitution because they considered it as applying only to the territorial term—and I barely gave my opinion without assigning for it any explanatory reason." Monroe, and Adams, would certainly have preferred a simple yes or no to this question, but the expression of reasons by the Southerners and the absence of reasons from Adams seemed to put the imprimatur on the Southern interpretation of Thomas's amendment. It had been no easier for the Southern cabinet officers to produce their opinions than it had been for Adams, as the concession implicit in the first question, that Congress could regulate slavery in territories, was more than most Southerners in Congress had been willing to concede. With those opinions in hand, Monroe signed the bill that day. Unfortunately, we cannot have the benefit of reading any of the opinions of the Southern cabinet officers—when the written versions were sought during the 1848 debate on the Oregon Territory, an entry was found showing that they had been properly filed in the State Department, but the opinions themselves had disappeared. The ultimate unanimity of the cabinet in 1820, however, was an important factor in the credibility and durability of the Missouri Compromise.[40]

The upshot was that the balance between slave and free states had been preserved. The North had conceded the admission of Missouri as a slave state, and the South had given way on the basic principle that had been its guiding light since the ratification of the Constitution, that Congress lacked authority to regulate slavery in either territories or states. The controversy was over, at least for that session of Congress, but the participants were still reeling from the ferocity of the contest. Monroe, for one, did almost too good a job of selling the compromise as a Southern victory in order to protect his back with the Richmond Junto and in the process created inevitable backlash in the North. John Quincy Adams confirmed this perception:

The most remarkable circumstance in the history of this transaction is that it was ultimately carried against the opinions, wishes and interests of the free States, by the votes of their own members. They have a decided majority in both houses of Congress; but lost the vote by disunion. The slaveholders, clung together, without losing one vote. Many of them, and almost all the Virginians, held out to the last even against the compromise—the cause of this closer union on the slavish side is that the question affected the individual interest of every slave holding member and of almost every one of his constituents—

Yet, though Adams and others characterized the compromise at the time as a Southern victory, he likely based his acquiescence not just on the immediate political imperative of protecting his candidacy for the presidency but also on an instinct that the compromise might preserve the Union long enough for the North to gather the conviction and the economic strength to uproot slavery. Though the Southern cotton economy grew sixtyfold between 1800 and 1860, it was still dramatically outstripped by the growth of the Northern manufacturing economy, especially when the latter was supplemented by the grain economy of the Old Northwest and the east-west transportation infrastructure. Besides, the North's economic growth supported the making of war, whereas wars are not fought with cotton.[41]

Thomas Jefferson, in retirement at Monticello, recognized the risk in proceeding with a compromise based upon a geographical dividing line and understood that establishing a line between slave and free would increasingly drive a wedge between the different sections of the country. He saw that such a compromise contained the seeds of its own destruction. To his visitors that spring, he described the Missouri Compromise as a hopeless conundrum that should have been avoided. The most famous, and vivid, statement of his views came in a letter, dated April 22, 1820, to John Holmes of the District of Maine, who had sent Jefferson a published statement of his reasons for voting for the compromise:

> This momentous question, like a fire bell in the night,
> awakened and filled me with terror. I considered it at
> once as the knell of the Union. It is hushed indeed for the
> moment, but this is a reprieve only, not a final sentence.

A geographical line, coinciding with a marked principle,
moral and political, once conceived and held up to the angry
passions of men, will never be obliterated; and every new
irritation will mark it deeper and deeper. . . . As it is we have
the wolf by the ear, and we can neither hold him, nor safely
let him go. Justice is in one scale and self-preservation in
the other. . . . [T]o regulate the condition of the different
descriptions of men composing a State . . . is the exclusive
right of every State, which nothing in the constitution has
taken from them and given to the General Government.[42]

From this very brief admission of the injustice of human bondage, Jefferson
retreated into the miasma of diffusion as his preferred solution for slavery and
an almost blind emphasis on states' rights.

In terms of the development of the U.S. Constitution, the Compromise of
1820 was an important precedent for congressional control over slavery in the
territories, but, as discussed earlier, there had been others. When slavery was
first excluded from the Northwest Territory by Article VI of the Northwest
Ordinance, the action was taken by the Continental Congress acting under
the Articles of Confederation, but the ordinance, with its Article VI, was then
ratified by Congress after adoption of the Constitution, and, when Congress
had subsequently created the Indiana, Michigan, and Illinois Territories, it
had specifically made the new territories subject to the Northwest Ordinance.
The second constitutional question at stake in the compromise was whether
Congress had the right to impose upon a state asking for admission into the
Union conditions that did not apply to other states already in the Union. At
least in Jesse Thomas's mind this question was answered in the negative by the
Missouri Compromise. On the other extreme were those like John Quincy
Adams, who thought the question had been answered in the affirmative. For
most, the question was simply left up in the air. The fact that it could be so
variously interpreted was, from a political point of view, one of the peculiar
beauties of what Thomas had wrought.

The compromise achieved one very important objective for Southerners—
no slaves had been, or would be, emancipated by action of the Congress. In
addition, the only areas of the Louisiana Purchase that were being actively
settled at the time of the compromise, namely Louisiana, Missouri, and Arkansas, were all going to be safely slave. As it turned out, Missouri was the

last of a spate of seven states admitted to the Union between the War of 1812 and 1821, and there was to be a lull of fifteen years after the Missouri controversy before anyone dared to tinker with the status quo. By the time Arkansas was admitted in 1836, the area north of the line was becoming settled and was clearly destined to yield more states than the area south of the line. The compromise had already begun its slow transformation from a Southern coup into a Northern line of defense against the expansion of slavery. Iowa was the first territory north of the line to be sufficiently settled to pursue statehood, and by the time it was admitted in 1846, the partisans of slavery were busy working on the repeal of the compromise.

Despite the important role played by Jesse Thomas in the Sixteenth Congress, the landscape of congressional power soon began to shift in ways that worked against him. The Republican Party was splitting into a faction that backed national development and a strong central government (National Republicans, many of whom later became Whigs) and a faction that argued for states' rights (Democratic Republicans who became Jacksonian Democrats). As this realignment occurred, Thomas found himself in an unfortunate position. On the one hand, he backed William Crawford, an incipient Democratic Republican, for the presidency, and he was also about to back a states' rights campaign to legalize slavery in Illinois, which was also a Democratic Republican issue. On the other hand, he was in irreconcilable conflict with Andrew Jackson, the future standard-bearer of the Democratic Republicans, who would never forget Thomas's unwavering support of William Crawford. He was also by nature and instinct a National Republican, and his involvement with the Michigan-Illinois Canal, the planned link between Lake Michigan and the Mississippi, and with business and real estate development generally made him more of a Whig every day, which was, in fact, what he eventually became. Like Clay, he was by instinct a Whig who was forced by circumstance into being a states' rightist. It is this twist of fate that was to spell the end of his political career in Illinois. The compromise that Jesse Burgess Thomas proposed and successfully shepherded through the U.S. Congress ultimately became his proudest political legacy, one that he regarded as probably the most important act of his life. As the Missouri Compromise, so hastily pasted together, weathered year after year and continued for thirty-four years as the central legal distinction permitting the country to deal with its deep divisions, he undoubtedly began to think of himself less as a politician and more as a statesman.[43]

CHAPTER 12

The Aftermath

ews of the Missouri Compromise reached St. Louis on March 25, and the night sky was lit by bonfires and illuminations. But the spirit of contention persisted. In a constitutional convention in which Richard Thomas, Jesse Thomas's older brother, was one of the leading figures, the old defiance reappeared as uniformly proslavery delegates voted for a provision requiring the legislature to pass a law denying free black people the right to enter the state "under any pretext whatsoever."[1] Because free black people were citizens of the states from which they came, this provision violated Article IV, §2, of the U.S. Constitution, guaranteeing that "the citizens of each state shall be entitled to all the privileges and immunities of the citizens of the several states." The provision therefore violated the enabling act provision requiring that nothing in the Missouri Constitution be repugnant to the U.S. Constitution. Richard Thomas was one of the few delegates who attempted to water down this reckless proposal, possibly because he understood from Jesse Thomas just how perilous this course of conduct might be. The exclusionary measure, amounting almost to insolence, brought on the second Missouri controversy when the Missouri Constitution was submitted to Congress in 1821.

Jesse Thomas played no significant part in the compromise that ended this second Missouri controversy. This time it was Henry Clay who engineered a settlement through the creative strategy of requiring that the Missouri Constitution be interpreted consistently with the U.S. Constitution. The compromise was based upon the Missouri legislature passing a solemn public act affirming its adherence to the U.S. Constitution—which it grudgingly did. Fortunately, Missouri's General Assembly chose not to pass the laws shutting out free black citizens that had been mandated in the new constitution and did not do so for twenty-six years.

Richard Thomas had received the second most votes to be president of the constitutional convention and, after losing out to David Barton, was given the very important role of chairman of the Committee on the Judiciary. In this capacity he became a champion for a very strong judiciary, which led to his ultimate fall from power. After the new government was established, Richard was appointed as one of the four circuit court judges mandated by the new constitution. The constitution had provided that those judges be paid the very ample annual salary of $2,000, not to be reduced during their tenure in office (which, incidentally, was the same salary as the governor and the state supreme court judges). Even though Richard had voted against salaries of that magnitude, he was branded as an opportunist for taking one of the high-paying judgeships he had helped to create. And although Richard Thomas and the other supporters of a strong judiciary had prevailed in the constitutional convention, stubborn resistance to judges soon emerged as the new state's most contentious issue. The particular points of aggravation were, predictably, the constitutional provisions setting the $2,000 salaries for circuit judges and protecting them from removal. No sooner had the ink dried on the new constitution than opposition sprang up to the article on the judiciary, and Missouri began the process of amending its constitution even before the original one was submitted to Congress for approval.

Meanwhile, Jesse's attention had shifted to land issues, which had always been of more vital interest to him. As a member of the Public Lands Committee in the Senate, Jesse was far more anxious about the Panic of 1819 and its effect on land values and the ability of settlers to pay for land they had already purchased, since many now found they owed more than their land was worth. While he was dealing with Missouri, Thomas, with the backing of William Harris Crawford, was drafting the most significant amendment of the public lands law since William Henry Harrison's initiative in 1800 and was pushing that and the Missouri Compromise through Congress simultaneously. At the same time, the contest between Thomas and Ninian Edwards was turning increasingly ugly. All of the mileposts in Jesse Thomas's career—his leadership on the Missouri question and on land reform, his upcoming campaign to be reelected in 1823, and the movement to legalize slavery in Illinois—were about to be caught up in, and even obscured by, his and Edwards's enmity for each other and their involvement in presidential politics.

Their confrontation began with the Bank of Edwardsville, which was about to implode amid accusations of impropriety. As the general economic situation deteriorated in the spring of 1821, Secretary of the Treasury William Crawford felt he was losing touch with what was going on in western land offices and banks and decided to appoint Thomas as a special inspector for the Treasury Department in the Old Northwest. Edwards and his allies, concerned about Edwards's involvement with the flailing Bank of Edwardsville, sensed danger from Thomas, who so well understood where the proverbial bodies were buried in Illinois. They immediately attacked his appointment in Congress as improper for a sitting senator and were especially critical of the extra pay and traveling expenses he received. They naturally asserted that Thomas's appointment was a thinly veiled stratagem of Crawford's to send a close ally out to the frontier at government expense armed with both carrots and sticks to support Crawford's candidacy for the presidency and Thomas's campaign for reelection to the Senate.

Thomas, as it turned out, did a comprehensive and competent job throughout the Northwest, ending his tour by focusing on the precarious financial situation in his hometown. His inspection of the land office and bank in Edwardsville, both of which were still under the control of Benjamin Stephenson, indicated that the bank was struggling to maintain sufficient specie to redeem its notes on demand. Stephenson's land office had not been keeping current in depositing its receipts into the bank or in making required reports to the Treasury Department. Stephenson's garbled accounts presented to Thomas, on a silver platter, the irresistible chance for political retribution against his main rivals in Illinois, who had been flinging charges at him since his appointment as special examiner. In the fall following Thomas's review of the books, the Bank of Edwardsville announced partial suspension of specie payment, and in early 1822 it closed its doors for good. Stephenson's juggling of the books in the final months only made the ultimate failure messier. As the end neared, Edwards apparently came to believe that his only option was to counterattack. Whatever financial expectations he and his friends may have had in the bank were gone, and his focus shifted from saving his investment to saving his reputation. Edwards, however, lacked the skills of a natural political infighter. The showdown between Illinois' first two U.S. senators played out on both the state and national level and ended with Edwards's national political career cut off.

As Thomas's initial four-year term in the Senate drew to a close in 1823, the Third Illinois General Assembly gathered in Vandalia to decide not only his political future but also whether Illinois would attempt to amend its state constitution to permit slavery, the question that had been subtly, but effectively, left open in the state constitutional convention of 1818. The Eighteenth Congress was set to open December 1, 1823, and it was advisable for the Illinois legislature to select a new senator in time for him to reach Washington by that date. Both Edwards and Thomas used their powers of federal patronage and local persuasion to ensure that their adherents ran for and won spots in that pivotal General Assembly. As the senatorial contest approached, however, Edwards, in typical fashion, could not settle on a candidate to support against Thomas. Edwards's forces tried to delay the election, but Thomas succeeded in having the election pushed up earlier in the session, to January 9, 1823, at which time he was reelected to a full six-year term.

Disappointed in Illinois, Edwards switched his focus to the national level, merging his vendetta against Thomas into John C. Calhoun's effort to unseat Crawford as the favorite for the presidency in 1824. Two weeks after Thomas's reelection in Vandalia, a frustrated Edwards threw down the gauntlet to him and to Crawford in Washington in what would come to be called the A. B. affair. On January 23, 1823, Edwards, signing himself anonymously as "A. B.," wrote the first of fifteen letters in the *Washington Republican* accusing Crawford of deceit and mismanagement.[2] The A. B. affair is usually discussed in the context of the 1824 presidential campaign, with Edwards acting as Calhoun's minion to undermine Crawford; but the affair was also, and perhaps more important, the final chapter in the struggle between the two early leaders in Illinois, with Edwards attacking Thomas in order to deflect public interest in the debacle of the Bank of Edwardsville. Edwards had resigned from the bank's board in 1819 but had managed to circulate his resignation letter only locally without sending the original on to its addressee, the secretary of the treasury. This tactic was apparently intended to deflect local criticism while leaving Edwards able to represent the bank in Washington.

Edwards had suffered a serious blow when, on October 10, 1822, Benjamin Stephenson died in Edwardsville at the age of fifty-four. Sources indicate the cause of Stephenson's death was malaria, but anxiety related to the failure of his bank and the tangled affairs at his land office must certainly have been a contributing factor. Stephenson had been the only witness to Edwards's suspect account of his resignation as bank director. Palemon Winchester, Stephenson's twenty-seven-year-old son-in-law and secretary, tried to step in to untangle his affairs and help Stephenson's thirty-four-year-old widow, Lucy, settle his accounts. Winchester, though a lawyer, proved extremely high-strung and fully as disorganized as his father-in-law, and as Stephenson's affairs unraveled, so did he. Meanwhile, Crawford's response to the accusations in the A. B. letters was to press his attack in Edwardsville based on Thomas's reports as special examiner. Crawford held off briefly because of Stephenson's death, but then, tiring of the delays in settling Stephenson's accounts and suspecting Edwards of being behind the A. B. letters, he instructed the district attorney in Illinois in late March 1823 to bring suit against the Bank of Edwardsville for arrears of $141,238.[3] Lucy lobbied hard to have Winchester appointed as Stephenson's successor, but the current state of the books he oversaw as Stephenson's secretary made such a choice politically impossible.

The collapse of the Bank of Edwardsville and the other troubles attendant on the Panic of 1819 were, however, overshadowed by the impending battle over slavery in Illinois. Missouri had succeeded in legitimizing slavery, and now the spotlight shifted to Illinois, where a movement was brewing to attempt the same thing, this time after statehood. Many believed that the admission of Missouri as a slave state meant that a referendum on slavery in Illinois was inevitable.[4] John Quincy Adams had been convinced on the eve of the Missouri Compromise that proslavery sentiment in Missouri and Illinois would prove insurmountable and that, even though he believed Congress had the power to restrict slavery, the citizens of those states so opposed restriction that slavery was inevitable there. Furthermore, he had believed that their right to choose slavery would be supported by a majority of the states in the Union and that slavery was so profitable that it would be difficult even to keep it out of Indiana.[5] The timing of the contest in Illinois was presaged by the two provisions quietly inserted into its constitution by Jesse Thomas and Elias Kent Kane, the first permitting slavery in the Salines only through 1825 and the second setting terms for the initial judges on the Illinois Supreme Court to expire in 1824 (so that life tenure judges could not overturn an amendment to the Illinois Constitution allowing slavery). The battle to permit slavery generally and indefinitely in Illinois climaxed in a call for a constitutional convention in 1823.

The economic downturn was a major reason slavery again came to the fore in Illinois, and the conventionist controversy can be seen as an effort to restore Illinois' faltering commerce by restoring the flow of well-heeled immigrant slaveholders into the state. With the phasing out of the saltworks indenture provision, Illinois would soon be a completely free state, and the slave states across both rivers from bottomland Illinois were perceived as magnets for immigrants from the South, drawing them away from Illinois. The poor white majority was convinced that it was the prohibition of slavery in the new state's constitution, rather than the general economic downturn, that was causing Illinois' problems. The movement to instate slavery in Illinois proved to be very contentious, with crosscurrents that had less to do with slavery than with class and political philosophy.[6] This movement was seen by its proponents as not just about slavery but also about states' rights and protecting so-called Southern culture from an increasingly diverse and industrial North that was growing at an exponential rate. The fight between Edwards and Thomas, however, had by that time become so consuming that both men were largely absent during the conventionist controversy. Thomas, for his part, probably sensed uncertainty on the horizon and was reluctant to join the fray, fearful that the issue would hurt his chances for reelection that year. However, as one of the authors of the plan in the 1818 constitutional convention to possibly revisit the issue of slavery five years after statehood, he probably also felt bound to join the effort, though the Missouri controversy may by that time have sapped some of his enthusiasm for the project.

The contest over slavery was exacerbated by the arrival in Illinois of Edward Coles. Coles, formerly secretary to President Monroe, was appointed by him in 1819 to be register of the new land office in Edwardsville. Coles was a liberal, well-educated, pro-emancipation Virginian. On his way down the Ohio River, he had emancipated twenty-six slaves he had inherited and settled them in Madison County, Illinois, donating to each head of family a quarter section of land. As an outsider and the recipient of perhaps the plum of all federal jobs in Illinois, he rapidly became the perfect target for proslavery activists. Coles decided to run for governor in 1822 at the same time that proslavery elements initiated their push to reconsider slavery in Illinois. He had not been the candidate of either of the two main political factions, but, owing to a three-way division of the proslavery vote, he was elected governor with only 2,854 votes, as opposed to the combined 5,752 votes of the three proslavery candidates opposing him.[7] In his inaugural address, delivered in early December 1822, Coles called for the abolition of slavery, including the liberation of slaves held by settlers who thought themselves protected by the "heretofore" language in Article VI of the 1818 constitution. He went even further by proposing the repeal of the indenture laws that supported Illinois' system of proto-slavery. Coles lectured the General Assembly with an arrogance typical of an affluent liberal, and the Illinois Senate immediately rose up to meet his challenge.

The senate named a committee to deal specifically with Coles's message, and that committee, in turn, chose as its spokesman the incendiary Theophilus W. Smith, who, though a senator, was not even a member of the committee but had the requisite training as an advocate, having read law with Aaron Burr in New York. Smith, an unreliable and fractious recruit to the Thomas faction, crafted a fiery response calling for a constitutional convention intended to amend the state's constitution to explicitly authorize slavery. Smith represented Madison County, a county normally expected to vote against slavery, and he recognized the leverage he could have if he threw in his lot with the proslavery southern counties. Smith managed to hold together this coalition and in the process became the architect of the nascent Jacksonian movement in Illinois, melding it with the proslavery movement and transforming it into a general attack against the "big folks." The movement to legalize slavery was thus transformed into an attack on established political elites. Smith managed to paint the big folks like Coles and Edwards as the nineteenth-century equivalent of limousine liberals; what offended him and his allies was not so much their position on slavery as it was their general pretension and self-importance. Jesse Thomas, aware that this new movement was welling up among his own followers, was forced into an uneasy alliance with this younger generation of firebrands. Thereafter, the conventionists, with Smith as their effective leader and Jesse Thomas their reluctant patron, started down a slippery slope to popular government in Illinois. Their stated objective was to seek some permanent accommodation allowing slavery, but their real purpose was to bring down the big folks.

During this fiery interlude in Illinois, the long slog of charge and counter-charge related to the Edwardsville land office and bank resumed in Washington. It took another year for the A. B. affair to finally wind down, and by that time Calhoun was no longer a candidate for the presidency and therefore less inclined to sponsor Edwards's unseemly marauding. Crawford, for his part, suffered a stroke-like malady in 1823 that effectively removed him from presidential contention. He was stricken ill while visiting his friend Senator James Barbour at his home in Virginia and was apparently mistreated by a local doctor who bled him twenty-three times, which could not have helped matters. The end result was that Crawford remained for months speechless, nearly blind, and mostly immobile. He had a serious relapse in May 1824, and his adversaries, feeling his candidacy might soon come to an end, were positioning themselves to pick up his supporters. Therefore, the remaining presidential contenders went out of their way to avoid giving offense to Crawford's allies, even if that meant abandoning Edwards. Monroe was especially upset with Edwards because he believed that Edwards's appointment as ambassador to Mexico late in the A. B. affair would now be interpreted as a reward for a hatchet job on Crawford that Monroe supported. Monroe had in fact drifted away from his support for Crawford but very much wanted to be viewed as impartial in the upcoming presidential struggle. Edwards finally ended the drama by resigning as ambassador just as Monroe was preparing to revoke his commission. This marked the end of Edwards's prominence on the national stage.[8]

As the A. B. affair was winding down in Washington, the campaign over the convention scheme accelerated in Illinois, extending through the summer of 1824. The campaign was conducted with fiery zeal on both sides, increasing in bitterness as the final round of voting approached. During much of this time Jesse Thomas was in Washington attending to the business of the Senate, but, when Congress adjourned for the summer on May 27, 1824, he immediately went to Illinois to participate in the pro-convention campaign. The campaign was particularly vicious: "In this spirit was the contest of 1823–4 waged. Old friendships were sundered, families divided, and neighborhoods arrayed in opposition to each other. . . . As in time of warfare, every man expected an attack, and was prepared to meet it. Pistols and dirks were in great demand [by] all those conspicuous for their opposition to the Convention measure." Thomas Ford wrote later that "the whole people for the space of eighteen months did scarcely anything but read newspapers, hand-bills and pamphlets, quarrel, argue and wrangle with each other whenever they met together to hear the violent harangues of their orators."[9]

In an outcome that could not have been predicted only a few months before, the convention scheme was voted down by the voters on August 2, 1824, by a resounding vote of 6,640 against to 4,972 votes in favor. The outcome was a stunning reversal of the gubernatorial election two years before, when the heavy preponderance of the combined votes for the proslavery candidates had seemed to preordain the defeat of any plebiscite to ban slavery. Likewise, the previous election in 1823 had voted in a General Assembly that was clearly in favor of calling a constitutional convention, an outcome that also indicated a majority in favor of slavery. But the proslavery sentiments of voters in Illinois had been overestimated by the conventionists, or perhaps the balance on this vital issue had shifted in the two years it took for the matter to come to a final popular vote, or possibly Smith's new anti–big folks party did not really care that much about slavery. In the end, the convention resolution was defeated, the murky status of slavery in Illinois was not resolved, and slavery was not legally barred in Illinois until 1845.[10]

The eighteen-month delay prescribed for constitutional amendments in Illinois almost certainly killed the convention scheme. Thus, not only had Thomas devised the 1818 compromises that gave rise to the conventionist controversy, but he also had engineered the constitutional provisions that had made it so difficult to amend that constitution. In the intervening years, he had been at the center of the national trauma over slavery and now had an appreciation of the dangers of disunion that his younger allies lacked. Jesse Thomas had carefully crafted the Missouri Compromise so that it applied only to territories and not to states. The conventionists had exploited that opening by attempting to change the status of slavery after statehood in Illinois, and they had failed. This made it less likely that rules on slavery would be changed after statehood in other states. Thomas may have heaved a sigh of relief—he would have had a lot of explaining to do in Congress had the conventionists succeeded. Demonstrating the equivocal nature of their support for slavery, the conventionists, despite being unable to amend the constitution, won a majority of the seats in the next General Assembly and controlled the next legislature, continuing to grow thereafter into an independent force in Illinois. But they did this independently of Jesse Thomas, and his own status declined as the conventionists emerged as a powerful new presence in Illinois, primarily loyal to Andrew Jackson. Ironically, Smith, Thomas's recent ally and the leading figure among the conventionists, and the man who, with Thomas's old ally Elias Kane, later led what was left of the Thomas faction, was soon to see his daughter marry Thomas's nephew, Richard's second son, named Jesse Burgess Thomas after his uncle.

Meanwhile, Richard Thomas was in trouble in Missouri, also caught up in the rising tide of Jacksonian democracy. The judiciary soon became the center of this storm, and Thomas himself became the lightning rod. He first brought trouble down on his head by trying to force the resignation of a perfectly competent clerk in his court in order to replace him with his eldest son, Claiborne. His biggest strategic error, though, was his role as a litigant in a number of complicated test cases challenging acts passed by the populist legislature to provide relief to citizens forced to the edge of ruination by the Panic of 1819. For this, he was impeached by pro-Jackson members of the Missouri House in 1825 and removed from office, despite being represented by his friend Edward Bates, Lincoln's future attorney general. Richard received some vindication the following year when the political pendulum swung back in a conservative direction and he was again elected as a state senator. Meanwhile, his personal finances fell apart while his test cases wound their way slowly to the U.S. Supreme Court. They were eventually decided in Richard's favor in decisions written by Chief Justice John Marshall[11]—but not before Richard's untimely death in 1828 following a fall from a horse while riding the circuit after being forced to return to the practice of law.

Jesse's political star began to set in 1823 at the same time as Richard's. The unsuccessful campaign to legalize slavery in Illinois was one setback, but, much more critical, it was becoming clear that his mentor William Crawford would never fully recover. When first stricken, Crawford was only fifty-one; he was in the prime of life, and his supporters had no hint that health issues would imperil his candidacy. It was difficult for the public to determine the seriousness of Crawford's ailment or the prognosis for his recovery, because his allies did a good job of disguising its seriousness. All Washington knew, however, that Crawford had suffered a relapse after retaking the reins of his campaign in March 1824 and attending one cabinet meeting in April and that at times he was quite deranged. Thomas, who knew the true situation, nonetheless made the decision to stick loyally, even stubbornly, to Crawford, and he ended by paying a price for that choice.

It is easy to forget the towering reputation of Crawford during the Madison and Monroe administrations. On account of his collapse, subsequent history has lost sight of his formidable political presence, and he has been defined by the major figures against whom he contended and their biographers, who have passed on to posterity a one-sided, negative account of a man who previously had been highly regarded. Albert Gallatin, certainly one of the ablest of the founding generation, thought highly enough of Crawford that he ultimately agreed to serve as his vice presidential running mate in 1824. Gallatin believed that Crawford united a powerful mind to "a most correct judgment and an inflexible integrity" and was, in his view, to be preferred over Calhoun, Clay, or Adams.[12]

In his years in Congress, Jesse Thomas had become a part of the national establishment in a way that no other contemporary figure in Illinois had done, but his membership in that establishment had been inextricably connected to Crawford. When Crawford's career was derailed, so was Thomas's. Thomas, so effective on the national stage, had lost touch with the pulse of Illinois politics.

It is ironic that a politician so often accused of saying whatever the electorate wanted to hear now felt uncomfortable being as protean as the times required.

Crawford's weakened condition made the presidency no longer a realistic possibility in 1824, but his campaign moved forward under its own momentum. In the previous seven presidential elections, the presidential candidates had been chosen by a joint congressional caucus of the members of each party, and then the presidential electors were chosen by the state legislatures. Even a weakened Crawford could have been elected using this machinery, but the system was increasingly under attack as undemocratic. It was a system that protected the interests of the older eastern states (with larger congressional delegations), but it flew in the face of developments in the western states, where a more broad-based democracy was taking root. By 1824, the territorial and state legislatures of the West were expanding the franchise to encourage immigration, and the eastern states were forced to expand their suffrage as well in order to keep their citizens from heading west. Eighteen of the twenty-four states had by then gone so far as to provide for the popular election of presidential electors. These new developments were a bellwether of the Jacksonian era.

Against this background the caucus system seemed particularly unfair because of the complete domination of the Republican Party. If a congressional caucus were allowed to nominate the Republican candidate that year, it seemed quite possible that the first truly popular election for president would have only one viable candidate. In the past there had been two such caucuses, one for each of the major parties, which had at least left the states with some real decision-making authority. If the choice had been only between a president chosen by federal legislators and one chosen by state legislators, there probably would not have been the dustup that occurred in 1824, but the irony of having a congressional caucus deprive the people of their power of choice in the first election in which they could directly participate was not lost on the voters, and they rose up against the caucus system so definitively that it was never used again.

Jesse Thomas may have been from one of the new, more democratic states, but he had a faith in the caucus system that showed him to be more naturally a member of the elitist political generation that was passing from the scene. He was also a steely realist and recognized that the caucus was the best, and possibly the only, way to win Crawford's nomination. With Crawford's health so precarious, Thomas and others worked assiduously to hold the caucus as soon as possible and were hoping to do so before the end of December. Thomas's excitement was tangible in a December 8, 1823, letter to his political ally Governor

Shadrach Bond: "I have as you will readily suppose been engaged in the great work—there is no doubt but a Congressional caucus will take place and that Mr. Crawford will be nominated and as little doubt of his ultimate success."[13]

Very few others were as sanguine as Thomas about either the caucus or Crawford's health. Thomas was one of the few in Congress pushing for a caucus, which was piquantly ironic given that his own quest for national office had been launched when he undercut a caucus in Indiana. A congressional caucus of Republicans was finally held February 14, 1824, and it chose Crawford; but it was attended by only sixty-six senators and representatives. Crawford's campaign went downhill from there, and in the fall voting he came in a distant third in the electoral college after Jackson and Adams but still ahead of Henry Clay. With no candidate receiving a majority, the election was thrown into the House of Representatives, where it was decided by each state delegation casting a single vote as required by the Constitution, which gave the representatives of small states enormous power. Both Daniel Pope Cook of Illinois and John Scott of Missouri, each the lone representative from his state, voted for John Quincy Adams, helping to put him in the White House. Since some states' House delegations felt bound to follow instructions received from their state legislatures, in the end the election was decided by an interaction of politicians at both the federal and state levels, just as had been the case before popular participation.

In Illinois, the presidential election, held three months after the crushing defeat of the conventionist campaign, was an anticlimax but equally devastating. The long continued excitement and acrimony of the struggle over the convention deflated the presidential election; only 4,707 votes were cast in the national election as opposed to an aggregate of 11,787 in the convention election. But that presidential election, although largely ignored in Illinois, was to have major repercussions for Senator Thomas, principally because he was so strongly identified with Crawford, the weakest candidate in Illinois, at a time when Andrew Jackson's star was rising rapidly. Of the four candidates for president in 1824, Illinois gave Adams 1,516 votes, Jackson 1,272, Clay 1,036, and Crawford a distant 847.

Crawford left Washington and returned to Georgia where he served as a circuit judge until his death in 1834. He continued to dabble in politics, corresponding with Thomas and others. Crawford had been the hammer to Thomas's nail, and, when the hammer was taken from the scene, the nail lost much of its relevance. Without Crawford's patronage, Thomas's slide from political power began, and he never recovered the power he had enjoyed when Crawford was in Washington. As a participant in the caucus and a supporter of another candidate, Thomas shared in the general opprobrium brought about by the widespread perception that Andrew Jackson had been cheated of his rightful claim to the presidency. The friction between Andrew Jackson and Jesse Thomas was made worse because Thomas made no secret of his dislike, even contempt, for Jackson, both personally and politically, and, as discussed earlier, Jackson had an equally cordial dislike of Thomas.

Thomas further isolated himself by being one of only fourteen senators voting against the confirmation of Henry Clay as secretary of state, influenced to some degree no doubt by the so-called corrupt bargain between Adams and Clay that deprived Jackson of the presidency. Thomas eventually became a supporter of the Adams administration but never a warm one. It was the only course open for someone who wanted to stand against Jackson. By so doing, Thomas completed his transition from Jeffersonian Republican to Crawford Republican and then, with Crawford no longer a national figure, to National Republican and backer of John Quincy Adams. But Adams lacked the instincts to stand against the rising tide of Jacksonian democracy. Gifted as a diplomat, Adams had no aptitude as a politician. He refused to tailor his objectives to what was politically possible and failed to reward his friends or punish his enemies. The one favor that Adams did for Thomas was to nominate his stepson John Francis Hamtramck to be Indian agent to the Osage tribe. Hamtramck was confirmed in the Senate on May 2, 1826 (over the stout resistance of Thomas Hart Benton), but this small favor became just one more piece of ammunition for the Jacksonians. Thomas's conversion to the cause of Adams helped him very little and, in fact, harmed him further with the Jacksonians. In particular, the growing hostility of Jackson's ally Thomas Hart Benton was to hurt both Jesse and Richard Thomas.[14]

On May 4, 1826, Benton, now Jackson's darling, submitted a report calling for a reduction in executive patronage and proposing a constitutional amendment intended to exclude senators and representatives from appointment to any civil office under the authority of the federal government. Though Benton did not identify Thomas by name, newspaper articles written to support Benton's campaign had already singled Thomas out as a recipient of supposedly tainted patronage, both for his appointment as special examiner for the Treasury and for his stepson's appointment as Indian agent. Adams decided to run for re-election in 1828, and Thomas did his best to nudge Adams onto a course that would make his reelection possible, but it was of no avail. Adams consistently took principled but unpopular positions on issues like tariffs and western land prices. Suffering from a kind of political death wish, Adams was swept from office a few months later, following which Thomas and other Adams Republicans could expect no mercy from the Jacksonians.[15]

The last Congress in which Thomas served was the twentieth, running from 1827 to 1829, and he did not make a speech in either the first or second session.[16] This silence from a senator who had earned both respect and seniority may possibly have evidenced a growing depression but certainly reflected his realization that the end of an epoch was approaching. As he left the U.S. Senate on March 3, 1829, his political career in Illinois was over, and such was the nature of those rancorous times that his life in Illinois was over as well. Since departing Indiana under a cloud in 1809, Thomas had put down deep roots in Illinois. Admittedly, ten of those twenty years had been spent largely in Washington, and even as early as 1823 he had apparently questioned the idea of continuing to live in Illinois. Still, Illinois had been his home more than anywhere else. Nonetheless, at the close of the Twentieth Congress, Thomas chose to settle in Mount Vernon, Ohio, without even returning to Illinois; as far as is known, he never went back. This decision to depart the state must have been a bitter pill for a man who had been instrumental in the formation of the Illinois Territory and then had served as a territorial judge during the entire territorial period, as president of the state constitutional convention, and finally as a U.S. senator during the first ten years of statehood.

Thomas was not alone in passing from the political stage in Illinois; it was a time when many of his old rivals also departed. Ninian Edwards returned to Illinois, where he practiced law and acquired additional interests in saw- and gristmills and other mercantile pursuits. After unsuccessful bids to regain a U.S. Senate seat in two elections in 1824, Edwards settled on running for governor in 1826 and was finally successful, winning narrowly over two insignificant opponents who split the pro-Jackson vote. He had a tumultuous but largely successful term. Illinois counties were named for Edwards and Nathaniel Pope while they were still alive, for Kane and even Stephenson shortly after their deaths, and, a bit later, for Cook. It is only Thomas among the group of early leaders who does not have one named after him, which speaks both to his self-effacing nature and to the rapidity of his eclipse in Illinois. It is only fitting that, instead of a faceless name of an Illinois county, he is better remembered for the Missouri Compromise.

CHAPTER 13

The Perspective of Ohio

ount Vernon was a prosperous and picturesque town, in a lovely setting on the Kokosing River, about thirty miles northeast of Columbus. Largely at Jesse Thomas's initiative, a substantial part of the town had been located on the 2,363 acres Rebecca had inherited from her first husband, and she and Jesse had a natural interest in promoting the town's growth. Thomas had set the town on this course by helping to have it designated as the county seat of Knox County twenty-one years before, and he had played an active role in the development of the town even during the years he and Rebecca had lived in Illinois. On his move to Mount Vernon in 1829, Judge Thomas, as he reverted to being called, rolled up his sleeves and got to work in earnest.

One of the first local property owners with whom he transacted business was the eccentric John Chapman, better known as Johnny Appleseed, who had established several orchards in Mount Vernon. At the time Thomas was preparing to settle in the town, Chapman was just winding down his nursery operations there preparatory to moving farther west. In 1828 Thomas purchased one of a number of lots he was putting up for sale. Chapman was a good businessman and had his own slant on real estate development; the lot he sold was on Main Street and had certainly increased significantly in value since he bought it.[1]

Thomas threw himself wholeheartedly into the development of Mount Vernon. In the time just before and after his decision to settle there, he was involved with two additions to the town, one in 1826 and the second ten years later. Several streets were added to the north of the existing town, including ones named Hamtramck and Burgess, and several more on the eastern edge, including ones named McKenzie, McArthur, and Ridgeley, all names coming from his and Rebecca's families. The younger John Francis Hamtramck was likely not directly involved in the first town addition, which was made in his name. He was twenty-eight years old when that occurred and was involved in his military career. After his graduation in 1819 from West Point, ranked fifteenth in a class of twenty-nine, he had started off on a career as an artillery officer and, with Jesse's support, had survived reductions in the peacetime army. A short time later, however, he resigned from the army. He had a short stint as a planter in Florissant, Missouri, and may have served briefly in the Treasury Department. In December 1825, Hamtramck married Eliza Clagett Selby at Shepherdstown, Virginia, in the area straddling the Potomac River in western Maryland, where his stepfather's family had come from, thus reestablishing the family's links with the East. He persuaded his new wife to return with him to the frontier and, again with the help of his stepfather, secured the post of Indian agent for the Osage tribe, which he held from 1826 to 1832.[2]

Jesse Thomas owned a number of buildings in Mount Vernon, and he amassed a considerable fortune in his years there, both for his stepson and for himself.[3] He also began to dabble in local politics almost as soon as he arrived in Ohio, but most of the officeholders he could have challenged were, like him, anti-Jacksonians. Besides, he no longer had the same interest in active involvement in politics, though he was as interested as ever in discussing the issues. In 1830 Judge Thomas made a preliminary canvass to assess his chances of winning a seat in the U.S. Congress from the Eighth Congressional District that encompassed Knox County. However, it turned out that the incumbent, William Stanbery, had such a firm hold on the seat that Thomas was discouraged from going further. Stanbery failed to win renomination two years later, but by that time Judge Thomas apparently had lost interest in pursuing the seat.

Although real estate investment and politics remained important for Thomas, his most important commitment in Mount Vernon was to St. Paul's Episcopal Church, and it was one he shared with Rebecca, who had been brought up an Anglican in Montreal. The Episcopal Church was a new arrival in the West and one that quickly became associated with wealth and social standing. Thomas's involvement was particularly interesting because of the church's strong stand against slavery. Some of the town's most prominent citizens were Episcopalians, including Henry B. Curtis, its leading lawyer and a close friend of Judge Thomas. The two of them worked with Philander Chase, the first bishop of Ohio, to purchase eight thousand acres of land four miles east of Mount Vernon in present-day Gambier as a site for an Episcopal seminary and Kenyon College. Although the seminary and college struggled in their early years, they had a strong symbiotic relationship with the parish in Mount Vernon, which was formally established as St. Paul's Episcopal Church in 1829, largely on the impetus of Curtis and Thomas. Many of the scholars who came to teach in the seminary in Gambier also served the church in Mount Vernon, and architects and builders who constructed the buildings for the seminary and college stayed on to complete notable buildings in Mount Vernon as well, many of which were constructed for Curtis.[4]

Jesse Thomas and Henry Curtis were among the four vestrymen elected at the first St. Paul's parish meeting on September 7, 1829, a position to which both were reelected many times and which Thomas apparently held almost continuously until his death. In 1836 the first St. Paul's Episcopal Church building was found to have a defective foundation, and by May of that year $4,000 had been subscribed for a new church ($500 of it from Judge Thomas). Although Jesse played an active role in the business of the parish, serving as vestry chair in 1830 and 1831 and as treasurer in 1832, he was not confirmed as a member until 1842. By contrast, Rebecca's name was the first on the list of members prepared in 1834 when the parish began to keep its own records. Of the nine people on the original list of communicants, it is interesting that eight were women, and it appears that women in general, and Rebecca in particular, continued to play an important role in the parish, perhaps also influencing their husbands to gradually adopt views more opposed to slavery.[5]

Rebecca and Jesse also established a family around them in Mount Vernon, which stood in place of the children they never had together. They continued their close relationship with Rebecca's children by her first marriage to John Francis Hamtramck and even with the children of her first husband's earlier marriage, and also with the children of Jesse's older brother, Richard, who had died the year before Jesse and Rebecca's move to Ohio. In 1837 Thomas and Rebecca built a tasteful house at 301 East Gambier Street, which still stands on a street of historic houses in Mount Vernon.[6] Like many of its neighbors, it is Greek Revival in design, built of brick with white shutters and trim. There are three bays of windows across the front in the main section with a handsome portico under the left-hand bay, supported by Corinthian columns and topped by an impressive entablature. Jesse and Rebecca created an ordered but unostentatious world in their East Gambier Street house. His carriage house was well equipped with a large carriage and a more sporty two-wheeled Rockaway carriage. They owned a few simple pieces of silver and some other small luxuries, but the two of them appear to have lived well within their means.[7]

From the time he moved to Ohio, Jesse Thomas threw in his lot with the Whig Party, as did Henry Curtis and others of his friends. Perhaps he felt freed for the first time from the necessity of having to conform his views to those of his political supporters, and his natural conservatism won out over whatever proslavery instincts he may have had left. Living in Ohio, a state distinctly less proslavery than Illinois, Jesse's views on slavery and on the Missouri Compromise began to shift as well, in ways that mirrored changing national thinking about the compromise. Thomas's shift was not that unusual; William Henry Harrison, his former colleague and adversary and future political friend, had already gone through a similar change.[8]

After a time when both men appeared to be in decline, Harrison reemerged on the national stage with Thomas as an ally. Mount Vernon was in a part of Ohio with strong loyalties to Henry Clay, and, following Harrison's close loss in 1836, Jesse Thomas helped convince that part of Ohio to support Harrison for the presidency in 1840. In the summer of 1838, Thomas probably had a hand in a convention of Ohio Whigs who presented Harrison as their first choice for the presidency and also in organizing a Young Men's Whig Convention in Mount Vernon that nominated Harrison for president without reservations, both moves that infuriated Clay.[9] Harrison's death after his first month in office must have shaken Thomas as much as Crawford's collapse had eighteen years before. Thomas also stayed in close touch with John McLean, one of the political movers and shakers in Washington, who had served as commissioner of the General Land Office, as postmaster general, and eventually on the Supreme Court. McLean had very pronounced antislavery views, and it is clear in their correspondence about slavery, the Wilmot Proviso, and the possible cession of territory from Mexico following the Mexican-American War that McLean considered Thomas to be a sympathetic ally who believed as he did.[10] It must have been deeply troubling to Thomas to realize that all the issues underlying the Missouri Compromise were once again coming to a boil.

Jesse Thomas's views on slavery were clearly affected by his involvement in St. Paul's Church. In the 1840s he increased his involvement in the church, with his interest now extending beyond the business of the parish to include issues of belief. In 1841 a new minister came to the parish. Rev. Dr. Joseph Muenscher had been a professor of Hebrew, Latin, and sacred literature at the seminary in Gambier for eight years before coming to St. Paul's and continued to teach at the seminary afterward. Jesse Thomas clearly respected his intellect and accomplishments, for it must have been Muenscher who persuaded him to be confirmed in 1842. Slavery was not the only pressing issue for the Episcopal Church in the 1840s, but it is certain that the clergy and most of the laity were opposed to the practice.[11] Muenscher, in particular, brought up in Massachusetts, trained at Brown and Andover Theological Seminary, and called to serve in three New England churches before coming to Ohio, must have been opposed to slavery. It seems inevitable that Jesse Thomas, through his increased involvement in the church and his friendship with Muenscher, would have further tilted his views against slavery. Rebecca may well have been applying gentle pressure in that direction for years, and it would have been satisfying to Jesse that this change in his personal views occurred at a time when the Missouri Compromise itself was coming to be seen as a mainstay of the antislavery movement.

Thomas likely adopted mildly antislavery views as a result of his natural pragmatism and his experience in the crucible of the Missouri controversy. This shift would be consistent with the idea that slavery had always been a subject of secondary interest to him and one that he could deal with in a much more unemotional and clinical way than could abolitionists or slave-owning Southerners. But the most important factor in changing the way that Thomas felt about slavery may well have been the pace of his life in Mount Vernon. Perhaps he allowed himself, for the first time, to think as a man and not as a politician. In his early adulthood, his political vocation had consumed him so completely he had had little time or space for contemplation. In Mount Vernon, life slowed, and he was able to think about himself as a father figure for his extended family. He had time to contemplate his brother's death and his own failures, and he had the necessary calm to think about life in spiritual terms. Whatever the reasons for the shifts, Jesse Thomas became in Mount Vernon a man quite different from the man who had brokered the Missouri Compromise.

Jesse remained deeply involved with all his brother's children, but a principal focus of his later years was the careers of the two nephews who had moved east from Missouri, one named Jesse Burgess Thomas after him and the other, eleven years younger, named Richard S. Thomas Jr. Both were able and energetic and established themselves in successful careers in Illinois under the watchful eye of the elder Thomas, sitting by that time as an Olympian statesman in Ohio. For him they became surrogate sons. Both nephews were shaped by their father's financial and political failures and by the example of their uncle's rise and fall. Both must have watched with keen interest as the Loan Office cases in which their father had been involved were, after his death, decided as he had argued they should be, first in Missouri and then in the U.S. Supreme Court. They certainly must have felt it to be a cruel fate that their father had died without knowing the outcomes.

The elder nephew became a distinguished public servant in Illinois, moving from post to post and serving several times as a justice on the state supreme court. He was assisted in his career by his marriage to Adeline Clarissa Smith, daughter of Theophilus Smith, the shrewd and fiery conventionist. The younger Jesse Thomas is best remembered for courageously presiding over the first part of the trial of the men who murdered Mormon founder Joseph Smith. He is also remembered as the butt of Abraham Lincoln's cruel mimicry after the younger Jesse, running for office against Lincoln, made some pointed comments about his adversary. Lincoln's partner and biographer William Herndon recalled the incident:

> Lincoln felt the sting of Thomas' allusions, and, for the first time on the stump or in public, resorted to mimicry for effect. In this . . . he was without a rival. He imitated Thomas in gesture and voice, at times caricaturing his walk and the very motions of his body. Thomas, like everybody else, had some peculiarities of expression and gesture, and these Lincoln succeeded in rendering more prominent than ever. The crowd yelled and cheered as he continued. Encouraged by the demonstration, the ludicrous features of the speaker's performance gave way to intense and scathing ridicule.
>
> Thomas, who was obliged to sit near by and endure the pain of the unique ordeal, was unusually sensitive, and . . . the exhibition affected him deeply.[12]

Herndon went on to say that "the next day Lincoln's performance was the talk of the town, and for years afterwards it was referred to as the 'skinning' of Thomas. . . . I heard him [Lincoln] afterwards say that the recollection of his conduct that evening filled him with the deepest chagrin." Herndon asserted that never again did Lincoln go to such lengths in a public address. Lincoln was a close friend and political ally of Jesse Thomas's younger brother, Richard S. Thomas Jr., who, unlike Jesse, became a Whig. It seems strange that Lincoln would do this to his friend's older brother, but it certainly helps to explain the extent of his remorse.[13]

The younger Richard S. Thomas was a charming and hard-working man who was a promoter of the town of Virginia in Cass County, Illinois, a land speculator in Cass County and Chicago, a railroad builder, and a friend and political colleague of Abraham Lincoln. Like his father and uncle, he was tall, dark, and distinguished and was known and admired for his good character. He became an able lawyer, an eloquent speaker, and a strong, effective writer with a simple, easy style.[14] Richard had a brief political career, serving in the Illinois House and running unsuccessfully for the Illinois Senate in 1852 in an election in which he spent more time helping his friend Richard Yates win election to the U.S House than he did on his own campaign.[15] In the end, Richard's interest in politics proved chiefly to be as a supporter of his political friends and allies, first Yates, who later became governor,[16] and later Lincoln. He was happier, as it turned out, as a real estate developer and businessman than as a politician and, after his involvement with the town of Virginia, moved on to real estate development in Chicago and to running the ultimately unsuccessful Illinois River Railroad.

His uncle had been an important figure in Richard's life, particularly after the death of his own father shortly after his eleventh birthday, and they remained very close over the years. Richard Yates, in writing Richard S. Thomas Jr. about a visit Yates had had with the elder Jesse in Washington, told his friend that his uncle "takes a deep interest in your welfare—in fact he seems wholly absorbed in you."[17] Looking back on the life of the second Richard Thomas, however, his most interesting connection was with the rising Abraham Lincoln. Lincoln was eight years older than Richard, and he took the younger man under his wing. Richard began serving his one term in the Illinois House in 1848 at the same time that Lincoln, returning to Springfield after his one term in the U.S. House, was establishing himself as one of the most powerful lawyers in Illinois. Thereafter, when both men were in private practice, they together rode the old Eighth Circuit, a region comprising fifteen counties centered on the Illinois River valley, and they shared many of the same experiences.

Lincoln had probably never known the original Jesse Burgess Thomas, who had left Illinois shortly before Lincoln arrived, but, possibly in part out of regard for the former senator's nephew, Lincoln put the author of the Missouri Compromise into his personal pantheon. Typical are the remarks he is said to have made in a speech, known as Lincoln's "lost speech," given in Bloomington, Illinois, on May 29, 1856, at the first Republican state convention: "We, here in Illinois, should feel especially proud of the provision of the Missouri Compromise excluding slavery from what is now Kansas; for an Illinois man, Jesse B. Thomas, was its father."[18] Lincoln's speech, a fervent attack on slavery, has never been recovered in the form delivered. It was said, by some, to have been so mesmerizing that all reporters and observers present ceased taking notes after the first few paragraphs, but it is more likely that the speech was intentionally downplayed because it was too advanced in its thinking for the time. Lincoln, however, must have delivered words something like those quoted because they are not the kind of thing that would be fabricated later from whole cloth. With this praise of Jesse Thomas, Lincoln contributed to the transformation of the Missouri Compromise into a bulwark of the Union.

CHAPTER 14

A Rest to the People of God

B y 1851 there were not many people left for Jesse Thomas besides his wife, Rebecca, and his nephews and nieces. The years had been filled with premature deaths: his brother Richard had died in 1828, and Richard's two oldest sons, Claiborne and Jesse, the senator's namesake, had followed in 1838 and 1850. Jesse and Rebecca lived on happily and predictably in Mount Vernon. They remained devoted to each other as they had throughout their marriage and continued so until her death on June 1, 1851, at the age of seventy-five. Rebecca's death was a cruel blow for Thomas, but he had at least the consolation of being surrounded by the families of two nieces in Mount Vernon and the devotion of his nephew Richard S. Thomas Jr., who frequently stopped in transit to or from railroad business in New York to spend time with his sisters and uncle. Jesse also had the day-to-day support of his stepdaughter Rebecca Harrison, who had been devoted to his wife and remained so to him.

However, all was not well with the former senator. He was depressed over his wife's death, and a creeping melancholy was gradually overtaking him. Certainly one of the factors affecting him was the gradual unraveling of the Missouri Compromise. With the passage of years, Thomas had become increasingly proud of the compromise at the same time that it was coming under incessant attack by a phalanx led by Stephen Douglas. When it passed in 1820, the compromise, shaped around his famous 36°30' line, had been promoted, and accepted, as a victory for the South, and Thomas, as a Southern-leaning Northerner, had been proud of it. But as he left the Senate, gave up his slaves and indentured servants, moved to Ohio, and became a Whig and a member of a church opposed to slavery, Thomas's attitude toward the compromise had changed into a truly national one.

At the same time, and in somewhat parallel fashion, the nation was changing its attitude to the compromise. The Missouri Compromise gradually took on a lasting identity, becoming far more fixed in the American historical psyche than was likely contemplated by its authors. Even Stephen Douglas, who would ultimately lead the effort to dismantle it, said in 1849 that it had become "canonized in the hearts of the American people, as a sacred thing, which no ruthless hand would ever be reckless enough to disturb."[1] The compromise had been negotiated in the context of the Louisiana Purchase and finalized at a time when no one knew the exact westward extent of the purchase or of American expansion. There proved to be more hospitable land in the purchase north of the Missouri Compromise line, and less south of it, than anyone imagined in 1820; but this relative advantage was soon offset by the acquisition of further territories from Mexico in the Southwest, which in turn was offset by the acquisition of the Oregon Territory from the British in 1846. Each of these acquisitions had its own dynamic, but all were affected by an awareness of a hypothetical extension of the Missouri Compromise line to the Pacific and a desire to keep lands north and south of the line in balance. California, admitted without slavery in 1850, was the first state to straddle the compromise line and perhaps contributed to undermining the line's importance. A principal reason for the compromise becoming so set in the American consciousness was that, after the bitterness of 1820, no other territories were brought forward for statehood until Arkansas and Michigan were paired sixteen years later as slave and nonslave candidates. This long lapse of time allowed the compromise to take root, and nearly another ten years went by before the first of five more states was admitted in the years after the Mexican-American War.[2]

Suddenly the line that Jefferson had so much feared had turned on its Southern makers and become a protection for the North. Thomas now saw starkly that the geographical dividing line he had helped to establish, and then had grown proud of, was pushing the country ineluctably toward civil war. In the end his pride apparently gave way to despair, or even guilt. The final demise of the Missouri Compromise did not occur until the year after Thomas's death, but the antislavery press had been sounding the warning for years.[3] Perhaps Thomas already sensed Bloody Kansas on the horizon, but in any event he certainly recognized that the world he knew and had helped to shape was falling apart. By identifying himself so strongly with the compromise, Thomas's own psychological well-being became wrapped up with its fate, which had been out of his hands since he left the Senate.

The exact nature and causes of Thomas's depression, and how long the final episode went on, will never be known. The only certainty is that, on May 3, 1853, Thomas, at the age of seventy-eight, committed suicide at his home in Mount Vernon by cutting his throat with a razor. Many sources, reflecting perhaps the sensitivity of the times on the subject of suicide, simply do not mention that he took his own life. Those that do indicate that he was suffering from some form of mental illness. Typical is the *Mount Vernon Democratic Banner*, which reported that it was well known in the community that he had "for several months been laboring under severe affliction of body and mind,— bordering on insanity."[4] From the vantage point of the twenty-first century, the obvious prognosis would be depression, and it seems likely it may have been a life-long affliction, perhaps for his brother Richard as well as for himself and for so many other highly motivated men and women. Certainly the death of his wife and other close family members and the impending demise of the Missouri Compromise would have been contributing factors to this disorder.

Jesse Burgess Thomas was buried next to Rebecca in Mound View Cemetery in Mount Vernon. There is an upright monument for both Jesse and Rebecca and then a very simple headstone for each of them. On the monument is a verse, the first part of which is illegible and the last part is "rest to the people of God." It is apparently the biblical passage from Hebrews 4:9 in the King James translation, "There remaineth therefore a rest to the people of God," which attests both to the hard work that went before and a very real yearning for a long-promised rest.

Epilogue

J esse Burgess Thomas was and remains an enigmatic figure. He was a Southern-leaning senator from a state that the vote counters considered a Northern state. Although he voted with the Southerners throughout the Missouri controversy, we know very little about his real views on slavery. Thomas himself, through happenstance or calculation, shielded his views from his contemporaries and thus from us. The delicate balancing between proslavery and antislavery in Thomas's life began with the geography of his birth. He was born either in the town of Shepherdstown—then in Virginia but later in West Virginia when that state joined the Union—or a few miles away in his mother's family's house near Frederick, Maryland, in the part of that border state least hospitable to slavery. Although he had patrician forebears endowed with the proslavery outlook of tidewater Maryland and Virginia, the locale of his childhood suggests a pragmatic antislavery outlook.

All politicians are by nature protean, but Thomas from the first was an extreme of the type. When he was first elected a representative from Dearborn County in the Indiana territorial legislature, his own constituents were largely antislavery, but those in power in the Indiana Territory, especially William Henry Harrison, were proslavery. Thomas successfully navigated this initial political challenge and was elected as the first Speaker of the territorial House. As the presiding officer in that body, Thomas had to vote only in the event of ties, of which there were few, so he could avoid displeasing both his antislavery constituents and his proslavery patron. As it became impossible to remain ambivalent on slavery in Indiana, Thomas managed to be elected territorial delegate by an unlikely mélange of antislavery advocates from southeastern Indiana and proslavery separatists from

Illinois. Appointed one of the original territorial judges in Illinois, Thomas was once again in a role where he could be impartial, and, in 1818, in his last role before coming to the U.S. Senate, he presided at the Illinois constitutional convention, where he could again cloak his views but achieve his objectives through his able lieutenant Elias Kent Kane. As a senator, he also largely kept his views to himself. During the Missouri debate in Congress, Thomas continued to hold his cards very close to his vest. He rarely spoke and was once again a conundrum, and as he pressed for a compromise he likely convinced his listeners on both sides of the issue that he was on their side. Thus, when the final tense negotiations occurred, it was Thomas who drafted the compromise language, was elected chairman of the Senate managers of the conference committee, and ultimately drafted the final report in his own hand. Fittingly, despite his proslavery votes over the years, Thomas died a Whig and almost certainly an opponent of slavery.

Thomas never needed the limelight. He was working closely with William Harris Crawford in an effort to hold the country together and to put the slavery problem behind them so that they could get on with issues they viewed as more important, such as public lands policy and the faltering economy. Looking back over what Jesse Thomas achieved, the feat of producing the Missouri Compromise was arguably the first test of resolve for the second generation of American political leadership, a generation that still remembered and revered what the Founding Fathers had wrought. As Thomas Hart Benton put it, it was a time when "the difference between a UNION and a LEAGUE [was] better understood . . . when so many of the fathers of the new government were still alive."[1] It is difficult to overestimate the importance of the 36°30′ line in permitting the unfolding of America's manifest destiny over the four decades after its passage. It created a momentum to maintain a balance in the number of states north and south of the line and thus had a critical impact on both the question of Texas annexation and the settlement of the Oregon question. It provided an acceptable mechanism for Northerners who did not like slavery but supported the idea of westward expansion. Even the Kansas-Nebraska Act, passed the year after Thomas's death and formally repealing his Missouri Compromise, did not spell the total demise of Thomas's concept of drawing a dividing line between slave and free. On the eve of the Civil War, John J. Crittenden, a senator from the border state of Kentucky, tried to revive the 36°30′ line in a last-ditch effort to save the Union and prevent the war. Crittenden failed, but Jesse Thomas's idea of a dividing line had played its part in history. It was now time to decide whether the Union would cease to be divided.

NOTES

SOURCES

SELECTED BIBLIOGRAPHY

INDEX

NOTES

Introduction

1. For original language of Jefferson's antislavery proviso and its subsequent amendment, see *Journals of the Continental Congress, 1774–1789* (Washington D.C.: Government Printing Office, 1904–37), 26:277. See also http://www.loc. gov/collections/thomas-jefferson-papers/articles-and-essays/the-thomas-jeffer-son-papers-timeline-1743-to-1827/1784-to-1789/ (accessed May 27, 2015).

1. From Maryland to Kentucky: First Steps toward Egypt

1. For the commercial interests of Thomas Thomas, see the Thomas Thomas Notebook, 10–11. For the bail incident, see June 11, 1772, entry, 41.

2. The spelling of Richard Simms Thomas's middle name was later changed to "Symmes." Some sources give Jesse Burgess Thomas's (hereafter JBT) birth year as 1777, but his gravestone gives it as 1775, which is presumed here to be correct. None of the sources gives a month or day for his birth, and even his place of birth is given differently in different sources, either as Shepherdstown, in what was then Virginia, or Hagerstown, Maryland. *A Register of Officers and Agents, Civil, Military and Naval, in the Service of the United States, on the Thirtieth Day of September, 1816* (Washington, D.C.: Department of State, printed by Jonathan Eliot, 1816), 16, https://www.google.books.com (accessed May 27, 2015), is one of the few authoritative sources including his place of birth, and it is there given as Virginia. The 1850 U.S. Census for Knox County, Ohio, also gives Virginia as his birthplace. Richard and Jesse may both have been born at Sabina's family's home, which was in the Antietam Valley in the general vicinity of both Shepherdstown and Hagerstown.

3. Snyder, "Forgotten Statesmen of Illinois," 514.

4. JBT to Ninian Edwards, March 23, 1812, JBT Papers.

5. Original authority for JBT's first marriage appears to be Morrison, "Biographical Sketch," but it also appears in Snyder's biographical sketch of JBT in "Forgotten Statesmen of Illinois," 514, which was presumably checked and approved by JBT's nephews who were friends of the author; none of them

noted his wife's name. As to the description of Washington, Kentucky, see http://washingtonky.com (accessed May 27, 2015).

6. As to the effect of his wife's death, see Snyder, *Adam W. Snyder*, 10. For JBT's departure to the Indiana Territory, see Morrison, "Biographical Sketch." The testimonial was dated November 25, 1803, and is in the JBT Papers.

2. *The Northwest Territory: Organizing an Expanding Nation*

1. Paul W. Gates, *History of Public Land Law Development* (Washington, D.C.: U.S. Government Printing Office, 1968), 50; Treat, *National Land System*, 325–40.

2. As to the antislavery provision, see "Plan of Government for the Western Territory, Revised Report of the Committee," March 22, 1784, *Papers of Thomas Jefferson*, ed. Julian P. Boyd et al., 45 vols. (Princeton: Princeton University Press, 1950–), 6:608–9, very nearly the same language as in the report of March 1, reprinted a few pages before. As to the vote, see letter from Jefferson to James Madison, April 25, 1784, in ibid., 7:118. Under the Articles of Confederation, each state had a single vote, determined by a majority of its delegates present. As to detractors, see Finkelman, "Slavery and the Northwest Ordinance," and in Jefferson's defense, see Merkel, "Jefferson's Failed Anti-slavery Proviso."

3. The Northwest Ordinance is more formally "An Ordinance for the Government of the Territory of the United States North-West of the River Ohio," adopted July 13, 1787, by the Second Continental Congress (National Archives Microfilm Publication M332, roll 9), Miscellaneous Papers of the Continental Congress, 1774–1789, Records of the Continental and Confederation Congresses and the Constitutional Convention, 1774–1789, RG 360, National Archives. Quotations from the Northwest Ordinance throughout the book are from this source. See also http://ourdocuments.gov (accessed May 27, 2015).

4. Virginia's Deed of Cession was accepted by Congress on March 1, 1784. The fourteen states proposed to be formed by Jefferson in 1784, which would have included southern ceded lands as well as northern, would, like Monroe's plan, have preserved rough balance between North and South; but it is important to note that these debates occurred while the United States was operating under the Articles of Confederation, which gave each state a single vote, so Jefferson's proposal would have given the western states one more vote than the original thirteen states combined. See also the discussion in Jay A. Barrett, *Evolution of the Ordinance of 1787* (New York: G. P. Putnam's Sons, 1891), 17–20.

5. Aldrich, "Slavery or Involuntary Servitude in Illinois," 117.

6. The three-fifths rule (original U.S. Constitution, Article I, §2, clause 3) remained in effect until the passage of the Thirteenth Amendment following the Civil War. As to the composition of the House in 1820, there were sixty representatives from Alabama, Georgia, Louisiana, Mississippi, North Carolina, South Carolina, Tennessee, and Virginia; twenty-one from Delaware, Kentucky, and Maryland; and eight from Illinois, Indiana, and Ohio. Thus, even if the South could ally with the three border states and the three new states of the Old Northwest, it would still be outweighed by the ninety-eight representatives from Connecticut, Massachusetts, New Hampshire, New Jersey, New York, Pennsylvania, Rhode Island, and Vermont. The view that the Missouri controversy was primarily a struggle for political power is best made by Leonard Richards in *The Slave Power: The Free North and Southern Domination, 1780–1860.*

7. Article I, §9, clause 1.

8. With the first division of the Northwest Territory, which resulted in the new state of Ohio and the new Indiana Territory, appointment by the Congress evolved into appointment by the president with the advice and consent of the Senate; see §3, An Act to Divide the Territory of the United States Northwest of the Ohio, into Two Separate Governments, 2 Stat. (1800).

3. In the Shadow of Slavery

1. Richard C. Knopf, ed., *Transcription of the Executive Journal of the Northwest Territory*, http://ww2.ohiohistory.org/onlinedoc/northwest/exjournal/, 551 for first appointment, 555 for second.

2. Snyder, sketch of JBT in "Forgotten Statesmen of Illinois"; Morrison, "Biographical Sketch"; Dunn, *Indiana: A Redemption from Slavery*, 327; Reynolds, *Pioneer History of Illinois*, 402; T. Ford, *History of Illinois*, 24.

3. Although the Northwest Ordinance had provided for the division of territories, it appears the Continental Congress had not considered that the division of a territory already in the second stage of territorial government would result in the creation of a new territory that would fall back into the first stage of territorial government. In recognition that frontiersmen were understandably discouraged and disappointed by losing newly won rights to representative government, Congress made the hurdles for moving to the second stage of territorial government progressively easier with each new territory it formed and eventually, beginning with Missouri Territory, eliminated the first stage of territorial government altogether. This evolution, interestingly, brought the

process of territorial government back into line with Jefferson's original aspirations in his Ordinance of 1784.

4. For Michael Jones's purchase of property, see Ellen Berry and David Berry, comps., *Early Ohio Settlers, Purchasers of Land in Southwestern Ohio, 1800–1840* (Baltimore: Genealogical Publishing Co., 1986). For James Hamilton, see *History of Dearborn and Ohio Counties*, 5150 For the founders of Lawrenceburg, see *History of Lawrenceburg*, unnumbered pages. For Vance's failure, see Dunn, *Indiana: A Redemption from Slavery*, 326.

5. See Paul Finkelman, "Evading the Ordinance," *Journal of the Early Republic* 9, no. 1 (1989): 21–51, for a good discussion of the petitions to suspend or revoke Article VI and for the growth of the indenture system in the Indiana and Illinois Territories. Petition is reproduced in Jacob P. Dunn, *Slavery Petitions and Papers*, Indiana Historical Society Publications (Indianapolis: Bowen-Merrill, 1894), 20–21.

6. "A Law Concerning Servants," September 22, 1803, in Philbrick, *Laws of Indiana Territory, 1801–1809*, 42.

7. Second paragraph of the U.S. Constitution, Article IV, §3; Louisiana Purchase Treaty, April 30, 1803, General Records of the U.S. Government, RG 11, National Archives.

8. As to the power to set rules, see Gary Lawson and Guy Seidman, "The First 'Incorporation' Debate," in Sanford Levinson and Batholomew Sparrow, eds., *The Louisiana Purchase and American Expansion, 1803–1898* (Lanham, MD: Rowman & Littlefield, 2005).

9. Roger G. Kennedy, *Mr. Jefferson's Lost Cause: Land, Farmers, Slavery, and the Louisiana Purchase* (New York: Oxford University Press, 2003).

10. Joseph J. Ellis, *American Creation* (New York: Alfred A. Knopf, 2007), 235.

11. For the requirements to move to the second stage, see §4, An Act to Divide the Territory of the United States Northwest of the Ohio, into Two Separate Governments, 2 Stat. (1800). For the petition, see Dunn, *Indiana: A Redemption from Slavery*, 320–24; and "Address to the Freeholders from the Citizens of Knox County," *Indiana Gazette* (Vincennes), August 28, 1804.

12. Reifel, *History of Franklin County*, 193.

13. For Harrison's preference for planter elites, presumably shared by JBT in the first part of his career, see Owens, *Mr. Jefferson's Hammer*, 145.

14. Morrison, "Biographical Sketch"; see also Elise Selby Billmyer and Lucy Mary Kellogg, comps., "Ancestry and Descendants of John Francis Hamtramck, First American Commandant at Detroit Michigan," *Detroit Society for Genealogical Research Magazine* 26, no. 1 (1962): 5–12.

15. Robert Munro to Harrison, June 14, 1805, in Esarey, *Messages and Letters*, 136.

16. For JBT's inclination against slavery, see Dunn, *Indiana: A Redemption from Slavery*, 367. For JBT's forcing rivals to take positions, see ibid., 369.

17. Harrison to Thomas, March 21, 1807, JBT Papers. For JBT's signature on laws, see Philbrick, *Laws of Indiana Territory, 1801–1809*.

18. For the full text of the revised indenture law, see Philbrick, *Laws of Indiana Territory, 1801–1809*, 463–67. In 1799 the New York legislature had passed An Act for the Gradual Abolition of Slavery with only token opposition; it provided for gradual manumission by allowing masters to keep their younger slaves in bondage for their most productive years, to recoup their investment. The law freed all children born to slave women, but only when the males became twenty-eight and the females twenty-five; till then, they would remain the property of the mother's master. Slaves already in servitude before July 4, 1799, remained slaves for life, though they were reclassified as indentured servants. The 1807 Illinois statute was discussed in great detail by Stephen Douglas in a letter to Edward Coles, February 18, 1854, in Johannsen, *Letters of Stephen A. Douglas*, 290.

19. For the House petition, see "Petition from Indiana, Slavery," in Esarey, *Messages and Letters*, 253–55. Under Article I, §9, clause 1 of the original U.S. Constitution, 1808 was the first time Congress was permitted to regulate the slave trade.

20. Thornbrough, *Correspondence of John Badollet and Albert Gallatin*, 93n5.

21. "General Washington" in this case was Johnston's given name. Johnston's report is set out in Thornbrough and Riker, *Journals of the General Assembly*, 23–28; and Dunn's characterization of it is in his *Indiana: A Redemption from Slavery*, 370–76.

22. *History of Warren County*, 297, indicates he was elected in three successive General Assemblies, but on 424–25, he is listed only in the fifth and sixth General Assemblies; the latter appears to be correct.

23. The vote was held on December 11, 1809. Thomas was edged out by Alexander Campbell, who received thirty-eight votes to Thomas's twenty-nine; three other candidates received one vote each.

24. For the recording of the plat, see Virgil E. Davis, *Through Our Years: The Story of Brookville, 1808–1958* (Brookville, Ind.: Whitewater Publications, 1958), 10. Burgess Street was later changed to Main Street, which it has remained since.

4. The Next Slippery Rung on the Political Ladder

1. For Parke's role, see April 11, 1808, *Annals of Congress*, House, 10th Cong., 1st sess., 2068. For Harrison's resistance, see Owens, *Mr. Jefferson's Hammer*, 188.

2. The presence of this Michael Jones along with the one who was Jesse Thomas's half brother is a coincidence that has caused some confusion; see Relf, "Two Michael Joneses." For Reynolds's quote, see his *Pioneer History of Illinois*, 352. Michael Jones of Kaskaskia is said to have been a relative of Nathaniel Pope, the first territorial secretary (see, e.g., Alvord, *Illinois Country*, 428), but the connection, if any, is distant.

3. Thornbrough and Riker, *Journals of the General Assembly*, 248n64.

4. Dunn, *Indiana: A Redemption from Slavery*, 355.

5. John Rice Jones to Michael Jones, JBT's half brother, November 1822, copy in JBT Papers, dated June 4, 1823. See also the *Vincennes Western Sun*, November 5, 1808.

6. Thornbrough and Riker, *Journals of the General Assembly*, 248–49.

7. Arthur Clinton Boggess, *The Settlement of Illinois: 1778–1830* (Chicago: Chicago Historical Society, 1908), 195.

8. Christopher Lloyd, *The Navy and the Slave Trade* (London: Longmans, Green and Co., 1949), appendix A.

9. U.S. Bureau of the Census, John Cummings, and Joseph Adna Hill, *Negro Population 1790–1915* (Washington, D.C.: U.S. Government Printing Office, 1918), 25.

10. Dunn, *Indiana: A Redemption from Slavery*, 358.

5. Into the Fray in Illinois

1. See the excellent discussion of this controversy in chapter 8 of Treat, *National Land System*.

2. For Varnum presenting the certificate, see *Annals of Congress*, House, 10th Cong., 2nd sess., 484. For Chambers's submittal letter, see ibid., 501. As to the seating of JBT, see ibid., 611.

3. Though there is no record of a roll-call vote on the measure in the Senate.

4. Davis, *Frontier Illinois*, 120–21.

5. For "property and honor," see Alvord, *Illinois Country*, 424. Rice Jones's letter, not formally addressed or dated but certainly to JBT, has notation on the cover indicating it was written in 1808, JBT Papers.

6. For comments on Jones and Bond, see Alvord, *Illinois Country*, 428. The quote from Dunlap's account after the duel is in the *Vincennes Western Sun*, August 27, 1808.

7. For the duel, see the *Vincennes Western Sun*, August 27 and September 10, 1808; Reynolds, *Pioneer History of Illinois*, 173; and Rees, "Bond-Jones Duel." For John Rice Jones's letter, see Edward G. Mason, ed., *Early Chicago and Illinois* (Chicago: Fergus, 1890), 276–77.

8. Morrison letter written within days of the event but evidently taken later to Kentucky and posted there December 25, 1808, JBT Papers. For issuance of demand, see Carter, *Territorial Papers*, 16:33.

9. For action on December 13, see *House Journal*, 10th Congress, 2nd sess., 385. For action on December 16, see ibid., 393.

10. *Annals of Congress*, House, 10th Congress, 2nd sess., 971–73.

11. Thomas's initiative was Bill H.R. 25, 10th Cong., 2nd sess. For the Indiana resolution, dated October 19, 1808, see Thornbrough and Riker, *Journals of the General Assembly of Indiana Territory*, 224.

12. For burning in effigy, see Rice Jones to JBT, November 7, 1808, JBT Papers. For his nomination as judge, see March 6, 1809, *Senate Exec. Journal*, 11th Cong., special session, 119, confirmed the next day.

13. JBT to Madison, February 11, 1809, JBT Papers. Boyle preferred to return to Kentucky, where he was appointed on April 4, 1809, to fill the vacancy on the Kentucky High Court of Appeals created by Ninian Edwards's resignation; the next year he became chief justice.

14. As to his father, see Ernest Macpherson, William Wirt, and Edward MacPherson, "Benjamin Edwards: The Father of Ninian Edwards, Governor of Illinois Territory," *Journal of the Illinois State Historical Society* 9, no. 3 (1916): 279–83; as to Edwards himself, see Pease, *Frontier State*, 92–93.

15. Edwards, *Edwards Papers*, 17–27.

16. See Pat Boyd Rumore, *From Power to Service: The Story of Lawyers in Alabama* (Montgomery: History and Archives Committee of the Alabama State Bar and the Alabama Bench and Bar Historical Society, 2010), chap. 1, identifying Obadiah Jones as "an intimate friend of Georgia's senator William Crawford" and a fellow member of the Broad River Georgians, who had immigrated together to Georgia from the Virginia piedmont.

6. Gathering Forces

1. Description given as of 1810 in an unidentified source quoted in Robert Freke Gould, *Gould's History of Freemasonry throughout the World*, revised by Dudley Wright (New York: Charles Scribner's Sons, 1936), 5:177.

2. For the location of the home, see Snyder, "Forgotten Statesmen of Illinois," 515. William Carr Lane, second cousin to Elvira and Harvey and also a doctor, was elected St. Louis's first mayor in 1823 and was reelected seven times.

3. Alvord, "Laws of the Territory of Illinois," 1. Indiana laws were supplemented mainly by Southern laws, reflecting the background of the governor and judges; Kentucky supplied five laws, Georgia three, Virginia two, and South Carolina and Pennsylvania one each. J. Davis, *Frontier Illinois*, 123.

4. *Combined History of Randolph, Monroe and Perry Counties, Illinois*, 105.

5. Alvord, *Illinois Country*, 427.

6. *American State Papers: Public Lands*, 2:104.

7. From governor and judges to the Secretary of State, February 2, 1810, written in JBT's hand, in Carter, *Territorial Papers*, 16:71–72.

8. Miller, *New States and Territories*, 81.

9. Foley, *History of Missouri*, 162–66.

10. Secretary of State of Missouri website, http://www.sos.mo.gov/archives/history/historicallistings/molegt.asp.

11. William R. Eddleman, *Abstracts of Cape Girardeau Deeds*, Deed Book D (Cape Girardeau: Cape Girardeau Co., 1998–2002), 9, 14.

12. For circuit court salaries, see Foley, *History of Missouri*, 194. For the description of the Southern Circuit, see Charless, *Charless' Missouri and Illinois Magazine Almanac for 1818*, unnumbered page, and Houck, *History of Missouri*, 3:9. After Missouri statehood, this circuit was further subdivided to include only the southwestern part of Missouri and came to be called the Fourth Judicial Circuit.

13. Houck, *History of Missouri*, 3:10n5.

14. Jacob W. Myers, "History of the Gallatin Salines," *Journal of the Illinois State Historical Society* 14 (1922): 3–4, 137–48; see also "Lucille Lawler Memoir," Oral History Office, Sangamon State University, Springfield, Illinois, 1979, 8–24.

15. Edwards, *Edwards Papers*, 95; Norton, *Illinois Census Returns*, xxx.

16. For the description of Brookville, see Miller, *New States and Territories*, 63, apparently the source drawn upon later by Reifel, *History of Franklin County*, 195. For the marriage, see Chris McHenry, *Marriages of Early Dearborn County, Indiana, Residents Not Found in Marriage Records* (Lawrenceburg, Ind.: self-published, 1983 [Indiana State Library, General 977.201 D 285 mm]).

17. JBT Papers.

18. Gallatin County Illinois, Land Records G–L, for Michael Jones, http://genealogytrails.com/ill/gallatin/index.html.

19. Buckskins were used as a form of currency on the frontier, hence the term "buck" in its current usage. For the original committee, see J. H. Burnham, "An Early Illinois Newspaper: Extracts from Its Files," *Transactions of the Illinois State Historical Society for the Year 1903*, Illinois State Historical Library (Springfield: Phillips Brothers, 1904), 182.

20. Simeone, *Democracy and Slavery in Frontier Illinois*, 109.

21. Undated petition in Edwards, *Edwards Papers*, 75.

22. J. Davis, *Frontier Illinois*, 141–42.

23. JBT Papers.

24. JBT to Edwards, February 21, 1812, ibid.

25. Pease, *Frontier State*, 94.

7. The Political Divide

1. Norton, *Illinois Census Returns*, xxx, xxxii.

2. For ownership by individuals, see Database of Illinois Servitude and Emancipation Records, http://search.ancestry.com/search/db.aspx?dbid=3749, maintained by the Illinois secretary of state and state archivist. The 1820 Illinois census confirms the makeup of JBT's household, including five "free people of Colour," which presumably referred to slaves indentured under the Black Code. For his stepdaughters' claim, see JBT to Robert Forsyth, November 12, 1810, JBT Papers. For conveyance from Thomas Ragland, see Ragland to JBT, June 21, 1814, JBT Papers. Only three of the slaveholders tabulated in the 1820 Illinois census owned more slaves than Edwards; Edwards also owned twenty-two slaves in Missouri at the time he voted in the Senate for the admission of Missouri as a slave state; see *Edwardsville Spectator*, July 4, 1820.

3. James, *Territorial Records of Illinois*, 8.

4. This and subsequent letters in the exchange are from JBT Papers; material in brackets is not decipherable.

5. "An Act to Suppress Dueling. Adopted from the Virginia Code," April 7, 1810, in Philbrick, *Laws of Illinois Territory, 1809–1818*, 36–38.

6. William Sprigg had been appointed a territorial judge in 1809 in place of Alexander Stuart.

7. Quoted in Buck, *Illinois in 1818*, 199, without citation of source.

8. Congressional action, Act of March 3, 1815, ch. 98, 3 Stat. 237; open letter, *Kaskaskia Western Intelligencer*, June 19, 1816.

8. Illinois Statehood

1. JBT to James Monroe, November 8, 1814, recommending that the young Hamtramck be made an officer, in Letters Received by Adjutant General, RG 94, National Archives; JBT to Monroe, February 27, 1815, recommending Hamtramck's appointment, ibid.; see also Register of the Officers and Cadets of the U.S. Military Academy, June 1818, showing he enrolled at West Point September 26, 1815, http://medamana.org:7086/wheelerg/pierre_thomas/wp_1818.pdf (accessed June 10, 2015). Hamtramck was appointed from the Indiana Territory, indicating that Harrison, recently resigned as governor but still living in Vincennes, likely sponsored him. The 1818 Illinois census for St. Clair County, which does not give gender or age except for white males over twenty-one, shows three white persons in the household in addition to JBT, who was the only white male over twenty-one, leading to the surmise that the three others were his wife, Rebecca; her son Alexander; and her daughter Rebecca. The 1820 Illinois census for Madison County, taken just two years later, includes two free white males over twenty-one years of age and three other white inhabitants; Alexander would still have been under twenty-one, so perhaps John Francis Hamtramck Jr. was home at the time of the census or was counted regardless. Jesse and his family do not appear in the 1820 federal census, perhaps because they were in Washington at the time of the enumeration.

2. Snyder, *Adam W. Snyder*, has JBT establishing a business in Cahokia in 1817, having moved there by that time, 13–14. It appears from the *Database of Illinois Servitude and Emancipation Records* that JBT also maintained a residence in Randolph County at least through the month of September 1817 but was in St. Clair County by the time the census was taken in 1818. Morrison, "Biographical Sketch," confirms the pattern of movement from Kaskaskia to Cahokia and then to Edwardsville.

3. Snyder, *Adam W. Snyder*, 16; Foley, *History of Missouri*, 167.

4. *Kaskaskia Western Intelligencer*, November 27, 1817.

5. *Journal of the Constitutional Convention*, reproduced in full in Carpenter, "Illinois Constitutional Convention," 357.

6. Ibid., 353–54.

7. Snyder, "Forgotten Statesmen of Illinois," 522.

8. Carpenter, "Illinois Constitutional Convention," 356.

9. See, for example, the speech of Representative Robert Reid, in Missouri debate, February 1, 1820, *Annals of Congress*, House, 16th Cong., 1st sess., 1027–30.

10. Louisiana Purchase Treaty, April 30, 1803, General Records of the U.S. Government, RG 11, National Archives; electronic version: www.ourdocuments.gov/doc.php?doc=18 (accessed June 10, 2015).

11. Indiana Constitution, Article XI, §7; Article VIII, §1.

12. Ohio Constitution, Article VIII, §2.

13. Ibid., Article VII, §5.

14. Simeone, *Democracy and Slavery in Frontier Illinois*, 25.

15. This hypothesis is further bolstered by Kane's unsuccessful effort in the constitutional convention to have Kaskaskia designated as state capital for only five years.

9. First Months in the U.S. Senate

1. Howard, *Illinois*, 117.

2. *Shawneetown Illinois Emigrant*, October 17, 1818. Other sources have the election going to a fourth ballot.

3. March 30, 1819, *Laws of the State of Illinois, 1819–*, published by authority of the General Assembly of the State of Illinois, 354.

4. *Annals of Congress*, House, 15th Cong., 2nd sess., 290–91.

5. All in this paragraph, ibid., 296.

6. Ibid., 297–98.

7. Ibid., 306–7.

8. November 23, 1818, ibid., 311.

9. U.S. Constitution, Article I, §3.

10. *Annals of Congress*, Senate, 15th Cong., 2nd sess., 38. The previously popular Edwards, up for reelection a few months later at the end of the Fifteenth Congress, was elected over a single opponent, Michael Jones of Kaskaskia, by the narrow margin of 23 to 19 (Buck, *Illinois in 1818*, 303–4).

11. The facts are not in dispute; but for a defense of Jackson's motives see Robert Remini, *Andrew Jackson and His Indian Wars* (New York: Viking Adult, 2001), and for a more critical view see Andrew Burstein, *The Passions of Andrew Jackson* (New York: Alfred A. Knopf, 2003).

12. *Annals of Congress*, Senate, 15th Cong., 2nd sess., 255–66.

13. To Andrew Jackson Donelson, January 31, 1819, in Bassett, *Correspondence of Andrew Jackson*, 2:408.

14. For Cook's quarters, see the *Kaskaskia Western Intelligencer*, April 20, 1816; and Burnham, "An Early Illinois Newspaper," 182. The name of this important newspaper was changed on May 27, 1818, to the *Illinois Intelligencer*; it was subsequently published in Vandalia and then in Edwardsville.

15. Ford, *History of Illinois*, 51.

16. Foley, *History of Missouri*, 114.

17. See Merton L. Dillon, *Slavery Attacked: Southern Slaves and Their Allies, 1619–1865* (Baton Rouge: Louisiana State University Press, 1991), 112–29, for a nuanced account of the roles of black people, abolitionists, and Southerners as pressure increased on the institution of slavery.

18. Alabama was admitted eleven days after Illinois, bringing the total to twenty-two states. A rough tally, using abbreviations, shows 115 representatives from generally antislavery states (Conn., Ind., Mich., Mass., N.H., N.J., N.Y., Ohio, R.I., Vt.) and 90 representatives from generally proslavery states (Ala., Del., Ga., Ill., Ky., La., Md., Miss., N.C., S.C., Tenn., Va.).

19. Under the direction of President Monroe, Congress approved a joint resolution March 27, 1818, directing the publication of the *Journal and Proceedings of the Constitutional Convention*, including the *Secret Journals of the Acts and Proceedings* and the *Foreign Correspondence of the Congress of the United States. Journals of the Continental Congress, 1774-1789*, ed. Worthington C. Ford (Washington, D.C., 1904–37), http://memory.loc.gov/ammem/amlaw/lwjc.html (accessed June 13, 2015). Debate at *Annals of Congress*, House, 16th Cong., 1st sess., 1051–64.

20. *Annals of Congress*, Senate, 16th Cong., 1st sess., 126.

21. For formation of the committee, see ibid., House, 15th Cong., 1st sess., 1391. For the action by Clay, see ibid., 1672.

22. *House Journal*, 15th Cong., 1st sess., 421.

23. For the vote to block admission, see *Annals of Congress*, House, 15th Cong., 2nd sess., 311. For statehood petition, see ibid., 418.

24. Ibid., 1166, for motion and subsequent debate.

25. January 12, 1819, ibid., Senate, 15th Cong., 2nd sess., 121.

26. *St. Louis Enquirer*, May 19, 1819.

27. *Annals of Congress*, House, 15th Cong., 2nd sess., 1178.

28. Although other sources suggest that the Mason-Dixon Line was not used as a geographical dividing line for slavery until later (see Mason, *Slavery and Politics in the Early American Republic*, 187), perhaps the first reference to that line in that context was in the famous antislavery report of General Washington Johnston to the Indiana territorial House.

29. March 2, 1820, *Annals of Congress*, House, 16th Cong., 1st sess., 1584.

30. For the vote on the Tallmadge amendment, see ibid., 15th Cong., 2nd sess., 1193. For Scott's threat, see ibid., 1201.

31. Ibid., 1204.

32. Ibid., 1214–16.

33. Ibid., 1222.

34. Ibid., 1223–24.

35. Ibid., 1228, 1235.

36. Crawford also had close, if not intimate, relationships with a number of the more constructive restrictionists in the Missouri controversy, including James Tallmadge and John W. Taylor. For example, Tallmadge wrote Crawford later that same year requesting him to intercede with President Monroe to secure a federal judgeship for Taylor. Crawford to Tallmadge, Washington, July 12, 1819, Taylor Papers. The loss of Crawford's papers to fire is one of the great disappointments to scholars of this period.

37. See debate over the sacrosanct nature of the Compromise between Stephen Douglas and William Seward on March 3, 1854, in *Congressional Globe,* 33rd Cong., 1st sess., appendix, 328.

38. *Annals of Congress,* House, 16th Cong., 1st sess., 1582.

39. Ibid., 15th Cong., 2nd sess., 1235–36.

40. Ibid., 1236.

41. Ibid., 1274.

42. Ibid., 1278.

43. For Taylor's proposal, see ibid., 1280. Thomas Hart Benton also recognized the geographical anomaly of two existing slave states north of the proposed line; see his *Thirty Years' View,* 5.

44. Article I of the Louisiana Purchase Treaty of 1803, http://www.ourdocuments.gov/doc.php?doc=18&page=transcript.

45. For Livermore's line, see *Annals of Congress,* House, 15th Cong., 2nd sess., 1280. For Harrison's line, see ibid., 1281.

46. Salma Hale to William Plumer, February 21, 1819, Plumer Papers, Library of Congress, as quoted in Moore, *Missouri Controversy, 1819–1821,* 49.

47. For the Missouri enabling bill, see *Annals of Congress,* Senate, 15th Cong., 2nd sess., 251. For the Arkansas enabling bill, see *Senate Journal,* 15th Cong., 2nd sess., 295. For the postponed vote on the Missouri enabling bill, see *Senate Journal,* 15th Cong., 2nd sess., 304.

48. For the Senate informing the House, see *Senate Journal,* 15th Cong., 2nd sess., 324–25. For the House vote, see *Annals of Congress,* House, 15th Cong., 2nd sess., 1433–34.

10. Maneuvering for Position

1. It is telling that the headline announcing the final compromise in Thomas Hart Benton's *St. Louis Enquirer* of March 25, 1820, was "Gratifying News from Washington.—King and Clinton defeated.—"

2. For the Senate admitting Alabama, see *Annals of Congress*, Senate, 16th Cong., 1st sess., 20–21. For the House admitting Alabama, see ibid., 710.

3. For Strong's notice, see ibid., 704. For Scott's bill, see December 9, 1820, ibid., 711.

4. Hale to Taylor, December 28, 1819, as quoted in Moore, *Missouri Controversy*, 86. For Taylor's remarks, see *Annals of Congress*, House, 16th Cong., 1st sess., 732. The *Annals* throughout are written in this peculiar combination of third and first person.

5. For Taylor restating the proposal, see December 28, 1819, *Annals of Congress*, House, 16th Cong., 1st sess., 802. For Taylor's proposal being tabled, see ibid., 732.

6. Ibid., Senate, 24.

7. Ibid., House, 735–36.

8. For Thomas's election to the Committee on Public Lands, see ibid., Senate, 26. For JBT's appointment to the Committee on Roads and Canals, see ibid., 368. For Thomas's committee assignments during his entire Senate career, see David Canon, Garrison Nelson, and Charles Stewart, *Congressional Committees, Historical Standing Committees*, web.mit.edu/~17.251/www/data_page. html (accessed May 31, 2015), which shows he was active as chairman of the Committee on Public Lands in both the 16th and 17th Congresses. For additional supporting evidence that he was chairman in the 16th Congress, see letter from Josiah Meigs of the General Land Office addressed to JBT as chairman of the Committee on Public Lands, February 2, 1821, *Annals of Congress*, Senate, 2nd sess., 330. For a general description of the committee system, see *Guide to Congress*, 5th ed. (Thousand Oaks, Calif.: CQ Press, 2000), 1:96. For discussion of committee elections and procedures, see Robert Byrd, *The Senate, 1789–1989, Addresses on the History of the United States Senate*, bicentennial ed. (Washington D.C.: Government Printing Office, 1981–87), 2:207–219. Senator Byrd also cites John Quincy Adams as source for procedure by which committee chairmen were chosen; see C. Adams, *Memoirs of John Quincy Adams*, 1:482. See also *Daily National Journal* (Washington, D.C.), December 9, 1826, col. A, indicating the practice continued until at least 1826.

9. *Annals of Congress*, House, 16th Cong., 1st sess., 76, 78, 313.

10. Ibid., 749.

11. Ibid., 801–2.

12. Reference to weather conditions here and later during the Missouri controversy are from letters of Taylor to his wife, Jane, in Taylor Papers.

13. *Annals of Congress*, House, 16th Cong., 1st sess., 831.

14. Ibid., 831–34.

15. Foote was elected to the U.S. Senate as an Adams Republican in 1826.

16. *Annals of Congress*, Senate, 16th Cong., 1st sess., 47.

17. Ibid., 54, 74.

18. Ibid., House, 966–67.

19. Hay letter, Series 1, James Monroe Papers, Manuscript Division, Library of Congress; on communication with John Quincy Adams, see entry of January 8, 1820, in C. Adams, *Memoirs of John Quincy Adams*, 4:498–99; on involvement of Biddle, see Ammon, *James Monroe*, 460.

20. January 10, 1820, Monroe Papers, New York Public Library.

21. For the vote against recommitment, see *Annals of Congress*, Senate, 16th Cong., 1st sess., 118. For notice by JBT, see ibid., 119.

22. Ibid., 105.

23. Ibid., 157–58. The first part of the line represents the United States' first attempt to appropriate part of Texas.

24. Ibid., 187–95.

25. Ibid., 232–33.

26. For Pinkney's speech, Friday, January 21, and Monday, January 24, see ibid., 233–36. For Taylor's letter, Washington, January 22, 1820, see the Taylor Papers.

27. For Otis's response, see *Annals of Congress*, Senate, 16th Cong., 1st sess., 236. For Taylor's motion, see ibid., House, 937–38.

28. Ibid., Senate, 243–44.

29. For Scott's motion to commit and Storrs's quote, see ibid., House, 940. For Taylor's motion, see ibid., 947.

30. Henry Meigs, "Speech of Mr. Meigs, of New York, on the Restriction of Slavery in Missouri," delivered in the House of Representatives, January 25, 1820, Miscellaneous Pamphlet Collection, Library of Congress.

31. For Clay's observations, see letter to Adam Beatty, January 22, 1820, in Hopkins and Hargreaves, *Papers of Henry Clay*, 2:766. For the vote against the amendment, see *Annals of Congress*, Senate, 16th Cong., 1st sess., 359.

32. *Annals of Congress*, House, 16th Cong., 1st sess., 949.

33. Ibid., 949–50.

34. Friday evening, January 28, 1820, Taylor Papers.

35. For Edwards's purported role, see Edwards, *History of Illinois*, 124. For Edwards's circle, Pease, *Frontier State*, 55.

36. *Annals of Congress*, Senate, 16th Cong., 1st sess., 360–61.

37. Monroe to Barbour, February 3, 1820, in "Missouri Compromise: Letters to James Barbour," 9. For good discussion of the role of Barbour in the Missouri debate, see Lowery, *James Barbour*, 113–31.

38. *Annals of Congress*, Senate, 16th Cong., 1st sess., 363.

39. Ibid., 1092.

40. Ibid., 1111.

11. The Missouri Compromise: The Final Struggle

1. Taylor to his wife, Washington, February 4, 1820, Taylor Papers. For Meigs's resolution, see *Annals of Congress*, House, 16th Cong., 1st sess., 1113–14. For the discussion postponed, see ibid., Senate, 367.

2. *Annals of Congress*, House, 16th Cong., 1st sess., 1167.

3. See Lowery, *James Barbour*, 119–23.

4. Monroe Papers, New York Public Library.

5. Hill to William King, February 9, 1820, quoted in Moore, *Missouri Controversy*, 235n73; Charles Yancey to James Barbour, February 10, 1820, in "Missouri Compromise: Letters to James Barbour," 10; Barbour to Monroe, February 10, 1820, James Monroe Papers, Library of Congress.

6. *Annals of Congress*, House, 16th Cong., 1st sess., 1172.

7. Ibid., Senate, 424, but full text only in *Senate Journal*, 16th Cong., 1st sess., 160–61.

8. Ibid.

9. Ibid., 426–27.

10. Ibid., House, 940.

11. Benton, *Thirty Years' View*, 5.

12. For adjournment and Thomas's amendment ordered engrossed and read a third time, see *Senate Journal*, 16th Cong., 1st sess., 161–67; for final passage, see *Annals of Congress*, Senate, 16th Cong., 1st sess., 426–30; for it being sent to the House, see *Annals of Congress*, House, 16th Cong., 1st sess., 1403–4.

13. *Annals of Congress*, Senate, 16th Cong., 1st sess., 424–30.

14. Ibid., House, 1406.

15. For remarks of Strother, Livermore, Storrs, McLane, and others, see ibid., 1406–9.

16. Taylor Papers.

17. *Annals of Congress*, House, 16th Cong., 1st sess., 1455–57.

18. Ibid., Senate, 444.

19. Ibid., 453.

20. Ibid., House, 1491.

21. Ibid., 1539.

22. J. Adams, *Diaries*, March 5, 1820, 31:279.

23. *Annals of Congress*, House, 16th Cong., 1st sess., 1540.

24. Ibid., 1554.

25. For this and the preceding paragraph, see ibid., Senate, 457–59. It is not absolutely clear that Thomas was the chairman, but he did make the motion for the conference and was listed first of the three senators elected by the Senate, which by accepted practice indicated that the senator so listed had received the most votes and would become chairman. In addition, the conference committee report, at least the one prepared for the Senate, was in his handwriting.

26. Ibid., House, 1558.

27. For Walker's avowal, see *St. Louis Enquirer*, March 29, 1820, quoted in Moore, *Missouri Controversy*, 100. For the vote on the House Missouri bill, see *Annals of Congress*, House, 16th Cong., 1st sess., 1573.

28. John Taylor wrote his wife, Jane, the evening of February 29 that he was one of the House managers and that the conference would be held the next day. In his next letter, the morning of March 3, he said he was "called off night before last to attend another meeting of the Committee of Conference." Taylor Papers.

29. *Annals of Congress*, Senate, 16th Cong, 1st sess., 467–69.

30. For Lowndes's remarks, see ibid., House, 1578; for the vote, see ibid., 1586.

31. Ibid., 1587–88; for the signing by Monroe, see *Statutes at Large*, 16th Cong., 1st sess., 545.

32. March 7 and 10, 1820.

33. Morning, March 3, 1820, Taylor Papers.

34. Thomas's version is in the National Archives; see Joint Committee of Conference on the Missouri Bill, 03/01/1820–03/06/1820, RG 128l, Records of Joint Committees of Congress, 1789–1989. It is available online at http://www.ourdocuments.gov/doc.php?flash=true&doc=22.

35. *Annals of Congress*, House, 16th Cong., 1st sess., 1586.

36. Ibid., 1589.

37. For the second conference committee report, see ibid., Senate, 471–72; Holmes to William G. King, March 2, 1820, John Holmes Papers, Maine Historical Society, Portland.

38. C. Adams, *Memoirs of John Quincy Adams*, 5:4–10. Even Adams, mindful of the upcoming 1824 presidential election, was not such a wholehearted restrictionist and almost certainly welcomed the compromise as a document that he could argue was consistent with his principles. Although earlier decidedly in favor of restriction, Adams changed his position about a week before the

final question was taken and said that though he had no doubt that Congress had the power to impose restriction on Missouri, he was convinced it could not enforce it and therefore should not make it a condition to statehood. See William Plumer Jr. to William Plumer, April 7, 1820, in E. Brown, *Missouri Compromises*, 16.

39. For the question asked, see March 5, 1820, J. Adams, *Diaries*, 31:279; for the question answered, see the next day, 280.

40. C. Adams, *Memoirs of John Quincy Adams*, 5:14–15. For the written opinions given Monroe by cabinet members, see W. Ford, *Writings of John Quincy Adams*, 7:1–2. For the quoted passage, see J. Adams, *Diaries*, March 6, 1820, 3:280. As to the lost opinions, Calhoun was arguing twenty-eight years later that Congress had no right to prohibit slavery in a territory, which was counter to his position in 1820, and also claimed to have no recollection of Monroe having asked for written opinions; he was reported by some as not wanting to give a written opinion in the first place (for example, Richard Taylor Stevenson, *The Growth of the Nation, 1809–1837*, The History of North America, vol. 12 [Philadelphia: George Barrie and Sons, 1905], 188). On that record, it is logical to suppose that Calhoun may have had something to do with expunging the records. As to the durability of the Compromise, see Benton, *Thirty Years' View*, 8.

41. Quote from J. Adams, *Diaries*, March 7, 1820, 31:280. For antebellum economic growth, see Charles Sellers, *The Market Revolution: Jacksonian America, 1815–1846* (New York: Oxford University Press, 1991); and Henry J. Sage, *American Economic Growth 1820–1860*, http://sageamericanhistory.net/antebellum_america/topics/EconomicIssues.htm, 2005–6, updated December 13, 2013.

42. P. Ford, *Works of Thomas Jefferson*, 12:158–59.

43. As to Jackson's dislike of JBT, see letter to Jackson from his lieutenant James Bronaugh, December 30, 1821, in Moser, Hoth, and Hoemann, *Papers of Andrew Jackson*, 5:125; as to JBT's legacy, see Morrison, "Biographical Sketch."

12. The Aftermath

1. Missouri Constitution, adopted July 19, 1820, Article III, §26.

2. The A. B. letters were all published in the *Washington Republican*, a paper published daily when Congress was in session and semiweekly at other times. There were fifteen letters in all, published January 20, 21, 23, 27, and 29; February 3, 6, 10, 17, and 24; and March 3 in the daily edition, and March 26 and 29 and April 2 and 9 in the semiweekly edition.

3. Mooney, *William H. Crawford*, 244, and sources mentioned there in footnote 74.

4. Moore, *Missouri Controversy*, 287.

5. As quoted in William Plumer Jr. to William Plumer, April 7, 1820, in E. Brown, *Missouri Compromises*, 16.

6. For an excellent discussion of class, politics, and slavery in Illinois, see Simeone, *Democracy and Slavery in Frontier Illinois*, chap. 4.

7. Snyder, "Forgotten Statesmen of Illinois," 520.

8. The A. B. affair and its aftermath are well described in the *Report of the Select Committee to whom was referred the Address of Ninian Edwards, May 23, 1824, read and allowed to lie upon the table*, Historical Society of Pennsylvania, closed stacks, Td* 1824 vol. 5.

9. For the first quote, see W. Brown, *Historical Sketch*, 24; for the second quote, see T. Ford, *History of Illinois*, 63.

10. In the case of *Jarrot v. Jarrot*, 7 Ill. 1, in *Reports of Cases Argued and Determined in the Supreme Court of the State of Illinois* (Chicago: Callaghan and Co., 1886), the Illinois Supreme Court finally declared that even the slaves introduced by the French were entitled to freedom under the Northwest Ordinance of 1787 and the Illinois Constitution. Even after this Illinois Supreme Court decision, various forms of legal discrimination against black people persisted until the passage of the Fourteenth and Fifteenth Amendments to the U.S. Constitution and the Illinois Civil Rights Act of 1885.

11. *Craig v. Missouri*, 29 U.S. 410 (1830); *Byrne v. Missouri*, 33 U.S. 40 (1834).

12. Stevens, *Albert Gallatin*, 368–69.

13. Letter in Senator Thomas's hand from the Senate Chamber, possibly a copy but not so marked, JBT Papers.

14. For vote against confirming Clay, see March 7, 1825, *Senate Exec. Journal*, 18th Cong., 2nd sess., 441. For Benton's opposition, see April 28, 1826, ibid., 19th Cong., 1st sess., 534. For attacks on JBT, see Wiltse, *John C. Calhoun*, 332.

15. For the proposed amendment, see *Register of Debates*, Senate, 19th Cong., 1st sess., appendix, 137. For the newspaper article, see the *Richmond Enquirer*, April 11, 1826.

16. *Register of Debates, 1824–1837*, Index to 20th Congress, 1st and 2nd sess., "Index to the Names of the Speakers in the Debates in the Senate, Alphabetically Arranged."

13. The Perspective of Ohio

1. Hill, *History of Knox County*, 225.

2. For JBT's support, see JBT to James Monroe, March 3, 1821, RG 94, Letters Received by Adjutant General, National Archives. For possible appointment in the Treasury Department, see the *Richmond Enquirer*, April 11, 1826. For Hamtramck in Shepherdstown, see Billmyer and Kellogg, "Ancestry and Descendants of John Francis Hamtramck," 10. For details of Hamtramck's military career, see Charles K. Gardner, *A Dictionary of All Officers, Who Have Been Commissioned, or Have Been Appointed and Served, in the Army of the United States* (New York: D. Van Nostrand, 1860), 212.

3. Porter, *Politics and Peril*, 81.

4. Hill, *History of Knox County*, 412–15.

5. Frederick N. Lorey, *St. Paul's Church, Mount Vernon, Ohio, 1829–1979, Mount Vernon, Ohio* (Mount Vernon: published by the author, n.d.). For the political and ideological situation in Ohio at the time of JBT's arrival, see Andrew Cayton, *The Frontier Republic: Ideology and Politics in the Ohio Country, 1780–1825* (Kent, Ohio: Kent State University Press, 1986).

6. Frederick N. Lorey, *History of Knox County, Ohio, 1876–1976* (Mount Vernon: Knox County Historical Society, 1992), 78.

7. For the details of the house, see the pamphlet *Historic Gambier Street, Mount Vernon, Ohio*, Mount Vernon Area Chamber of Commerce, 23; and inventory of the Estate of Jesse B. Thomas, Ohio Historical Society, Columbus, Microfilm GR 2890, 324.

8. Owens, *Mr. Jefferson's Hammer*, 194–95.

9. *Scioto (Ohio) Gazette*, June 7, 1838.

10. McLean to JBT, December 9, 1847, JBT Papers; the referenced war was the Mexican-American War.

11. Porter, *Politics and Peril*, 41, indicates that most who worshipped at St. Paul's c. 1830 were antislavery.

12. Herndon and Weik, *Herndon's Lincoln*, 1:188–89.

13. See Glenn H. Seymour, "'Conservative'—Another Lincoln Pseudonym?" *Journal of the Illinois State Historical Society* 29 (July 1936): 135–50; Glenn H. Seymour, "Lincoln—Author of the Letters by a Conservative," *Bulletin of the Abraham Lincoln Association*, no. 50 (December 1937): 8–9; and Burlingame, *Inner World of Abraham Lincoln*, appendix, 365–67.

14. Snyder, "Forgotten Statesmen of Illinois," 525.

15. Yates to Richard Symmes Thomas Jr., Washington, November 18, 1852, RST Jr. Papers, 1852–1865.

16. Yates was a member of the Illinois legislature from 1842 till 1849. In 1850 he was elected to the U.S. House of Representatives, where he was the youngest member of the 32nd Congress. In 1852 he was reelected to the 33rd Congress. In 1860 he was elected governor and was reelected for a second term in 1862 and so served as governor of Illinois throughout the Civil War.

17. Yates to Richard Symmes Thomas Jr., Washington, January 4, 1852, RST Jr. Papers, 1852–1865.

18. For general discussion, see Crissey, *Lincoln's Lost Speech*. The most famous version of this speech is the one offered by Henry Clay Whitney, a lawyer and Lincoln biographer, in *McClure's Magazine* in September 1896. This version has been questioned because it was made forty years after the speech, but Whitney said that it was based on notes he had taken as the speech was being delivered. Despite the fact that Joseph Medill, editor of the *Chicago Tribune*, confirmed the accuracy of Whitney's version, it is generally thought to be unreliable. The language quoted here comes from a reproduction of Whitney's version printed by the De Vinne Press for the Republican Club of the City of New York for its annual dinner on February 12, 1897, 33–34.

14. A Rest to the People of God

1. Speech before the Illinois Legislature, October 23, 1849, cited in Forbes, *The Missouri Compromise and Its Aftermath*, 274, and also in Allen Johnson, *Stephen A. Douglas: A Study in American Politics* (1908; New York: Da Capo Press, 1970), 235.

2. Florida and Texas in 1845, Iowa in 1846, Wisconsin in 1848, and California in 1850.

3. Wilentz, *The Rise of American Democracy*, 672–73.

4. *Mount Vernon Democratic Banner*, May 10, 1853. The account of the suicide and the means by which it was achieved is repeated in Snyder, "Forgotten Statesmen of Illinois," 523. One indication of the accuracy of the account is that the inventory of Thomas's estate lists all the other shaving paraphernalia (shaving mirror, shaving brush, and razor strop) but no razor.

Epilogue

1. Benton, *Thirty Years' View*, 4.

SOURCES

Sources not listed below or in the bibliography are described in full
when first cited in the endnotes and thereafter appear in short form.

The most frequently cited sources for this book are the *Annals of Congress*, the *Senate Journal*, and the *House Journal*, all of which are available online in *A Century of Lawmaking for a New Nation: U.S. Congressional Documents and Debates, 1774–1875*, http://memory.loc.gov/ammem/amlaw/lawhome.html. Documents relating to Jesse B. Thomas at the Abraham Lincoln Presidential Library in Springfield, Illinois, "Papers, 1785–1866," Manuscript SC 1531, are referred to as the "JBT Papers." Documents relating to his nephew Richard Symmes Thomas Jr., also at the Abraham Lincoln Presidential Library, "Letters, 1852–1865," Manuscript SC 1533, are referred to as the "RST Jr. Papers." The papers of John W. Taylor at the New-York Historical Society, New York, titled "Correspondence and Papers, 1804–1846," are referred to as the "Taylor Papers."

Historians' interpretations of the Missouri controversy have always reflected the concerns of the times in which they lived and worked. Though eclipsed by subsequent scholarship, the views of Avery Craven in *The Repressible Conflict, 1830–1861* (Baton Rouge: Louisiana State University Press, 1939) and J. G. Randal in *Civil War and Reconstruction* (Boston: D. C. Heath & Company, 1937) echo in the present. Craven and Randal wrote during the Depression era, a time when the wastefulness of war seemed particularly painful; working in the years between World War I and World War II, they were heavily influenced by the carnage of the former and the looming irrationality of the latter. They believed that the Civil War was a sectional clash over economic issues that could have been resolved by more skillful legislators. The idea that a national tragedy of such dimensions could result from a lack of political will to find a workable solution has fresh appeal in a time when Americans are again challenged to find principled compromises to preserve and protect our Republic.

Whatever their viewpoint, however, historians have always appreciated that our nation was founded on a series of fragile compromises and was thus susceptible to disunion when the art of compromise declined; Peter B.

Knupfer's *The Union as It Is: Constitutional Unionism and Sectional Compromise, 1787–1861* (Chapel Hill: University of North Carolina Press, 1991) is a good recent example of this view.

As a biography of arguably the most important legislator behind the Missouri Compromise, this book focuses on the legislative history of the compromise and the ways in which the legislative skills, or lack thereof, of those charged with resolving the crisis altered its outcome. Robert V. Remini takes a similar approach in his biographies of political figures of the period (*Martin Van Buren and the Making of the Democratic Party* [New York: Columbia University Press, 1959]; *Henry Clay: Statesman for the Union* [New York: W. W. Norton and Co., 1993]; and *Daniel Webster: The Man and His Time* [New York: W. W. Norton and Co., 1997]), emphasizing the legislative expertise of his subjects while downplaying the larger political, economic, and social forces that shaped events. This biographical approach elevates the art of compromise, which is necessary to move forward but which often fails to fully resolve the contested issue. We need to remind ourselves that the congressional machinations leading to the Missouri Compromise were not a political game but rather a delaying tactic that still left millions of people enslaved.

The seminal study of the compromise has been Glover Moore's *The Missouri Controversy, 1819–1821* (Lexington: University of Kentucky Press, 1953), which makes good use of primary sources and provides an accurate narrative of events, focusing on the critical role played by the middle states and the new states of the Old Northwest. Like his predecessors, Moore portrays the main proponents of the antislavery cause as former Federalists and allies of the renegade Republican governor of New York, DeWitt Clinton. Since then the trend has been to take a more discriminating look at the participants on both sides of the debate. Sean Wilentz, in his article "Jeffersonian Democracy and the Origin of Political Antislavery in the United States: The Missouri Crisis Revisited" in the *Journal of the Historical Society* (Fall 2004), 4:375–401, successfully argues that the critical sparks igniting the antislavery cause came not from Federalists and disaffected Clintonians but rather from Republicans who harked back to Jefferson's insistence that preserving the self-evident rights of all citizens, black as well as white, must take precedence over the rights of individual states (389). His masterful survey *The Rise of American Democracy: Jefferson to Lincoln* (New York: W. W. Norton and Co., 2005), published the following year, puts that argument in a broader context. Daniel Walker Howe, in *What Hath God Wrought* (New

York: Oxford University Press, 2007), continues the expansion of the scope of the debate by suggesting that the Tallmadge amendment, modeled on New York's emancipation laws, was actually a viable alternative for a state like Missouri, with its relatively small slave population, rather than just a tactical provocation as Moore and others had portrayed it. The Missouri Compromise has been most recently and thoroughly studied by Robert Pierce Forbes in his 2007 study, *The Missouri Compromise and Its Aftermath: Slavery and the Meaning of America* (Chapel Hill: University of North Carolina Press), which further expands the cast of characters involved behind the scenes in the debate. Forbes presents a convincing though necessarily circumstantial case that President Monroe had a greater involvement than previously supposed, an interpretation suggested by Harry Ammon in *James Monroe: The Quest for National Identity* (Charlottesville: University of Virginia Press, 1990) and Noble E. Cunningham Jr. in *The Presidency of James Monroe* (Lawrence: University of Kansas Press, 1996).

As historians moved away from the idea that slavery issues were decided by small groups of elites at the national level, they put increased emphasis on the importance of regional and local politics. In particular, historians examined more closely the role of regionalism in the rapidly expanding American Republic. Leonard L. Richards, in *The Slave Power: The Free North and Southern Domination, 1780–1860* (Baton Rouge: Louisiana State University Press, 2000), posits that the Missouri controversy, like many other crises in the pre–Civil War period, is more constructively viewed as part of a long political struggle between the North and the South, with the North growing increasingly resentful of the outsized power conceded the South in the early years of the Republic. John Craig Hammond, in *Slavery, Freedom and Expansion in the Early American West* (Charlottesville: University of Virginia Press, 2007), argues that the struggle between North and South became explosive only after the expanding West had committed itself to the Union, presumably on the Northern side, thus assuring the North the firepower necessary to break the Southern grip. The fifteen essays collected by Hammond and Matthew Mason in *Contesting Slavery: The Politics of Freedom and Bondage in the New American Nation* (Charlottesville: University of Virginia Press, 2011) further examine this proposition.

Vital record evidence is lacking for Jesse Burgess Thomas and his forebears, but there is much family narrative and circumstantial evidence, most of it not readily available. These include the following:

1. The Thomas Thomas Notebook, manuscript notebook, containing commercial and family records, dated from April 16, 1746, to April 8, 1808, by Thomas Thomas (1713– c. 1774), his son Thomas Thomas (1737–96), and his son Thomas Thomas (1778–1861), in the possession of Robert Bernard Thomas

2. The will of Richard S. Thomas, written June 21, 1823, and filed with the Fourth Circuit Court, June 9, 1831, Box 82, Bundle 1523, Cape Girardeau County Archive Center, Cape Girardeau, Missouri

3. Inventory of the Estate of Jesse B. Thomas, Ohio Historical Society, Knox County Estate Records, Microfilm GR 2890: 324

4. "Biographical Sketch of the Hon. Jesse Burgess Thomas," by Samuel Morrison, originally published in the *Lawrenceburg Press* shortly after Jesse Thomas's death in 1853 and reprinted May 9, 1872, in the *Franklin Democrat* in Brookville, Indiana, as well as in the 1887 edition of Reynolds, *Pioneer History of Illinois*, 401n2

5. John Francis Snyder, "Forgotten Statesmen of Illinois: Hon. Jesse Burgess Thomas, Jesse Burgess Thomas, Jr., Richard Symmes Thomas, Jr.," *Illinois State Historical Society Transactions* 9 (1904): 514–25

6. The obituary of the third Richard S. Thomas, written by his brother Henry Theodore Thomas for the Yale Alumni Office (Thomas, Richard Simms, '87, Manuscripts and Archives, Sterling Library, Yale University, record unit 830, Accn 2000-A-007/1, Box 63)

7. Elizabeth Rigby, "Maryland's Royal Family," *Maryland Historical Magazine* 29 (1934): 212, for Kittamaqund

8. Harry Wright Newman, *The Maryland Semmes and Kindred Families* (Baltimore: Maryland Historical Society, 1956)

9. Query in the *Maryland Genealogical Society Bulletin* 4, no. 2 (April 1963): 14, describing Sabina Symmes as a descendant of Baker Brooke and the Calvert family

10. Wayne Van Leer Jones, Genealogy Collection, Special Collections, Deering Library, Northwestern University

11. W. Cary Anderson, *The Descendants of Thomas Thomas and His Wife, Elizabeth, Daughter of James Knott* (Wyandotte, Okla.: Gregath Publishing Company, 1996)

SELECTED BIBLIOGRAPHY

Adams, Charles Francis, ed. *Memoirs of John Quincy Adams, Comprising Portions of His Diary from 1795 to 1848*. 12 vols. Philadelphia: J. B. Lippincott and Co., 1874–77.

Adams, John Quincy. *Diaries*. 51 vols. Boston: Electronic Archive, Massachusetts Historical Society, Adams Family Papers, http://www.masshist.org/jqadiaries, 2008.

Aldrich, O. W. "Slavery or Involuntary Servitude in Illinois Prior to and after Its Admission as a State." *Journal of the Illinois State Historical Society* 9, no. 2 (1916): 117–32.

Alvord, Clarence Walworth. *The Illinois Country, 1673–1818*. Centennial History of Illinois, vol. 1. Springfield: Illinois Centennial Commission, 1920.

———, ed. "Laws of the Territory of Illinois, 1809–1811." *Bulletin of the Illinois State Historical Library* 1, no. 2 (June 1906): 1–34.

Barnhart, John D., and Dorothy L. Riker. *Indiana to 1816: The Colonial Period*. Indianapolis: Indiana Historical Bureau and Indiana Historical Society, 1971.

Basler, Roy P., ed. *The Collected Works of Abraham Lincoln*. 9 vols. New Brunswick, N.J.: Rutgers University Press, 1953.

Bassett, John Spencer, ed. *Correspondence of Andrew Jackson*. 6 vols. Washington: Carnegie Institution, 1926–35.

Benton, Thomas Hart. *Thirty Years' View; or, A History of the Working of the American Government for Thirty Years, from 1820 to 1850*. New York: D. Appleton and Company, 1854.

Breese, Sidney. *The Early History of Illinois*. Chicago: E. B. Myers and Company, 1884.

Brown, Everett Somerville, ed. *The Missouri Compromises and Presidential Politics, 1820–1825, from the Letters of William Plumer, Jr., Representative from New Hampshire*. St. Louis: Missouri Historical Society, 1926.

Brown, William H. *An Historical Sketch of the Early Movement in Illinois for the Legalization of Slavery*. Chicago: Fergus Printing Company, 1876.

Buck, Solon Justus. *Illinois in 1818*. Springfield: Illinois Centennial Commission, 1917.

Burlingame, Michael. *Abraham Lincoln: A Life*. Baltimore: Johns Hopkins University Press, 2008.

————. *The Inner World of Abraham Lincoln*. Urbana: University of Illinois Press, 1997.

Burnet, Jacob. *Notes on the Early Settlement of the North-Western Territory*. 1847. Reprint, New York: Arno Press, 1975.

Canon, David T., Garrison Nelson, and Charles Stewart III. *Committees in the U.S. Congress, 1789–1946*. Washington, D.C.: CQ Press, 2001.

Carpenter, Richard V. "The Illinois Constitutional Convention of 1818." *Journal of the Illinois State Historical Society* 6, no. 3 (1894): 327–54.

Carter, Clarence Edwin, comp. *The Territorial Papers of the United States*. 28 vols. Washington: U.S. Government Printing Office, 1934–75.

Charless, Joseph, ed. *Charless' Missouri and Illinois Magazine Almanac for 1818*. St. Louis: Missouri Gazette, 1817.

Cleaves, Freeman. *Old Tippecanoe: William Henry Harrison and His Times*. New York: Scribner's, 1939. Reissue, Port Washington, N.Y.: Kennikat Press, 1969.

Collins, Lewis. *Historical Sketches of Kentucky*. Maysville, Ky., 1847; revised and brought down to 1874 by his son, Richard H. Collins. Covington, Ky.: Collins and Co., 1878.

Combined History of Randolph, Monroe and Perry Counties, Illinois. Philadelphia: J. L. McDonough and Co., 1883.

Crissey, Elwell. *Lincoln's Lost Speech: The Pivot of His Career*. New York: Hawthorn Books, 1967.

Davidson, Alexander, and Bernard Stuvé. *A Complete History of Illinois from 1673 to 1873*. Springfield: Illinois Journal Co., 1874.

Davis, James E. *Frontier Illinois*. Bloomington: Indiana University Press, 1998.

Dunn, Jacob Piatt, Jr. *Indiana and Indianans: A History of Aboriginal and Territorial Indiana and the Century of Statehood*. 5 vols. Chicago: American Historical Society, 1919.

————. *Indiana: A Redemption from Slavery*. Boston: Houghton Mifflin, 1905.

Edwards, Ninian W. *The Edwards Papers*. Edited by E. B. Washburne. Chicago: Fergus Printing, 1884.

————. *History of Illinois from 1778 to 1833; and Life and Times of Ninian W. Edwards*. Springfield: Illinois State Journal Company, 1870.

Esarey, Logan, ed. *Messages and Letters of William Henry Harrison*. Vol. 1, *1800–1811*. New York: Arno Press, 1975.

Finkelman, Paul. "Evading the Ordinance: The Persistence of Bondage in Indiana and Illinois." *Journal of the Early Republic* 9, no. 1 (Spring 1989): 21–51.

———. "Slavery and the Northwest Ordinance: A Study in Ambiguity." *Journal of the Early Republic* 6, no. 4 (Winter 1986): 343–70.

Foley, William E. *A History of Missouri, 1673 to 1820.* Vol. 1, *Missouri Sesquicentennial History,* edited by William E. Parrish. Columbia: University of Missouri Press, 1971.

Ford, Paul Leicester, ed. *The Works of Thomas Jefferson.* 12 vols. New York: G. P. Putnam's Sons, 1904–5.

Ford, Thomas. *A History of Illinois from Its Commencement as a State in 1818 to 1847.* Chicago: S. C. Griggs & Co., 1854. Reprint, Urbana: University of Illinois Press, 1995. Citations are to the 1854 edition.

Ford, Worthington Chauncey, ed. *The Writings of John Quincy Adams.* 7 vols. New York: Macmillan Company, 1913–17.

Goebel, Dorothy B. *William Henry Harrison: A Political Biography.* Indianapolis: Historical Bureau of the Indiana Library and Historical Department, 1926. Reprint 1973.

Goodspeed's History of Southeast Missouri. Chicago: Goodspeed Publishing Company, 1888.

Green, James A. *William Henry Harrison: His Life and Times.* Richmond, Va.: Garrett and Massie, 1941.

Green, Philip Jackson. *The Life of William Harris Crawford.* Charlotte: University of North Carolina at Charlotte, 1965.

Guasco, Suzanne Cooper, ed. "The Deadly Influence of Negro Capitalists: Southern Yeomen and Resistance to the Expansion of Slavery in Illinois." *Civil War History* 47, no. 1 (March 2001): 7–29.

Hammes, Raymond H. "Land Transactions in Illinois Prior to the Sale of Public Domain." *Journal of the Illinois State Historical Society* 77, no. 2 (Summer 1984): 101–14.

Hamtramck, John Francis, and Josiah Harmar. *Outpost on the Wabash, 1787–1791: Letters of Brigadier General Josiah Harmar and Major John Francis Hamtramck, and Other Letters and Documents Selected from the Harmar Papers.* Vol. 19. Vincennes: Indiana Historical Society, 1957.

Harris, Dwight N. *The History of Negro Servitude in Illinois and of the Slavery Agitation in That State, 1719–1864.* New York: Haskell House, 1969.

Hemphill, W. Edwin, ed. *The Papers of John C. Calhoun.* Columbia: University of South Carolina Press, 1975.

Herndon, William Henry, and Jesse Weik. *Herndon's Lincoln: The True Story of a Great Life.* 2 vols. New York: D. Appleton and Co., 1909.

Hill, N. N., Jr. *History of Knox County, Ohio.* Mount Vernon, Ohio: A. A. Graham and Co., 1881.

Hinchey-Cochran, Katherine J. "A History of Jackson, Missouri." *Jackson Sesquicentennial, 150 Years of Progress,* Souvenir Historical Program. Jackson, Mo.: Jackson Sesquicentennial, Inc. and Jackson Chamber of Commerce, 1965.

History of Dearborn and Ohio Counties, Indiana. Chicago: F. E. Weakley and Co., 1885.

History of Jackson, Missouri and Surrounding Communities. Paducah, Ky.: Turner Publishing, 2002.

History of Lawrenceburg, Indiana, Sesquicentennial Edition, August 23–29, 1953. Lawrenceburg, Ind.: Lawrenceburg Historical Society, 1953.

The History of Warren County. Chicago: W. H. Beers and Co., 1881.

Hopkins, James F., and Mary W. M. Hargreaves, eds. *The Papers of Henry Clay.* 6 vols. Lexington: University of Kentucky Press, 1959–81.

Houck, Louis. *A History of Missouri, from the Earliest Explorations and Settlements until the Admission of the State into the Union.* 3 vols. Chicago: R. R. Donnelley and Sons, 1908.

———. "Recollections of One of Cape Girardeau's Great Public Figures, Louis Houck, 1840–1925." *Cape Girardeau Southeast Missourian,* April 21–June 30, 1969, series of newspaper articles from privately owned manuscript.

Howard, Robert P. *Illinois: A History of the Prairie State.* Grand Rapids, Mich.: Eerdmans, 1972.

Hunt, James B. *A Brief History of the Circuit Court of Cape Girardeau County, Missouri.* Cape Girardeau, Mo.: Cape Girardeau County Court, 1965.

"The Illinois Constitutional Convention of 1818." *Journal of the Illinois Slate Historical Society* 6, no. 3 (October 1913): 327–424.

James, Edmund J., ed. *The Territorial Records of Illinois.* Springfield: Illinois State Historical Library, 1901.

Johannsen, Robert W., ed. *The Letters of Stephen A. Douglas.* Urbana: University of Illinois Press, 1961.

Journal of the Missouri State Convention. St. Louis: I. N. Henry and Co., 1820.

Kane, Elias Kent. Papers, 1808–1835. Chicago History Museum, NUCMC MS 61–2189.

Kenney, David, and Robert E. Hartley. *An Uncertain Tradition: U.S. Senators from Illinois, 1818–2003.* Carbondale: Southern Illinois University Press, 2003.

Knox, John Jay. *History of Banking in the United States.* New York: Bradford Rhodes and Company, 1900.

Leichtle, Kurt E. "The Rise of Jacksonian Politics in Illinois." *Illinois Historical Journal* 82, no. 2 (Summer 1989): 93–107.

Leonard, Gerald. *The Invention of Party Politics: Federalism, Popular Sovereignty and Constitutional Development in Jacksonian Illinois.* Chapel Hill: University of North Carolina Press, 2002.

Lowery, Charles D. *James Barbour, a Jeffersonian Republican.* Tuscaloosa: University of Alabama Press, 1984.

Lusk, David W. *Politics and Politicians: A Succinct History of the Politics of Illinois.* Springfield: H. W. Rokker, 1884.

March, David D. "The Admission of Missouri." *Missouri Historical Review* 65, no. 4 (July 1971): 427–49.

Mason, Matthew. *Slavery and Politics in the Early American Republic.* Chapel Hill: University of North Carolina Press, 2006.

Mateyka, Karen Campe. "Lucy Swearingen Stephenson." *The Volunteer: A Newsletter for the Volunteers of the 1820 Col. Benjamin Stephenson House* 2, no. 3 (February 2008): 1, 6–8.

McCandless, Perry. *A History of Missouri.* Vol. 2, *1820–1860.* Columbia: University of Missouri Press, 1971.

Merkel, William G. "Jefferson's Failed Anti-slavery Proviso of 1784 and the Nascence of Free Soil Constitutionalism." *Seton Hall Law Review* 38, no. 2 (2008): 555–603.

Miller, Andrew. *New States and Territories or the Ohio, Indiana, Illinois, Michigan, North-Western, Missouri, Louisiana, Mississippi and Alabama in their Real Characters in 1818.* Keene, N.H.: n.p., 1819.

"Missouri Compromise: Letters to James Barbour." *William and Mary Quarterly* 10, no. 1 (July 1901): 5–24.

Mooney, Chase C. *William H. Crawford, 1772–1834.* Lexington: University Press of Kentucky, 1974.

Morrow, Josiah. *A Brief History of Lebanon Ohio: A Centennial Sketch.* Lebanon, Ohio: Western Star Publishing, 1902.

Moser, Harold D., David R. Hoth, and George H. Hoemann, eds. *The Papers of Andrew Jackson, 1821–1824.* Vol. 5. Knoxville: University of Tennessee Press, 1996.

Moser, Harold D., Sharon McPherson, and Charles F. Bryan, Jr., eds. *The Papers of Andrew Jackson, 1804–1813.* Vol. 2. Knoxville: University of Tennessee Press, 1984.

Munroe, John A. *Louis McLane, Federalist and Jacksonian.* New Brunswick, N.J.: Rutgers University Press, 1973.

Norton, Margaret Cross, ed. *Illinois Census Returns 1810, 1818.* Collections of the Illinois State Historical Society, vol. 24, Statistical Series, vol. 2. Springfield: Illinois State Historical Library, 1935.

Oaks, Dallin H., and Marvin S. Hill. *Carthage Conspiracy: The Trial of the Accused Assassins of Joseph Smith.* Urbana: University of Illinois Press, 1979.

Otten, William L. *Col. J. F. Hamtramck—His Life and Times, 1756–1783: Captain of the Revolution.* Port Aransas, Tex.: Otten Publishing, 1997.

———. *Col. J. F. Hamtramck—His Life and Times, 1783–1791: Frontier Major.* Port Aransas, Tex.: Otten Publishing, 2003.

Owens, Robert M. *Mr. Jefferson's Hammer.* Norman: University of Oklahoma Press, 2007.

Pease, Theodore C. *The Frontier State, 1818–1848.* Centennial History of Illinois, vol. 2. Chicago: A. C. McClurg and Co., 1922.

Peterson, Merrill D. *The Great Triumvirate, Webster, Clay, and Calhoun.* New York: Oxford University Press, 1987.

Philbrick, Francis S., ed. *Laws of Illinois Territory, 1809–1818.* Collections of the Illinois State Historical Library, vol. 25, Law Series, vol. 5. Springfield: Illinois State Historical Library, 1950.

———, ed. *Laws of Indiana Territory, 1801–1809.* Collections of the Illinois State Historical Library, vol. 21, Law Series, vol. 2. Springfield: Illinois State Historical Library, 1930.

Porter, Lorle. *Politics and Peril: Mount Vernon, Ohio in the Nineteenth Century.* Zanesville, Ohio: New Concord Press, 2005.

Preston, Daniel. *A Comprehensive Catalogue of the Correspondence and Papers of James Monroe.* Westport, Conn.: Greenwood Press, 2001.

Putnam, James William. *The Illinois and Michigan Canal: A Study in Economic History.* Chicago: University of Chicago Press, 1917.

Rees, James D. "The Bond-Jones Duel and the Shooting of Rice Jones by Dr. James Dunlap: What Really Happened in Kaskaskia, Indiana Territory on 8 August and 7 December 1808." *Journal of the Illinois State Historical Society* 97, no. 4 (Winter 2004): 272–85.

Reifel, August J. *History of Franklin County, Indiana.* Indianapolis: B. F. Bowen and Company, 1915.

Relf, Frances H. "The Two Michael Joneses," *Journal of the Illinois State Historical Society* 9, no. 2 (July 1916): 146–51.

Reynolds, John. *My Own Times: Embracing Also the History of My Life.* Chicago: Chicago Historical Society, 1897.

———. *The Pioneer History of Illinois*. Belleville, Ill.: N. A. Randall, 1852; Chicago: Fergus Printing Co., 1887.

Roberts, James H. "The Life and Times of General John Edgar." *Transactions of the Illinois State Historical Society for the Year 1907*, 64–73. Springfield: Illinois State Historical Library, 1908.

Rohrbough, Malcolm J. *The Land Office Business, the Settlement and Administration of American Public Lands, 1789–1837*. London: Oxford University Press, 1968.

Rothbard, Murray N. *The Panic of 1819: Reactions and Policies*. New York: Columbia University Press, 1962.

Shinn, Josiah H. *Pioneers and Makers of Arkansas*. Washington, D.C.: Genealogical and Historical Publishing Company, 1908.

Shipp, John Edgar Dawson. *Giant Days, or the Life and Times of William H. Crawford*. Americus, Ga.: Southern Printers, 1909.

Shoemaker, Floyd C. "The First Constitution of Missouri," *Missouri Historical Review* 6, no. 2 (January 1912): 51–63.

———. *Missouri's Struggle for Statehood, 1804–1821*. Jefferson City, Mo.: Hugh Stephens Printing, 1916.

Simeone, James. *Democracy and Slavery in Frontier Illinois*. DeKalb: Northern Illinois University Press, 2000.

Smythe, George Franklin. *A History of the Diocese of Ohio until the Year 1918*. Cleveland: Diocese of Ohio, 1931.

Snyder, John Francis. *Adam W. Snyder, and His Period in Illinois History, 1817–1842*. Virginia, Ill.: E. Needham, 1906.

Stevens, John Austin. *Albert Gallatin*. Boston: Houghton Mifflin, 1883; Whitefish, Mont: Kessinger Publishing, 2006.

Suppiger, Joseph E. "Amity to Enmity: Ninian Edwards and Jesse B. Thomas." *Journal of the Illinois State Historical Society* 67 (April 1974): 201–11.

———. "Jesse Burgess Thomas: Illinois' Pro-slavery Advocate." Ph.D. diss., University of Tennessee, 1970. Abraham Lincoln Presidential Library, F896.3 T458s.

Thomas, Jesse B. (born 1806). Papers, 1830–1844. Abraham Lincoln Presidential Library, Springfield, Ill., Manuscript SC 1532.

Thomas, Jesse B. *Report of Jesse B. Thomas as a Member of the Executive Committee Appointed by the Chicago Harbor and River Convention, of the Statistics Concerning the City of Chicago*. Chicago: R. L. Wilson, 1847.

Thornbrough, Gayle, ed. *The Correspondence of John Badollet and Albert Gallatin, 1804–1836*. Indianapolis: Indiana Historical Society, 1963.

Thornbrough, Gayle, and Dorothy Riker, eds. *Journals of the General Assembly of Indiana Territory, 1805–1815.* Indiana Historical Collections, vol. 32. Indianapolis: Indiana Historical Bureau, 1950.

Tice, Nancy Jo. "The Territorial Delegate, 1794–1820." Ph.D. diss., University of Wisconsin, 1967.

Treat, Payson Jackson. *The National Land System, 1785–1820.* New York: E. B. Treat and Co., 1910.

Verlie, Emit Joseph, ed. *Illinois Constitutions.* Vol. 13. Springfield: Illinois State Historical Library, Collections of the Illinois State Historical Library, 1919.

Whitney, H. C. *Abraham Lincoln's Lost Speech.* New York: De Vinne Press, 1897.

Wilson, Woodrow. *Congressional Government: A Study in American Politics.* Boston: Houghton Mifflin, 1900.

Wiltse, Charles M. "John C. Calhoun and the 'A.B. Plot.'" *Journal of Southern History* 13, no. 1 (February 1947): 46–61.

———. *John C. Calhoun, Nationalist (1782–1828).* Indianapolis: Bobbs-Merrill, 1944.

INDEX

Page locators in italics refer to maps and photographs.

Matthew W. Hall is a former general counsel of the University of Pennsylvania and has practiced law for many years in the natural resources area. He was a recipient in 2007–8 of a grant from the Richard S. Brownlee Fund of the State Historical Society of Missouri to support his research for this book.